Shakespeare, Catholicism, and Romance

Shakespeare, Catholicism, and Romance

Velma Bourgeois Richmond

CONTINUUM
NEW YORK   LONDON

2000

The Continuum International Publishing Group Inc
370 Lexington Avenue, New York, NY 10017

The Continuum International Publishing Group Ltd
Wellington House, 125 Strand, London WC2R 0BB

Printed in the United States of America

Library of Congress Cataloging-in-Publication Data

Richmond, Velma Bourgeois.
Shakespeare, Catholicism, and romance / Velma Bourgeois Richmond.
p.   cm.
Includes bibliographical references and index.
ISBN 0-8264-1209-2 (alk. paper)
1. Shakespeare, William, 1564–1616—Tragicomedies.   2. Shakespeare,
William, 1564–1616—Religion.   3. Christian drama, English—History and
criticism.   4. Catholic Church—In literature.   5. Romances, English—
History and criticism.   6. Medievalism—England—History—16th
century.   7. Medievalism—England—History—17th century.   8. Christianity
and literature—England—History—16th century.   9. Christianity and
literature—England—History—17th century.   10. Tragicomedy.   I. Title.
PR2981.5 .R53 2000
822.3'3 21—dc21   99-040184

Contents

Illustrations

Preface

Every book about Shakespeare is indebted to the many who have read, performed, discussed, and written about him. I have named a few influences in my notes, but here it is appropriate to thank those who have been closest to my writing this book. First, Evander Lomke, my editor at Continuum, who from the first conversations about the subject has been encouraging and helpful, and who made many careful and useful editorial suggestions. Second, my husband Hugh Richmond, who has generously supported all of my work; but with this project his expertise and many years of sharing his love of Shakespeare and dedicated work, scholarly and in performance, have been immeasurably helpful. With a topic so controversial their pervasive spirit of tolerance has been reassuring, and I am deeply grateful. Finally, given the subject, I think it right, with gratitude and humility, to dedicate the book to the two Catholic parish communities that are so much a part of my life: St. Mary Magdalen in Berkeley, California, and St. Lawrence, Gairloch, Scotland.

Introduction

One dimension of current literary theory is the reexamination of texts to place them in cultural history, both the circumstances that helped to shape them and the responses of subsequent readers. The postmodern challenge to, if not the dismantling of, the canon opens many new possibilities. In Shakespeare studies, the dominant emphases in recent decades have been upon feminism, performance, and new historicism, which does not usually spring from any point of religion (particularly an affinity with Catholicism). This procedure signs our own rather than a contemporary emphasis, since anyone living in England during Shakespeare's life, between 1564 and 1616, had to be concerned with religious convictions and practices. The nation moved through great denominational and political changes; personal religion could literally be a matter of both physical and spiritual life and death. Parallel to changes in literary studies have been those in history, where increasingly more data, especially analyses of local archives, have enhanced knowledge. Recent revisions in histories of the sixteenth century that focus on the English Reformation are of especial significance.

When Elizabeth became queen in 1558, Tudor parishes in England faced the third major religious revision in twelve years. Henry VIII's youthful defense of orthodoxy in "The Defense of the Faith" (1521), a reply to Luther, led to a papal conferring of the title "Defender of the Faith" that is still held by the British monarch. Although his divorce from Katherine of Aragon in 1530 led to a formal break with Rome in the spring of 1533, Henry's opposition to those who wanted theological changes from conservative religion persisted until his death in January 1547. With the accession of Edward VI, Thomas Cranmer was free of a restraining royal hand, and changes in the period 1547 to 1553 were substantial. Visitations enforced Injunctions to effect a sweeping away of the old religious view of life, with its external signs of images, processions, lights, fasts and feasts, saints, pilgrimages, Purgatory, concern for the dead. Official *Homilies* and the prayer books of 1549 and 1552 replaced the old Sarum primers that had been so much a part of lay devotions. English replaced Latin, and the new texts made liturgical music obsolete and also reduced lay participation. The 1550 Act enforced the stripping of the altars and reduced reverence of the Sacrament of the Eucharist. The Reformers tried to secure their changes with Queen Jane Grey, but by the end of July 1553 the succession of Queen Mary Tudor was assured, as were efforts to restore Catholicism for the next five years. The return was easier than most Reformation historians have described because of a combination of strong survivals of the old religion, a discreet continuation of some reforms, especially *Homilies* that echo Cranmer and preaching, and an attempt to avoid disputations. But for Mary's death without children in 1558 England would have been Catholic; indeed Elizabeth's Church of England is quite different from continental Protestantism. This interpretation is a reassessment of the English Reformation that has accepted too absolutely the case of Fox's *Book of Martyrs* for its condemnation of Catholicism and a view of history that emphasizes progress, new reforms over the bad past. The many switches and the pacing of change, as well as the role of official Injunctions, Visitations, and mixed acceptance and avoidance, indicate the strength of the old religion and intense tensions that accompanied such extraordinary changes. The leading revisionist historian Christopher Haigh states the complexity in his title *English Reformations*, which both indicates a series of changes and their different nature as religious and political, and sets the experience in England apart from the development of Protestantism on the Continent. Official laws and practical responses are not the same. The latter are now more widely available because of many accumulations of data and analyses of local and national public records, previously unpublished manuscripts that include accounts of civic cases and churchwardens as well as careers at court. In the last forty years, a much richer knowledge of how people reacted and behaved has developed. A greater inclusiveness that recognizes cultural or social history as well as intellectual, legal, royal, and military history has altered the understanding of both historians and literary critics. William Shakespeare is a part of such revisions, and recent biographical studies include new information.

Shakespeare's parents belonged to the generation that lived through the reversals of the initial twelve years, which were followed by Elizabeth's final control. The Act of Uniformity in 1559 abolished the Mass and reauthorized a slightly modified version of the Prayer Book of Edward VI; it passed by a mere three votes in Parliament, a sign of how uncertain was the preferred religious direction for England. This is one reason for the severity of the Elizabethan Injunctions of 1559, which exceeded Edwardian demands. Not surprisingly, the 1570s and 1580s saw the reformed religion taking over traditional religion and concomitant disputations. Thus the usual view of Elizabeth's success in following a path of compromise and moderation is a far too simple assessment of religion in Shakespeare's England and Shakespeare's own possible affinities.[1] At the very least, the old interpretations of inevitable changes that marked the progress from an unpopular and outmoded Catholicism to a vital and individual Protestantism should be modified to recognize a long struggle and dissenting views.

The variety and depth of evidence for a vital late-medieval church, and for the continued association of the Shakespeare family with it, support serious consideration of Shakespeare and Catholicism. Eamon Duffy's *The Stripping of the Altars: Traditional Religion in England 1440–1580* (1992) is a solid reassessment of Catholic and Protestant experience, a substantial demonstration of the richness of medieval Christendom as lived in England and its survival through much of the sixteenth century. His only reference to Shakespeare is the often-cited fact that he could have seen one of the last performances of the Coventry Corpus Christi plays, which survived into the mid-1570s. The diocese of Lichfield and Coventry were unusually slow to implement Reformation changes. In 1565, the Court pressured the bishop to urge the people, ''daily,'' to ''cast away . . . their beads (rosaries), . . . Mass-books, . . . and all other books of Latin service'' and no longer to burn candles or recite Psalms for the dead.'' In short, the faithful were to rid themselves of the practices of Catholicism. In a later article, ''Was Shakespeare a Catholic?,'' Duffy concludes: ''Whether or not Shakespeare can be claimed as a Catholic writer, he was certainly not a Protestant one.'' This historian's evaluation echoes that of bibliographer Alan Keen, one of the first to connect Shakespeare with Catholic Lancashire: ''One point immediately stands clear: Shakespeare's youthful sympathies were predominantly Roman Catholic: he would seem to have been educated in that faith'' (95).

Shakespeare has long been identified primarily as a poet dramatist of the Renaissance and Reformation, and as a key to English (and American) Protestant identity. The case for his Catholic elements has been a lesser theme, although proponents of it date from the seventeenth century. In 1611, the historian John Speed linked Shakespeare with the Jesuit Robert Persons in an often-quoted phrase, ''this papist and his poet.'' More recent discoveries tie Shakespeare to recusants in northern England. The Star Chamber called a group of recusant players, who had performed miracle plays, *Pericles*, and *King Lear* in Yorkshire, to appear before them in 1610, and a recusant Yorkshire gentleman was convicted. In 1695, the Reverend Richard Davies, rector of Supperton, Gloucestershire, echoed Speed when he recorded that William Shakespeare ''dyed a papist.''

John Dryden, in his own life expressing the continuing tension between Anglicanism and Catholicism, praised Shakespeare with universals like ''the largest and most comprehensive soul'' and all the ''Images of Nature'' in *An Essay of Dramatic Poesie* (1668). And Alexander Pope, whose Roman Catholicism inhibited his career, went no further in his *Preface to the Works of Shake-speare* (1725) than to compare them with "an ancient majestic piece of Gothick Architecture . . . more strong and solemn" than "a neat Modern building . . . more elegant and glaring." In France in 1801 François René de Chateaubriand, a Romantic emerging from the Age of Reason, affirmed, "if Shakespeare was anything at all, he was a Catholic." Thomas Carlyle, a Scots Calvinist, in *The Hero as Poet* (1840), remarked "as rather curious, that Middle-Age Catholicism was abolished, so far as Acts of Parliament could abolish it, before Shakespeare, the noblest product of it, made his appearance." In 1850 in a review of Haw-thorne, a New England Calvinist, Herman Melville compared him with Shake-speare: "And if I magnify Shakespeare, it is not so much for what he did do as for what he did not do, or refrained from doing. For in this world of lies, Truth is forced to fly like a sacred white doe in the woodlands; and only by cunning glimpses will she reveal herself, as in Shakespeare and other great masters of the great Art of Telling the Truth—even though it be covertly and in snatches."

Early in the twentieth century, beginning with E. K. Chambers in the 1930s, scholarly evaluators began to raise questions about possible Catholic affinities, and increasing evidence supports this case. Proponents range from measured arguments that the family and the young Shakespeare himself were Catholic to full arguments against Protestant and Puritan affinity, with many in the middle positing a beginning Catholic that moved to a moderate Reformed church as Elizabeth's reign progressed and shifting the focus from belief to artistry, the transformation of a papist to a poet. Writers about "the lost years" in Shake-speare's biography have long included the "William Shakeshafte theory," plac-ing his lost years as a teacher in Lancashire with a Catholic family that had strong connections to the theater. Jesuits, especially Peter Milward, have con-tributed greatly to our knowledge, especially about recusancy, Jesuit influence, and Shakespeare's affinity for the Counter-Reformation religious order. Bio-graphical evidence for the recusancy of the Shakespeare family gives a context for interpretation; studies of contemporary religious practice and belief buttress this personal context. But the available printed sources for the religious contro-versies of the Elizabethan and Jacobean periods, described in Milward's bibli-ographical surveys, indicate a dauntingly substantial evidence for the extent and variety of published sources regarding the ongoing religious and political ar-guments during Shakespeare's lifetime. There was much to read; the extent of influence is hard to gauge, but religion was clearly a major concern, and there was great disagreement.

Most modern scholars, however, have given little attention to Shakespeare's Catholic connections, and there are relatively few interpretations of the rela-tionship between Shakespeare's plays and Catholicism. Samuel Schoenbaum's

William Shakespeare: A Documentary Life (1975) illustrates the arbitrariness of interpretation; he professes ''secular agnosticism'' and being an ''admittedly skeptical writer,'' but shows his bias by underrating the significance of religion in the sixteenth century and ''exalting the artist over the votary''; he also frequently expresses anti-Catholic sentiments.[2] Revisionist history and interpretation require an alternative, both an expansion of contexts for documentary evidence and attempts to reach a level of meaning not entirely circumscribed by modern experience and values, which leads to naturalistic readings that rely on psychological insights or are limited to a noting of specific connections with historical events or texts.

Paralleling current revisions of religious change and biographical materials is an increased interest in the late plays, the so-called romances, as they were identified by Edward Dowden in 1877, when he created a category to distinguish *Pericles, Cymbeline, The Winter's Tale*, and *The Tempest* from the First Folio designations of comedies and tragedies. Although the theatrical history of the late plays has often been substantial and successful, for many these plays have remained illogical, full of strange actions and inconsistencies, most notably concluding in forgiveness, resolution, and reconciliation, and a discernible but not easily defined plenitude and joy that is suffused with sadness. In fact, qualities of and episodes from romance are significant throughout Shakespeare's career, not just at the end, and show his fascination with this kind of storytelling. I have previously argued that the medieval romance is an expression of a Catholic *habit of mind*, and Shakespeare's increasingly heavy reliance upon it shows a vision of life that the Tudors systematically tried to destroy. This tradition, I will show, indicates that the roles of poet, playwright, and ''papist'' are not incompatible.

The implications may be clarified by brief allusion to studies of children's literature and to autobiographical recollections of writers, which consistently acknowledge that childhood experience—what is read and learned early—remains most vividly remembered. The Catholic experiences of the Shakespeare family, including official citations for recusancy and execution of relatives, I believe are part of this memory. Another approach is to consider what makes a ''Catholic writer,'' a question often put to contemporary Catholic novelists such as Flannery O'Connor, Graham Greene, Walker Percy, and Muriel Spark. Two examples from Spark will illustrate. In one novel the hero resents being questioned about how he feels ''as a Catholic'' and replies, ''To me, being Catholic is part of my human existence. I don't feel one way as a human being and another as a Catholic.'' And a heroine observes, ''Well, either religious faith penetrates everything in life or it doesn't.''[3] Being Catholic informs the entire being, and this includes being a writer who is Catholic. Literary critics note profound Catholic influences even in writers, such as James Joyce and Eugene

O'Neill, who explicitly separate themselves from the tradition. Hillaire Belloc puts the case well: "the plays of Shakespeare were written by a man plainly Catholic in habit of mind." As a less polemical view, Belloc's analysis avoids partisan claims and the concomitant emphases on the cleavage with Protestantism that came with the Reformation. This analysis is helpful in a study of the relation between Shakespeare's religious views and the romance tradition since it emphasizes ways of perceiving and believing.

Identification of "a habit of mind" is a crucial, and not easily denied, recognition that Shakespeare lived in a world still permeated with a Catholic vision of life expressed through traditions developed over centuries, and in the sixteenth century affirmed through published writings and the Jesuit Mission to England. One of the seminal and most crucial aspects of the cultural tradition is the romance, a widely popular literary mode closely tied to religious beliefs in the Middle Ages. Shakespeare used the romance throughout his career but with increasing complexity and exclusivity in the later plays. Changes in performance—from outdoor to indoor theaters with their more refined staging and elaborate spectacle—explain part of the attraction of romance, an imaginative genre in which, as with God, everything is possible (Matthew 19.26 and Mark 10.27). This applies to the experiences presented in the plays, to human life, and most poignantly to the moment in which the survival of even recusant Catholicism in England was uncertain.

The medieval romance is unlike other modes in its special relation to Christianity, whose essential characteristic is the triumph that comes through the Crucifixion—belief/faith/joy in the face of loss and despair. The message of the Cross challenges human intellect; in the words of St. Paul:

> For the preaching of the crosse is to them that perish, foolishnes: but vnto vs, which are saued, it is the power of God. For it is written, I wil destroye the wisdome of the wise, and wil cast away the vnderstanding of the prudent. Where is the wise? where is the Scribe? where is the disputer of this worlde? hathe not God made the wisdome of this world foolishnes?
> (I Corinthians 1:18–20).

For those who do not believe, the Cross's paradox of transcendence through suffering is an absurdity, or a naive optimism: an escapism from present reality, a wish-fulfillment that ignores rational evidence—precisely the descriptions often made of romance. Thus the romance became the appropriate literary mode to sustain Catholic values at the time that the Reformation was being implemented in England. Contemporary evidence supports the connection of Catholicism and romance; there were strong humanist and Reformation prejudices— typified by Roger Ascham in England and Michel Montaigne in France—against the romance as old-fashioned, papist, and immoral.[4] These objections to a highly popular literary form are analogous to the more obviously religious and political objections to Corpus Christi plays, which represented the events of Christendom, from Creation to Doomsday, with special emphasis upon the Passion of Christ and much attention to Mary, and thus overtly expressed the piety of Catholicism before the community. The plays and processions were a vital part of the popular lay experience of the old religion, and in the later sixteenth century performances were systematically made illegal, as Harold Gardiner showed in *Mysteries' End* (1946). The extraordinary popularity of *Guy of Warwick*, the medieval romance that most effectively combines chivalry and hagiography to tell the legend of the local hero of Shakespeare's shire, increased in the sixteenth century with the richest variety of texts in its centuries of development.[5] They indicate that the old favorite hero sustained popular values, with minimal adjustments, at a time when Renaissance styles and Reformation beliefs and customs were urged as alternatives. The romance, which was constantly available in many printed versions, did not suffer the fate of medieval drama. Medieval romances such as *Guy of Warwick* and *Bevis of Hampton* appeared in different and new versions, while Richard Johnson's *The Seven Champions of Christendom* was a new romance (1596, 1608, 1610) that exploited the popular tales of national heroes, the medieval warrior saints. Edmund Spenser, the most brilliant non-dramatic poet of the sixteenth century and an intense Protestant, deployed the traditions of romance in *The Faerie Queene*, most obviously in Book I where the Red Cross Knight is both Holiness and the Anglican Church. And his hero in Book II, Sir Guyon, owes much to Guy of Warwick, as was explicitly recognized by John Lane, a friend of John Milton's father and ''a fine old Queen Elizabeth gentleman,'' who rewrote Guy's romance in Spenserian style.[6]

The romance was more elusive than plays or legends of the saints; in the terminology of the thriller (which it resembles in many ways), the romance could be a ''cover'' for recusant Catholicism.[7] Catholics living under Elizabeth were constrained in language and actions from expressing religious affinity with the old faith; they had every incentive to find a mode that would allow an escape from the realm of historical fact into one of wishful thinking. For Shakespeare and his audience, the romance is an especially apt choice. In the romance, extraordinary perils are transcended, often by an explicit divine intervention. The plots are filled with excitement and danger—exile, quests, shipwrecks, lost children, rescues of maidens in distress, magic potions, strange creatures, mistaken identity, quick reversals and reconciliations, and they inspire wonder. My most personally exciting experience of a performance of *The Winter's Tale* was with our then-seven-year-old daughter, to whom I had not told the story. When she saw the statue revealed, she grabbed my hand and whispered, ''Mummy, she's alive!'' The actress was utterly still, so that the child's understanding was not an observation of reality but of mystery.

Northrop Frye argues that the romance is a literary form that provides an integrated vision that acknowledges the demonic and the divine, with man as the hero as God is the hero of sacred Scripture. Frye's broad theoretical framework, based on many texts, finds that "romance is the structural core of all fiction: being directly descended from folktale, it brings us closer than any other aspect of fiction, considered as a whole, as the epic of the creature, man's vision of his own life as a quest."[8] Romances also have contexts, and many printed and read in sixteenth-century England are Catholic.

A commonplace analysis of Shakespeare's plays is that they are a search for the reality beneath outward appearances; and religion, at least a religious habit of mind, is an appropriate addition to the analyses of ethics and character. The exact nature of Shakespeare's religious faith, its quality and practice, can never be "proved." But revisionist Reformation history encourages a consideration of a surviving vital Catholicism in England, as does increasing interest in Shakespeare's last plays—his romances, both in performances and critical evaluations, many of which puzzle over the "improbable." My study of medieval romances, and of Catholicism and of Shakespeare, finds a strong affinity in a habit of mind, which this book explores.

Part 1
THE CHRISTIAN VISION AND LIVING IN SHAKESPEARE'S WORLD

1
MEDIEVAL CHRISTENDOM

istorical periods are a convenience for academic exploration, but a too great focus on a single time can mean less knowledge and sympathetic response to other periods. Setting the borders and deciding whether to emphasize rooting in the past or expanding into the future is always complex. More than other eras, the "Renaissance" has usually been exalted as forward-looking, the way into modernity, a getting beyond "the dark ages," the aberration of the "Middle Ages" between the magnificence of Classical Greece and Rome and Renaissance Europe. Similarly, many have viewed the "Reformation" as the progressive development of Christianity, a phenomenon that evolved from the inherent limitations of Catholic religious beliefs and practices in the sixteenth century. With increased knowledge and challenges in both literary and historical interpretation, these oversimplifications are being revised. The idea of "rebirth" is now largely discredited, even if the past that is privileged in much study of the Renaissance remains classical antiquity, not medieval Christendom. Since classical literature and thought were widely disseminated in the Middle Ages—as a glance at Chaucer, medieval romances, and philosophy show—even the term *renaissance* is a misnomer. New historicists have more recently insisted upon the name "Early Modern," in part to avoid earlier elitist privileging, but also to assert their own dominance over previous literary history.[1] Consensus about changes in religion is slower; but the length and complexity of the process, the strength of medieval Catholicism, and of the economic and political forces behind the English Reformation, are now acknowledged. The earlier views of the period are partially a nineteenth- and twentieth-century favoring of originality and change, a commitment to an evolutionary view of human experience that sees development from a primitive time of the race or nation to understanding and sophistication.

There have also been recognitions of the "medieval heritage"—a phrase from Willard Farnham's definitive study of narrative backgrounds for Elizabethan tragedy[2]—that argue close continuity with the immediate past. In Shake-speare studies, most attention has been on drama. Craft guilds of towns—mostly Northern: York, Wakefield, N-Towne or Ludus Coventriae (possibly Lincoln), and Chester—performed cycles of plays for the feast of Corpus Christi, a late addition to the liturgical calendar. This holy day is the Thursday after Trinity Sunday, which is the Sunday after Pentecost/Whitsunday. Thus it follows the rich period of Lent and Easter, and it gives a focus in a part of the liturgical calendar that has few main celebrations. The choice of Thursday echoes Holy Thursday, the day of the Last Supper when Jesus instituted the Eucharist; Corpus Christi marks the Catholic belief in the transubstantiation of the bread and wine into the Body and Blood of Christ. Since this theological point was one most attacked by Protestant reformers, there was an automatic objection to the Cath-olic feast, and the plays associated with it were suppressed. The fate of medieval romances was more complicated and less disastrous. Although they have much in common with overtly didactic writings—many are exemplary or homiletic—romances are secular narratives. Their popularity in printed editions suggests that they, like books of religion, were a way of sustaining the ideals of medieval Christendom, with its pervasive imaginative constructs and daily and varied devotions.

The persistence of that religious ethos has been a subject of several recent studies, and resulting controversy because of their more fully and sympatheti-cally argued revisionist history of Catholicism in the late medieval and Tudor periods. The thesis of Johan Huizinga's *The Waning of the Middle Ages* (1927) is no longer the archetype; F. R. H. Du Boulay's *An Age of Ambition* (1970) seems nearer the mark. Eamon Duffy's *The Stripping of the Altars* (1992) es-tablishes the strength and vibrancy of a popular late-medieval religion that en-compassed the entire society, in which dissidents like the fourteenth-century Lollards were marginal, for all the importance given to them by later Protestant apologists. Anne Hudson demonstrated this in her study of manuscripts of Lol-lard Bibles and tracts—few of which were copied after 1430—in *The Premature Reformation* (1988). Many other more current studies of historical data show the need to rethink the story of the English church. As recently as 1967, William Matthews included among "Inherited Impediments in Medieval Literary His-tory" the disproportionate attention given to Wycliffe followers and deletion of "eremitical contemplatives firm in the orthodoxies of monastic Catholicism," and he suggested that the *Cambridge History of English Literature* (1911) gives some mystics brief coverage only because of R. W. Chambers's "religious de-velopment and his growing absorption in the saintly Thomas More."[3] Literary history of medieval writers has somewhat shifted. William Langland was called a precursor of Protestantism, a Lollard; now his indignation over failures and deep religious conviction are recognized as a mark of extreme orthodoxy. And

Chaucer's friendship with Lollard knights and his Parson in *The Canterbury Tales* are no longer readily accepted as signs of incipient Protestantism.[4]

Far from a church in decline, fifteenth and early sixteenth-century Catholicism was a religion in which clergy, the educated elite, and ordinary people shared a rich liturgical tradition that was the basis of the community. Late medieval parish churches, not monastic establishments, were the locus of building and decoration, of education, of civic/religious activities and celebrations usually organized by guilds, and of gentle adapting to changing circumstances without decline or violent disruption. The long-held view that the Reformation was widely welcomed as a solution to clerical corruption, ignorant superstition, and decadence is no longer axiomatic. Catholic scholars find both appealing and reassuring the late-medieval evidence that supports an interpretation of the Reformation as inspired more by politics and economic greed than by religion. But the case is not simply partisan, for the reinterpretation of the Reformation originates with G. R. Elton's introduction of the themes of coercion and conflict. Duffy's archetypal historian for the aggressively Protestant interpretation of the Reformation is A. G. Dickens; and he shows how a counterargument for Catholicism can be made from the same evidence, for example, of formulas in wills.

The physical remains of Catholicism are very substantial, particularly in parish churches, even after so much Protestant destruction of images—statues, glass, pilgrimage sites, vestments, ecclesiastical furniture. These help to focus some of the characteristics of medieval Catholicism, which was largely taught through a world of images, since many people could not read. Such external signs were simply a way to interpret and to express a vision of human experience that is based on faith and centered in the divine, yet rooted in a perception of the material world. In this vision the sacred and the profane coexist in the human person, as is articulated most frequently in allegorical combats between the Vices and Virtues that are objectifications of human behavior in an unending *psychomachia* (battle for the mind). Pictures both of divine beauty—most frequently shown in Jesus Christ, God become man—and of bodily torments or decaying cadavers offer similar contrasts. Doomsday pictures are potent in their combination of the saved and damned; the horrors of the latter can be contemplated because at the center is Christ, who died to save the world. Moreover, the figures in the stories of the Bible that fill churches and books are recognizably of the world; there is comfort in Noah as a medieval shipwright, or the shepherds at the Nativity who come from English fields, shown in the garb and gesture of the makers or craftsmen. Catholics do not worship such images but use them as outward signs to lead toward that which is beyond human delineation. At first glance, the multiplicity of images is dizzying, but there is a remarkable consistency of iconography from church to church, and the images tell sacred stories that can be read like the Bible or saints' legends. But however successful pedagogically and familiarly appealing the images were, the vision is most cogent in the prayers and sacraments that were essential as the church helped the human being to salvation. Understanding the rich and encompassing nature of late-medieval Christendom must precede a recognition of the relation of Shakespeare to Catholicism and romance.

Seven Sacraments

A start is to recognize that medieval Christendom was a complete and rich way of living spiritually and imaginatively, not just pragmatically. The limited expression of weekly or brief daily devotion that is characteristic even among churchgoers today—the modern world in which Cardinal Newman saw the greatest challenge because "Christianity has never yet had the experience of a world simply irreligious"—is a far cry from the Middle Ages. That time was marked as a complex liturgical year with its cycle of feasts and fasts, a constant involvement both physical and symbolic, and the parish church as the locus of social as well as religious life. The medieval Church's development of seven sacraments expresses a wish to provide for all the dimensions of present life and into eternity. In classical Latin *sacramentum* means *that which binds*; in Christian Latin it translated the Greek word for *mystery*. To frequent notings of Shakespeare's many allusions to Scripture should be added his references to the sacraments, which Christ instituted and entrusted to the Church, and that mark the believer's pilgrimage of life and make the mystery of salvation a reality. The Thirty-Nine Articles of the Anglican Church recognize only Baptism and the Supper of the Lord. Article XXV explains that the other five "are not to be counted for Sacraments of the Gospel, being such as have grown partly out of the corrupt following of the Apostles, partly are states of life allowed in the Scriptures; but yet have not like nature of Sacraments with Baptism and the Lord's Supper; for that they have not any visible sign or ceremony ordained of God." The Catholic Church cites precedents for all seven sacraments, and Shakespeare's precise knowledge and respectful treatment tell us something about his relation to Catholicism. As we will see, the plays include all except Confirmation.

Baptism, Confirmation, Penance (Confession), Eucharist, Holy Orders, Matrimony, and Extreme Unction—these mark the passages from beginning life in the Church through entry into eternal life. That comprehensive quality is especially marked in late medieval paintings of *The Seven Sacraments*: one by Roger van der Weyden (c.1400–1464), whose works are profoundly religious, in Antwerp; another, similar in style, by van der Stockt in Madrid. Because the Eucharist is the most essential sacrament, the Crucifixion, repeated in the sacrifice of the Mass, is the center of each painting and larger than the surrounding scenes that show the other sacraments. Viewed today, divorced from their original religious settings in church or chapel, these paintings still inspire responses of devotion as well as aesthetic pleasure. Such works of master artists belonged to kings and nobles, but countless representations by anonymous artisans or craftsmen express the same need to have a visible sign of the sacramental, the experiencing of eternity while living in the world. Many have survived, and they are to be found sometimes in museums but often still in modest parish churches. Those in stone, glass, and wood have survived better than wall paintings to show more simply—some judge primitively—how the sacraments were a part of everyday living.

Their importance is evident in Catechisms like that of John Thoresby (1357), and in John Mirk's *Instructions for Parish Priests*, written in verse, at the end of the fourteenth century and preserved in later manuscripts. Nearly two-thirds of Mirk's text (1,223 of 1,923 lines) explain the sacraments, with Confession, including explanations of sins, taking more than half of the total (1,023 lines). As in *Festial*, a collection of sermons, later printed by Caxton, Mirk urges the necessity of understanding so that teaching is in English: "Lo here the seuene and no mo, / Loke thow preche ofte þo" (534–35).[5] The instructions are combined with exhortations to virtuous behavior by the priests and very pragmatic reminders about usage. A fifteenth-century sermon by Dan John Gaytryge in the Thornton Manuscript (Lincoln Cathedral MS 91) shows the range of instruction provided in obeying the bishop's command: "Opynly, one ynglysche, apone Sonondayes, to preche and teche þaym þat þay hase cure off, þe lawe and þe lare to knawe God Almyghty."[6] Gattrynge presents "six things" to his flock, "if we sall knawe God Almyghty, and come till His Blysse" (14): the fourteen points made in the Apostles Creed, the Ten Commandments, the Seven Sacraments, the Seven Works of Mercy, the Seven Virtues, and the Seven Deadly Sins. A review of the Catholic sacraments shows the teaching that underlies Shakespeare's references to them.

Baptism is "(not the putting awaye of the filth of the flesh, but in that a good conscience maketh request to God) by the resurrection of Iesus Christ" (1 Peter 3:21). This first sacrament makes one Christian, washing away original sin and making salvation possible. Mirk concentrates upon the words—"I crystene þe, or elles I folowe, .N. In nome of þe fader and the son and the holy gost. Amen."—and counsels priestly propriety and care in details of water, oil and creme, and in conditional Baptism. Gaytryge repeats these points. His sermon explains briefly that Confirmation is for the baptized to whom bishops thus give "þe grace and þe gyfte of þe Haly Gaste, to make þaym mare stalleworthe þan þay ware be-fore, to stande agaynes þe fende and dedly syn" (8), but Mirk offers few instructions about this second sacrament. Both Mirk and Gaytryge devote greatest attention to Penance, or "sothefaste forthynkynge þat we have of oure syn, with-owtten will or thoghte to turne agayne to it" (8). Three things are necessary: sorrow, shrift or confession, and satisfaction or penance. Mirk emphasizes that the penance should lead the sinner to learn the basic articles of faith and prayers, if he does not know them, and that the reconciliation should be in his own parish. Much of the *Instructions* details the nature of sins and remedies for them; Mirk gives full texts in English for Confession and Latin for absolution. Medieval penitential literature, both religious instruction and romances, informs the plays, from seekings of the sacrament in *Romeo and Juliet* and *Measure for Measure*, to the quick regret of Valentine in *The Comedy of Errors* and Claudio in *Much Ado*, to a long living of penance by Prospero and Leontes, to a rich thematic consideration of penance and pardon in *Cymbeline*.

Gaytryge's explanation of "þe Sacrament of þe Autyr" includes Catholic belief in Transubstantiation: "cristes awen body in lyknes of brede, als hale as He tuke it of þe blysside mayden" (8). Holy Church requires that every man and woman receive the Sacrament of Eucharist once a year at Easter, after being cleansed of sin through Penance: "For he þat tase it worthily, tase his saluacyone; and wha-so takes it vnworthily, tase his dampnacione" (8). Mirk similarly urges that a priest teach this belief:

> That þey receyue in forme of bred,
> Hyt ys goddes body þe soffered ded
> Vp on the holy rode tre,
> To bye owre synnes & make vs fre"
>
> (244–47)

Mirk explains that all should kneel in reverence before the Host that is the Body of Christ, and he warns that the reserved Host should be protected so that no rat or mouse can eat it. A compelling analog is *The Play of the Sacrament*, which dramatizes a popular legend to show failed attempts to destroy the Host; the Jews who try are led to conversion. This English play ascribes the events to the year 1461, the manuscript (Trinity College, Dublin, F.4.20, Catalogue no. 652) dates from the end of the century, and is preserved in a collection of miscellaneous texts from the sixteenth and seventeenth centuries.

The Lay-Folks Mass Book; or, Manner of Hearing Mass, encouraged devotion to the Blessed Sacrament and fostered greater participation by the laity, giving the appropriate prayers, especially meditation on the Passion at the Elevation that stressed the Risen Body, and physical gestures. English verse translations of the twelfth-century Norman original survive in three separate forms, in manuscripts from the later fourteenth to the early sixteenth century. John Lydgate, prolific and esteemed court poet in the fifteenth century, sustains the tradition in *Merita Missae*: "svme worde to telle / To the lewde that can not rede, / But the pater noster and the Crede'' (3–4). Lydgate, whose *Troy Book* (printed 1513) was a source for Shakespeare, urges a fight against those who do not believe the Gospel: "thou arte a knyghte, / That dare fyght in this lordis right" (61–62). He introduces heroes of history and romance—Godfrey of Bouillon, Charles the Great, Arthur—as Christian exemplars to be preferred before those "That wylle not to the sacrament" (168), another illustration of the explicit tie between romance and Catholic devotion. Perhaps this is also a conjunction for Protestant derision like that expressed in Article XXXI: "The sacrifices at Masses ... were blasphemous fables and dangerous deceits." Shakespeare's only specific reference to the Mass is Juliet's question, "Or shall I come to you at evening mass?" (IV.i.38), but there are many references to receiving "the sacrament," and one to the doctrine of Transubstantiation. In *As You Like It* Rosalind, in the midst of a teasing exchange about love with Celia, declares: "And his kissing is as full of sanctity as the touch of holy bread" (III.iv.13). The specific image is closer to the Catholic custom (until Vatican II) of the priest's placing the Host on the tongue, not in the hand as is the Protestant custom.[7] Although Shakespeare's plays contain echoes of the *Book of Common Prayer*, not many are from the Communion Service. Critics often note the drama inherent in the Catholic Mass—spectacle of costume and gesture, dialogue in antiphonal singing, and representation in the bread and wine (from a Protestant point of view). For a Catholic, who believes in Transubstantiation, each Sacrifice of the Mass is a reality, not a dramatic imitation, albeit there is no change in the physical appearances of bread and wine. This habit of mind, of being, well suits the ethos of romance, in which as with God everything is possible.

The fifth sacrament is Extreme Unction or "þe laste Enoyntynge with oyle" of one who is near death. Mirk reviews the questions to be asked and Latin prayer to be said and then offers practical descriptions for offering the sacrament (1600–1748, 1839–92). The murdered King of Denmark expresses a Catholic longing for the Last Sacrament when he complains to Hamlet that he was "*unhouseled, disappointed, **unaneled" (*did not receive Eucharist, **not anointed, I.v.77). Sacraments ease the passing of a soul, and deprivation at the time of death occasions grief and regret. The so-called cult of Death—offerings of masses and prayers, generous benefactions, Dances of Death, Doomsday paintings, a morality play like *Everyman*—shows a preoccupation but also a belief in the blessed as well as the damned.

These five sacraments are for all Catholics; the final two depend upon a choice of life—Orders for priests and Matrimony for women and men who wed. With Holy Orders a priest is empowered "to synge messe, and for to mynstere þe Sacramentes of Haly Kirke." Mirk's *Instructions* are a handbook for priestly actions; he strongly urges against immoral or careless behavior: "Hyt ys I-made hem to schowne / þat haue no bokes of here owne, / And oþer þat beth of mene lore, / þat wolde fayn conne more'' (1923–26). Shakespeare's Friars—Patrick in *Two Gentlemen of Verona*, Lawrence in *Romeo and Juliet*, Francis in *Much Ado*, Thomas and Peter (and Duke Vincentio) in *Measure for Measure*—fully illustrate a worthy and compassionate carrying out of priestly duties; however, John of Lancaster's identification of the role of a Bishop best puts the Catholic view of the priest as intercessor: ''To us th'imagined voice of God himself, / The very opener and intelligencer / Between the grace, the sanctities, of heaven / And our dull workings'' (*2 Henry IV*, IV.ii.19–22). Protestants favor a direct approach to God without the mediation of priests—or saints or Mary. Gaytryge defines Matrimony as a ''lawefull festynnynge be-twyx man and woman at þaire bathere assente, for to lyffe samen with-owtten any lowssynge, whills þaire lyfe lastes, in remedy of syn and getynge of grace, if it be tane in gude Entente and clennes of lyfe'' (9). Shakespeare explores ''holy . . . blessed . . . honorable marriage'' in many ways.

The Seven Sacraments are often represented on medieval fonts, where Baptism takes place. Thus at the time of the infant's entry into the Church, there is a reminder of the Church's nourishing through the sacraments for the key events throughout life and in death. More than forty octagonal fonts, most in Norfolk and Suffolk, show the Seven Sacraments carved around the bowl. The precision of the representations indicates an orthodoxy, indeed a commitment to catechetical teaching. Their frequent occurrence in two counties, Norfolk and Suffolk, is a considered response to Lollard opposition to the Seven Sacraments. Most date from the late fifteenth century, but one from after Henry VIII's break with Rome. Fonts were generally the gift of laity, with donors having some role in the choice of subject and presentation, so that they are evidence of lay reinforcement of the Church's teaching. Shakespeare's one reference to ''the consecrated fount'' (*Measure for Measure*, IV.iii.98) is as likely to be church furniture as a spring, since the play explores many Catholic issues.

Fonts are but the most substantial survival of images of the Seven Sacraments. They also are in stained glass windows; for example, at Doddiscombsleigh in Devon and Crudwell in Wiltshire, and surviving panels at Melbury in Dorset. There are references to incomplete windows of the Seven Sacraments in Lincolnshire, Lancashire, Gloucester, Yorkshire, and Somerset. A wall painting at Kirton, Lincolnshire, survived until the nineteenth century. Confession, which always elicits the fullest commentary, is found even on misericords at Ely Cathedral and at New College, Oxford. Amidst carvings of the Seven Deadly Sins (also at Norwich Cathedral), devils (one being exorcised), wildmen, many beasts, and much natural foliage, the subject is apt. A surviving roof boss at Southwark, formerly a priory, is a Seven Deadly Sins. Roof bosses, stone or wooden sculptures placed at the keystone of vaults, are a common feature of Gothic architecture. They are very often placed in sequences to tell stories, but single bosses also contain narratives, and several include the Sacraments. The John the Baptist series in the transepts at Norwich has three Baptisms: in the Jordan and two of Christ's Baptism. One at St. Mary Redcliffe, Bristol, shows Penance; a priest hearing Confession raises his right hand as though giving absolution. Most interesting are bosses with narratives of the Eucharist, also at Norwich, site of the most comprehensive use of bosses in England. In the cloister is a beautiful representation of the vision of St. Edward the Confessor, who beholds a priest celebrating Mass. Another is the story of the Jew of Bourges. The altar is being used for Mass; there is a chalice with corporal cover and an open Sacramentary, and the priest gives the Eucharist to three boys. On the side the boy's Jewish father pushes him into an oven, from which the Virgin Mary delivered him in the legend.[8]

Fonts and windows are quite public, but misericords and bosses are part of an almost hidden world—below the seats or scarcely visible high on the vaulting. To find the sacraments in obscure locations, as well as prominent places for teaching, suggests their significance in the lives of the community; it also reiterates a view of the Church as God's house in which God—Who sees and knows all—is honored, and provides for His people. The art of the Middle Ages expresses the pervasive quality of Catholicism that thus shows itself as enfolding without being restrictive and confining. However delightful, deeply moving— or inadequately sophisticated—the typically modest artistic achievements of individual items may be to a modern eye, they are also a reminder that the aesthetic (which varies with the era and the viewer) is not the primary reason for art. Many late-medieval images in English churches reflect the import of sermons and religious drama, which instructed and delighted. Let us further apply these concepts of a sacramental life to Shakespeare. To see the sacraments pictured in the church is a parallel to being instructed by a priest, and in the sixteenth century images still reinforced learning from a primer or Book of Hours. Printing made these books available in great numbers and in a variety of editions. From the beginning of the thirteenth century, English bishops urged their use as supplementary guides. There were many manuals to assist priests in their teaching and to explain to the laity who could read both dogma and practice so that liturgies, already inherently appealing and accessible, could be more fully understood. Characteristic and pertinent to Shakespeare is the *Lay Folk's Catechism* that was established in 1357 and continued up to the Reformation. Its core was the three prayers most frequently said—the Lord's Prayer, Hail Mary, and Apostles' Creed. There was also an explanation of tenets of belief, presented in the order of the professions of faith in the Apostles' Creed. Caxton's *Golden Legend* (1483) presents lives of the saints, but he begins with a review of principal feasts, litanies, and main histories from the Old Testament with the Sundays they are to be read, and he concludes with the History of the

Mass and Twelve Articles of the Faith. Mirk's *Instructions for Parish Priests* is a typical English example of advice about how to carry out duties that include both education and pastoral care—knowledge of Scripture and what is needed for confession and to assist the dying. He demonstrated the use of Scripture and preaching in *Festial*, a popular collection of homilies for main feasts and occasions like funerals. Wynkyn de Worde (d.1534), Caxton's assistant and successor, printed it. De Worde was exclusively a businessman who served the general public; and he expanded with religious titles, including works like Hilton's *Scale of Perfection*, to strengthen his basic list of grammatical texts for schools. He and his rival Richard Pynson (d.1530), who printed a splendid edition of *The Canterbury Tales* and Henry VIII's works against Luther, were the principal early printers in England.

Both Caxton and de Worde were religiously conservative and printed romances. Thus, early English printers sustained the medieval juxtaposition of religion and romance, as an increasingly large numbers of books served the clergy and the needs of a growing literate laity. The same combination of titles occurs with continental printers. In England's pre-Reformation years of the 1520s and 1530s, François Regnault in Paris produced most of the Sarum primers and included significant English sections. He also printed the first edition of the French prose version of the romance *Guy de Warvich* (1525). His books are attractive; the type is clean, and woodcut illustrations engage the reader's attention and gloss the text. A printed *Horae* looks very like a medieval manuscript; some, though comparatively simple, were fine examples of printing. Others were very small sized with few pictures, usually to explain the text, and sold cheaply. The Act of 1534 against foreign printers led to native control. Regnault corresponded with Cromwell; Grafton and Coverdale made a plea on his behalf, but Regnault's market in England was closed.[9] Catholic needs were to give continental printers another role later in the century, in supplying primers and other Catholic texts.

Much more impressive than Regnault's rather simple primers are the *Horae* of Simon Vostre, a printer in Paris who produced at least six editions of the Sarum Hours before 1512 and a fine series of the Hours of Rouen usage. The continuity of medieval devotion and iconography persists in Vostre's beautiful texts, printed on vellum with an extraordinary range of illustrations on every page that puts these books in the first rank of early printing and engraving. Like the illuminations in many devotional manuscripts, the pictures display the exuberance and comprehensiveness of medieval art that embraces subjects from legend and everyday life—whose only immediate relevance is as part of God's creation—and images to illustrate Scriptural stories and church practice. The Seven Sacraments are for the user's meditation. I will base my description on my own copy of an edition of Rouen usage, of 1515, from which I also include photographs.

The first page carries Simon Vostre's name and device, and the reverse is an almanac for fifteen years, 1515–30. This faces a full-page anatomical man represented as a skeleton with the figure of a Fool who kneels between the leg bones (Figure 1). His cap and bells and jester's staff are proper costume to appear as Feste, Touchstone, or Lear's Fool; the surrounding images of star, sun, and moon are signs that appear in the Heavens of the Globe Theatre. There are 127 leaves of vellum, each richly illustrated with woodcuts, and the initials are colored in red or blue with gold. Twenty full-page illustrations with brief captions introduce the Offices, the sections of the *Horae*, but most pages combine fascinating borders with text in Gothic type. The borders are in French, while the Offices are in Latin. Their interest is early signaled in the calendar pages, of which April, "plus ioli," is pertinent (Figure 2). Its thirty days include St. George's feast. At the top are seasonal images of falconry and the zodiacal sign of Aries the ram, and the lower area is filled with a larger cut of pilgrimage (note on the hats the shell of St. James of Compostella and the shrine toward which they proceed), celebrated in Chaucer's *Canterbury Tales*. Along the right side are three smaller images: a Church father, St. Jerome seated in his scriptorium with his lion, the Pope (triple crown) and cardinals (wide hats) at prayer, a noble man and woman and their attendants kneeling in prayer. Other calendar pages similarly juxtapose secular activities with devotional images, and Vostre repeats cuts throughout the volume.

The Seven Sacraments come fairly early. The first section begins with the opening of John's Gospel ("In principio erat verbu[m][10] / In the beginning was the word"), followed by Luke's account of the Annunciation and marriage of Mary. The story continues with Matthew's telling of the journey of Mary and Joseph to Bethlehem, the birth of Jesus, and the coming of the Magi. The final passage is a theological summary from Mark: the twelve disciples, the necessity of baptism for salvation, Jesus' casting out demons, dying to save mankind, and assumption into heaven to sit at the right hand of God. The conclusion is "Illi aute[m] profecti predicaueru[n]t v[er]biq[ue] domino cooperante et sermonem confirmante sequentibus signis. Deo gratias." A full page woodcut introduces the Passion of Our Lord Jesus Christ according to John. There follows a brief prayer to Christ, and then longer devotions to the Blessed Virgin Mary.

At the opening between the first and second prayers to Mary the iconography becomes entirely theological; on four pages the Seven Sacraments are represented with the Seven Virtues, seated female figures that trample underfoot named persons, who epitomize the Vices, in the lower border of each image (Figure 3). The three Theological Virtues come first: "foy" (Faith) holds the

1. Skeleton man with Fool,
Simon Vostre, *Horae* (1515)

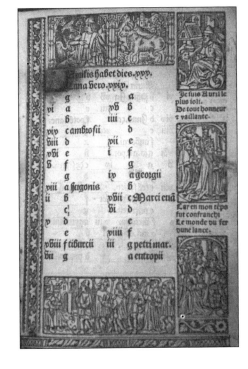

2. Calendar for April,
Simon Vostre, *Horae* (1515)

3. Virtues and Sacraments (Baptism, Confirmation, Exteme Unction), Simon Vostre, *Horae* (1515)

4. Virtues and Sacraments (Holy Orders, Eucharist, Penance, Marriage), Simon Vostre, *Horae* (1515)

Church and tablets of Moses and sits above Mahomet; "esperance" (Hope) holds the traditional anchor and a spade, sign of Adam's labor, while Midas with his bag of gold tries to rise; "charite" touches her heart on her breast and holds a bright star in her left hand; below is a flattened "heres" (Ares). The three Theological Virtues and four Cardinal Virtues combine to make Seven, a union of Platonic and Christian principles for living a virtuous life that dates from at least the fourth century with St. Ambrose. In English the phrase "Cardinal Virtues" was current as early as the *Cursor Mundi* (1300); the four turrets of the Castle of Love and Grace are so identified as part of a Marian iconography. In the fourth space is "justice," first of the four Cardinal Virtues, who holds the scales and sword, while "neron" (Nero) struggles to emerge. The lower border has four images, a panel of two on each page. Three sacraments mark the ages of man: Baptism, Confirmation, Extreme Unction. Shakespeare used this popular concept in its expanded form of seven ages for Jaques's speech in *As You Like It* (II.vii.138–65). The fourth image is of a priest with a book on an easel and a finger raised—emblems of his study and preaching. And printings of Vostre's *Horae* indicate that the laity increasingly exercised the former role.

The second opening has the remaining four sacraments: Holy Orders, Eucharist, Penance, Matrimony (Figure 4). Again the sequence is schematic because it shows the arc of a priest's service. The detail is precise: a Bishop, identified by the mitre, gives the sacraments of Confirmation and Holy Orders; priests offer or preside at the other five sacraments. The outer borders complete the Cardinal Virtues: "force" (Fortitude), a bare-headed female figure grasps the head of a dragon emerging from a tower that is balanced by a banner with a cross; below is Holofornes, Assyrian general and rapist slain by Judith in the Old Testament. Opposite is "prudence," whose emblems are a lighted candle to indicate vigilance and a book of Scripture surmounted by a cross; she has pressed down Sardenapolis, an effeminate prince in Greek legend who burned himself and his wives when under siege. The lower panel shows "atrenp[er]ace" (Temperance), who holds a skull and an image of the Virgin Mary; this iconography is a triumph over death, made possible by Christ's Passion and more accessible through the intervention of the Virgin Mary. The figure underfoot is Tarquin, legendary Roman leader(s) and emblem of rape, whether of the Sabine women or Lucrece. It is worth noting that one of Shakespeare's early works is *The Rape of Lucrece*, a poem about heroic chastity, and that he uses the name "Holofernes" for the pedant, who plans the pageant of Worthies, heroes of romance, in *Love's Labour's Lost* (V.i.114ff). The fourth panel, "lerimite" (hermit), shows a kneeling penitent praying to Christ as Salvator Mundi (Savior of the World), Who blesses and holds the orb.

In this edition Vostre places the Seven Sacraments very precisely to give a clear lesson.[11] At strategic points, he repeats: four leaves along (d1), in the Office of the Virgin (Stabat Mater, Ave Maria, Vera Virgo) Baptism and Confirmation, along with Faith and Hope, are on the verso page. The facing page here carries exclusively secular woodcuts: lovers across the bottom and figures in foliage along the side. The following page has Extreme Unction, with Charity and Justice, also on the opposite side from the initial placement, and here faced by a border of grotesques, weird animals and men riding stick horses. There are also repetitions of separate sacraments. The Penitential Psalms come in about the center of the *Horae*; in a vivid narrative sequence of pictures and captions that tell the story of Susannah and the elders, are Extreme Unction and the studying and preaching priest; thus there is an effect of *memento mori* that anticipates the Hours of the Dead. A second border tells the narrative story of the Prodigal Son; here the sacrament is Communion, a way of returning to the Church. Opposite the picture is of the Bridegroom and the Foolish Virgins, another warning about being always ready to be called to Christ.

The most compelling illustrations are for the Office of the Dead, which is preceded by the Litany of the Saints, with images of Doomsday—rising souls, Hell's mouth, the blessed, a judging God (Figure 5). The remarkable sequence shows the coming of Death (a skeleton with his scythe) to all in a rich encyclopedia of age, gender, class, professions—more comprehensive than the *danse macabre* that originated in France and flourished in wall paintings.[12] The sequence forms the side borders of thirty-five pages, three figures to the page and then two for the last third. The lower borders begin traditionally with the story of Job. Almost exactly midway, the Seven Sacraments are repeated in the lower borders with Death's taking persons from different stations in the borders (Figures 6 and 7). The page after the many comings of Death has two pictures: the Last Judgment, Christ on the rainbow and the souls below, and a standing pilgrim with a lower decorative border. The pertinence of this imagery in the sixteenth century is evident in the success of Hans Holbein the Younger: his *Dance of Death* had many editions, and *The Ambassadors* (1533) includes images of mortality—a Crucifix, broken string, and the skull that gives perspective to a painting of wealth, brilliant science, and art. John Stow described the Dance of Death at St. Paul's in *A Survey of London* (1598), and he added a note to Leland's *Itinerary* (1535–42) about another example at Stratford-upon-Avon.[13] The account of death in *Measure for Measure* (III.i.5–40) is very like such renderings. The attempted destruction of Catholic devotion to prayers for the dead had much to contend with.

The ubiquity of sacred images encourages a sense of signs, that there is a greater reality behind surface appearances. Baptism, a giving of a name and welcoming into the community that is the Church, is a triumph over Satan, an exorcism in which all participate. The priest questions, ''Do you renounce Satan?'' and an affirmative answer comes before the baptism—itself preceded by

5. Doomsday, Litany of the Saints, Simon Vostre, *Horae* (1515)

6. Dance of Death, Sacraments, Simon Vostre, *Horae* (1515)

7. Dance of Death, Sacraments, Simon Vostre, *Horae* (1515)

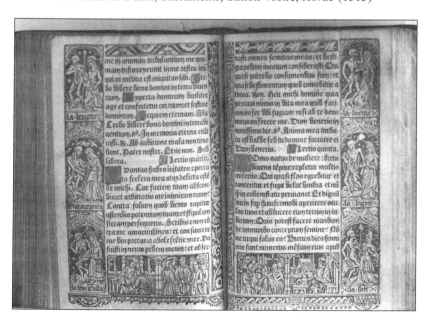

the blessing of salt and water, items that are crucial to human life that is both bitter and sweet. There are three uses of Baptism in Shakespeare's plays. Most famous is at the end of *Henry VIII*, when the King puts a suit to Cranmer for "a fair young maid that yet wants baptism" (V.iii.161). The other two are statements of dogma. Henry V compares right conscience with "Washed / As pure as sin with baptism" (I.ii.32), and Iago thinks Othello's love great enough for him "to renounce his baptism, / All seals and symbols of redeeméd sin" (II.iii.337–38). *The Merchant of Venice* refers to a custom: "In christening thou shalt have two godfathers" (IV.i.399). These are all orthodox views of Baptism, recognized in the Thirty-Nine Articles as well as Catholic dogma.

To begin a life in the Christian community with the banishing of the devil establishes an ongoing need for distinguishing between Vices and Virtues, which are so much a part of medieval theology and art. They are the basis for the simplest allegory, the core of morality plays that echo in Shakespeare's characterizations of Richard III and Falstaff. And such allegory persists in the great Protestant prose epic, *Pilgrim's Progress* by John Bunyan (1628–88), who owes much to the tradition of romance that he knew through chapbooks. He is their only humble reader to record enthusiasm, particularly for *Bevis of Southampton*, which contributed much to the imaginative sweep of his story, its quest and monsters.[14] When knights fight against dragons, or serpents, as in Chrétien de Troyes's *Yvain* and *Guy of Warwick*, when the hero intervenes to save the lion, they are entering the combat between good and evil. The subject is popular in English; for example, in illuminations for the Smithfield *Decretals* and misericords in the cathedrals of Chester, Carlisle, Gloucester, Lincoln, Worcester, Norwich, and Priory Churchs at Lancaster, or Beverley and Ripon.

To see the struggle played out in the human being acknowledges deep human needs on the way to salvation. Penance admits sin and declares the choice to abandon it. Confession to a priest became an annual requirement for lay people in 1215 as part of the reforms of the Fourth Lateran Council. Like all sacraments Penance brings grace, but the process of Confession involves a sustained review of behavior, so that the intention of requiring it was in part educational, to establish an occasion to develop the knowledge of the laity. Penance opens consideration of all Church dogma and how the individual is living his faith, and it is the sacrament that Shakespeare most frequently mentions and in greatest detail.

He introduces Confession in a somewhat orthodox way in *Romeo and Juliet*. Deeply concerned about his son's melancholy, Montague withdraws so that Romeo can talk alone with Benvolio, to whom he may make "true shrift" or reveal the causes of his distress and concurrently ease his isolation. Romeo's religious confessor is Friar Lawrence, who defines a good confession: "Be plain, good son, and homely in thy drift. / Riddling confession finds but riddling shrift"

(II.iv.55–56), and in this world it is a familiar sacrament. Romeo bids the Nurse to tell Juliet to "devise / Some means to come to shrift this afternoon, / And there she shall at Friar Lawrence's cell / Be shrived and married" (II.iv.176–79), but no device is needed since Juliet already "has leave" to go to shrift (II.v.66). The relation of the two sacraments, Penance and Matrimony, is natural, as implied in the Nurse's description when she returns, "See where she comes from shrift with merry look" (IV.ii.15). But there are grave difficulties; Penance is private between penitent and confessor, but Matrimony is to be celebrated before the community and witnessed by the priest. The irony of the Nurse's remark expands when Juliet says that through her confession she has "learned me repent the sin / Of disobedient opposition" to her father's will, and she asks Capulet's forgiveness. One of the ten commandments is to honor father and mother, but with mutual understanding, like that shown in the early family scenes. Capulet's initial solicitude for his daughter (I.ii) and Juliet's obedience and cooperation when she talks with her mother about the engagement to Paris (I.iii) indicate a respectful family. Yet as the play shows, hasty actions, concealment (even those of well-intentioned ecclesiastics), and human assumptions of providence, have fatal consequences. Montague and Capulet seem to be reconciled, after the Prince identifies their fault: "See what a scourge is laid upon your hate, / That heaven finds means to kill your joys with love" (V.iii.292–93). But they are still competing, this time in the grandeur of monuments to be built. The final image is of tombs in a time of "glooming peace," and the play's darkness continues with the Prince's injunction, "Go hence to have more talk of these sad things" (306). The survivors remain centered in the world and self-images.

In *Measure for Measure*, the conclusions are quite different and more hopeful. This may reflect the change in the monarchy. James VI was the son of Roman Catholic Mary Stuart and husband of Anne of Denmark, who had Catholic sympathies. He became king in 1603, and the play was probably presented in 1604. Its title and theme come directly from Scripture, the Sermon on the Mount: "with what iudgment ye judge, ye shal be iudged, and with what measure ye mette, it shal be measured to you againe" (Matthew 7:2). There are other more overt Catholic details, like references to religious orders. Duke Vincentio assumes the guise of a Franciscan friar. Friars Thomas and Peter, whose names evoke the meanings of doubt (twin to humans) and of solid rock, help the Duke in penitence for sloth, a spiritual failure, and in his attempt to make Vienna a place less given to sin. Isabella is a postulant, a young woman about to take vows to become a novice in the order of St. Clare (I.iv), also a Franciscan community.

There is an interesting point about the heroine's name. An Isabel Shakespeare (d.1504) was prioress at Wroxhall Priory, located some twelve miles north of Stratford-upon-Avon. It was founded in 1135 by a knight imprisoned in the Holy Land while on the Crusades; in answer to his prayers, he found himself returned to his own Warwickshire forest. The religious house was among those Henry VIII dissolved early in the century. Another explanation is that "Isabella" was the conventional name for a serious and competent woman's part because of the talents of the distinguished Italian player Isabella Andreine.

Saint Francis founded his order in the thirteenth century to meet current needs in the cities that were rapidly developing in Europe, since monastic religious communities, like the Benedictines and Cistercians, were usually in isolated places. Shakespeare again chooses the Franciscan order, a pre-Reformation community that began in reaction against worldly corruption and has been noted for its spirituality, care for the poor and needy, and its founder's peacemaking, rather than intellectual or political endeavors like those of the Jesuit order that answers Counter-Reformation needs. Shakespeare's specifying Franciscans may indicate a wish to be circumspect about Jesuit influence on Roman Catholics in Elizabethan England, but it may just as well be a comment of longing for an earlier and simpler Catholicism than that developing in response to the Protestant Reformation.

Indeed the setting of *Measure for Measure*, Vienna (really an alterity for London), alludes to a center for Catholic and Protestant debate; it is beset with evil that stems in part from misunderstanding, or ill-advised choosing, of religious principles and consequent exploitation for personal gain. Duke Vincentio begins by reacting against a self-defeating combination of "strict statutes and most biting laws" and laxity in their enforcement (I.iii. 19–31). He assumes the role of Franciscan Friar Lodovico, after receiving a habit and instruction from Friar Thomas so that he may "formally in person bear [himself] / Like a true friar" (47–48). In this he echoes the not unusual choice of nobles to become a part of a religious community after an active life in the world, or to live a quasi-monastic life as did Philip II at El Escorial. Vincentio's first effort is a corporal work of mercy, to visit those who are in prison, a service that presents him with many who need the instruction and comfort of confession. But it is important to recognize that the Friar/Duke, although he identifies himself as "confessor to Angelo" (III.i.169), does not blaspheme by a mock conferring of sacraments; rather, his work in the prison becomes an embodiment of the spiritual works of mercy: he counsels the doubtful, instructs the ignorant, admonishes the sinner, comforts the sorrowful, forgives injuries, bears wrongs patiently, and prays for the living and the dead. The corporal and spiritual works of mercy are the Church's formulations of the message of the Gospels, a plan for living in the material world. The Sermon on the Mount, which as already noted Shakespeare glosses in *Measure for Measure*, specifies actions needed for the second of the great Commandments: "Thou shalt loue thy neighbour as thy self" (Matthew 22:39).

A frequent reading casts the Duke as a sleeping but awakened Justice tempered by Isabella's Mercy. Mercy and Justice, two of the four daughters of God (Psalm 85), are here united, as they are in the morality play *The Castle of Perseverance*, but without a simple breaking into separate allegorical characters. The Friar/Duke leads penitents (even the reluctant) to contrition and a course of action that restores good to the community. He first speaks to Juliet—a notable repetition of name from the early tragedy—beloved of Claudio: "Repent you, fair one, of the sin you carry?" (II.iii.19), and she replies with the directness and brevity that Friar Lawrence described to Romeo as best shrift: "I do, and bear the shame most patiently" (20). Claudio's Juliet acknowledges the lovers' "mutual" consent and accepts that as a woman—the gender that traditionally upholds the ideal of moral sexual behavior—her sin was greater. A brief theological education discerns a sorrow for the sin because of shame from sorrow in offending God, a sorrow of love, not of fear (31–37), and Juliet makes a good confession, as the Duke's parting words mark: "Grace go with you. *Benedicite!*" (40). Even the news of Claudio's impending execution does not alter her patience.

Claudio, whom the Duke next visits, shares Juliet's penitence and conviction; but he falters when there is a prospect of pardon. For this searing human conflict—the same love of life that makes even the best knight put aside honor in the romance *Sir Gawain and the Green Knight*—Shakespeare wrote one of his most compelling and provocative scenes. Friar Ludovico intervenes between chiding Isabella and cringing, frightened Claudio. Although he has heard Claudio's most memorable speech about death—"Ay, but to die and go we know not where, / To lie in cold obstruction and to rot"—his counsel to the doomed young man is, "prepare yourself for death. . . . Tomorrow you must die. Go to your knees and make ready" (III.i.119–20,170–72). This is the message of the Hours of Death, of pictures of the *danse macabre*, of the Summoning of Death in *Everyman*, and countless Doomsdays, like that on the wall-painting (c.1500) of the Guild Chapel in Stratford. Medieval Christendom expresses the belief in Heaven and Hell, and no sympathy for Claudio's youth and essential good intentions, or uneasiness about the virulence of Isabella's resentment against his willingness to sacrifice her chastity for his life, can alter the reality. Thus Claudio's third response is to accept his human failing and to try to make amends, "Let me ask my sister pardon" (173). Initially, he seemed to understand and embrace the consolation of the Duke's advice, when he properly stated, "To sue to live, I find I seek to die, / And, seeking death, find life. Let it come on" (42–43). But given a possibility of escape, Claudio lets fears and self-interest win out over patience and faith.

The success of the Duke's second attempt to teach and lead the sinner shows the efficacy of ongoing efforts like annual confession. Indeed there is no end to God's grace. Even the long imprisoned and impenitent Barnardine—careless, drunken, having no fear of death (IV.ii.142–46; IV.iii.67–69)—is given another chance to prepare for death when he is not needed as the substitute for Claudio's corpse because another prisoner dies: "O, 'tis an accident that heaven provides!" At the end, the Duke forgives all his faults, with reliance upon the offices of the Church: "Friar, advise him; / I leave him to your hand" (V.i.496–97). Similarly, the Duke perseveres with a bawd like Pompey, recommending "correction and instruction," the way of penance (III.ii.33). His "Go mend, go mend" echoes Christ, Who quietly transformed sinners like the woman taken in adultery (John 8.3–11).

Even those who are holy need the grace of the sacraments. When the Duke turns to Isabella he descries a beauty of soul to match her physical beauty, outer fair showing inner good. However, this can be sustained only by the divine: "grace, being the soul of your complexion, shall keep the body of it fair" (184–85). And Isabella has yet to complete a thorough examination of conscience, to experience contrition, and to manage the difficulty of penance that turns thought into action. Explaining his intention, "To the love I have of doing good a remedy presents itself," the Duke assures Isabella that she will "do no stain to your own gracious person" (103–04) and further declares, "Virtue is bold, and goodness never fearful" (210). He then proposes the bed-trick—a Shakespearean addition to the source—a material act that will lead to the sorting out of the mismatches between sex and marriage that provide the surface or worldly deeds of *Measure for Measure*, which is his severest study of the sacrament of Matrimony in this most overtly Catholic play.

It is well-identified as a "problem play" because understanding the issues and Shakespeare's treatment of them is unusually difficult. Unlike other sacraments, Matrimony is not conferred by the priest, but by the man and woman upon each other. The priest's role is witness, and that is a late formulation in the history of the medieval Church. Angelo, easily seen as a Puritan in his excessive zeal and severity, is an extremist in following the letter of Mosaic law that makes death the penalty for adultery. In fact, he misreads by equating fornication with adultery to condemn Claudio. The relation between Juliet and Claudio was mutually agreed and based on "a true contract . . . she is fast my wife," but for a formal declaration "of outward order" not carried out "for propagation of a dower" (I.ii. 142–46). While money was the occasion of the concealment, its purpose was to secure friends' approbation (148–50), that is, to celebrate within the community Matrimony, the sacrament which is both most private and the foundation of society. In contrast, the marriage contract between Angelo and Mariana failed because of Angelo's avarice. Although "affianced to her by oath, and the nuptial appointed," he "swallowed his vows whole, pretending in her discoveries of dishonor" (III.ii.216, 228–29), when her dowry was lost in her brother's shipwreck. Angelo's self-interest, his greed, pride, and hypocrisy in protecting his reputation, make him the greater sinner. These are the reasons for Isabella's agreeing to appear to receive the lustful Angelo so that he will finally consummate the marriage with a willingly substituted Mariana. Assured of the Friar's respect and that Angelo is her "husband on a pre-contract / To bring you thus together, 'tis no sin, / Sith that the justice of your title to him / Doth flourish the deceit" (IV.i.52–53, 71–74), Mariana will gain her husband and free Isabella's brother Claudio without dishonor (III.ii. 245–60). The third marriage is that of Lucio to Mistress Kate Keepdown. Again there was a contract; she "was with child by him in the Duke's time; he promised her marriage" (III.ii. 194–95). At the end of a long fifth act of resolving promises, Lucio is compelled to marry her (V.i.520–24, 529), just as Friar Peter completed the marriage ceremony between Angelo and Mariana (382–86), after she faced Angelo with their "vowed contract" and the consummation of the marriage (214–18). Not the least significant dimension is that the women consistently accept the men, forgiving grave mistreatment and disloyalty. This is an imitation of the Virgin Mary's acceptance of her role as the mother of Jesus, expressed at the Annunciation in the Magnificat, which is a supreme act of obedience that is not passive self-resignation but an opening to the possibility of future activity, the salvation of the world: "Beholde, the seruant of the Lord: be it vnto me according to thy worde" (Luke 1.36).

Whether the Duke's promise to Isabella and request that she accompany him means that there will be a fourth marriage, is a problem that much exercises current directors of the closing scene. His last words suggest Matrimony: "I have a motion much imports your good, / Whereto if you'll a willing ear incline, / What's mine is yours, and what is yours is mine.—" (V.i.546–48). At very least there is a delay. But Vincentio and Isabella, neither of whom has managed very well unmarried, have advantages over the other couples that are far beyond social rank. Each has faced and admitted personal limitations and transcended them through service for the well-being of others, as the sorting out of the marriages shows. In a play so unrelenting in its consideration of sexuality, but also an allegory of the union of Mercy and Justice, the final focus is on charitable deeds. The Duke, who has learned as much as he taught through his work in the prison, returns the initiative of clerical ministry to Friar Peter, making him the chief agent in bringing the characters together (V.i.158–64) and speaking the truth publicly. Friar Peter introduces Isabella to the Duke (V.i.20), who sends her to prison so that she becomes one in need of mercy. This is a prelude to her response to Mariana's cry, "Sweet Isabel, take my part!" (438). Isabella's case is worthy of a confession manual, a distinction between thought and deed in the defining of sin. But the key point is that she pleads for Angelo, even though she believes that he had Claudio killed; this act of compassion acknowledges the arbitrariness of justice and law and that humans survive only with mercy. Thus the Duke forgives Lucio, who wrongfully, ostentatiously, and cruelly attacked him with lies and flaunted his authority and character.

Men and women should imitate the sacrifice of the Crucifixion, an event that is not just, but freely chosen by Jesus and repeated in every Mass in the sacrament of the Eucharist. In the history plays, a special case because they chronicle England's part in medieval Christendom, Shakespeare sustains many signs of Catholicism, but the oath "by the mass," occurs fifteen times in Shakespeare's plays, and not only in the history plays where "Christ" and "Christendom" are named. *Measure for Measure* has many echoes of Scripture, some already mentioned. To Escalus, an ancient lord wiser and more virtuous than most in Vienna, the Duke's initial greeting is "Bliss and goodness on you!" (III.ii.210), and he parts with the "Pax vobiscum" of the Mass, "Peace be with you!" (253). There are plays on *Grace* (noble title) and *grace* (of God), and Angelo fuses these at the end when he says to the Duke, "Your Grace, like power divine / Hath looked upon my passes" (377–78). Friar Peter reports, "Twice have the trumpets sounded" (IV.vi.12) to announce the final act, in which there is a kind of Judgment Day, when both Mercy and Justice are satisfied. There are many convincing critical arguments for the play as allegory, both general and historical, but the contexts favor an emphasis upon religion and the importance of the sacraments.

The self examination of Penance is readily transformed into modern psychology. The process of review and choice is exacting, and analogous to the technique of soliloquy, when a character speaks his mind aloud. It is most familiar in Hamlet's "To be, or not to be, that is the question" (III.i.57), usually seen as ultimately derived from the Book of Job with some influence from Montaigne. Although *Hamlet* is nominally set in the early medieval world of saga and chronicle, Shakespeare also makes observations about Elizabethan England. The play has been tied to the tradition of preaching, so crucial in Protestantism, that encouraged thought and repentance. All of the Seven Deadly Sins are in *Hamlet*—lechery, gluttony (especially drunkenness), envy, anger, covetousness, sloth, and pride from which the others spring. No play has provoked more controversy or varied interpretations: the hero's near-damnation, the appealing personal archetype of all thinkers, a cultural history of the changes from medieval to Renaissance and Reformation mentality, Shakespeare's lament for the Catholic cause.

I want briefly to suggest how I see the play's relation to Shakespeare, Catholicism, and romance. *Hamlet* contains many inherited beliefs and forms from Catholicism. Perhaps most obvious is concern with the souls departed. The ghost's uneasy wandering expresses anxiety about Purgatory, which Hamlet's father cannot describe to the living (I.v.10 23). Ophelia's ravings offer flowers in remembrance of the dead (her father Polonius) and conclude with a song that

ends in a prayer followed by her own prayer, " 'God ha' mercy for his soul!' /
And of all Christian souls, I pray God. God b' wi' you'' (IV.v.202–3). Hamlet's
macabre jesting about the corpse of Polonius (IV.iii) anticipates the vivid *ars
moriendi* in the gravediggers scene, where the two clowns engage in a theological debate about "Christian burial" in "Christian ground"; they too combine
the macabre and comic detachment, showing a thorough familiarity with attitudes toward death in a construct of the Corpus Christi plays from Adam to
Doomsday; the conclusion is a prayer for Ophelia, "One that was a woman,
sir, but rest her soul, she's dead'' (V.i.136). Laertes asks for more "ceremony,"
and the Priest explains the complexity of Church decisions about burial, noting
a generous interpretation—because the state intervened when Claudius ordered
enlargement of her obsequies—and also the ideal of "the service of the dead /
To sing a requiem and such rest . . . to peace-parted souls" (225–38). When
Hamlet dies, Horatio pronounces, "Good night, sweet Prince, / And flights of
angels sing thee to thy rest!'' (V.ii.361–62), a line that echoes the Catholic
requiem—"In Paradisum deducat te angeli . . . aeternam habeas requiem" (May
the angels bear thee to paradise . . . and mayst thou have eternal rest). In romance
angels bear away the souls of heroes, such as Guy or Lancelot, or Roland in
the earlier *chanson de geste*.[15] Shakespeare puts this on the stage in *Henry VIII*,
when Katherine has a vision that she sees as angels: "*as it were by inspiration,
she makes in her sleep signs of rejoicing, and holdeth up her hands to heaven*"
(IV.ii.82 stage direction). In romance and on the stage the audience beholds
virtue rewarded by Heaven, the last of the Four Last Things.

Hamlet initially is tied to Protestant ideas because he anachronistically at-
tends the university at Wittenberg (I.ii.113, 119, 164, 168). There Martin Luther
(1483–1546), then a Catholic monk, in 1517 posted his Ninety-five Theses on
the door of the castle church. These challenges about current practices in the
Catholic Church culminated in the Reformation. But Hamlet's Protestant education does not ultimately prevail; he does not return to Wittenberg, and Catholic
ideals are reiterated as he approaches death. After initial fury against the corruption of the world and a proud aggression about his role—"The time is out
of joint. O cursèd spite / That ever I was born to set it right!'' (I.v.197–98)—
to both know and enforce the truth, Hamlet's last actions are very different. He
acknowledges "in my heart there was a kind of fighting / That would not let
me sleep," but early "indiscretion" has taught that "There's a divinity that
shapes our ends, / Rough-hew them how we will'' (V.ii.4–10). Horatio's warnings against treachery are cast aside when Hamlet echoes Christ's words (Matthew 10:29), "There is a special providence in the fall of a sparrow" (217–18).
Death is part of the divine plan, and man's only role is how to respond to an
event that is inevitable and that he cannot control: "The readiness is all" (220).
At the end of *Hamlet* there are more dead bodies on stage than in any other

play, as the cycle of murder and revenge concludes. Yet there is reconciliation. After the hero's revenge by killing Claudius, a violent and ugly act, and Laertes' revenge and treachery in carrying out the King's plot by using the envenomed sword, the two dying young men "exchange forgiveness" after admitting their guilt, like a confession of sin, consistent with the sacrament of Extreme Unction, received as part of a good death. Much has been made of Hamlet's concern that he be understood and well remembered, a kind of Renaissance cum Scandinavian saga wish for fame. He enjoins Horatio, "Report my cause aright" (341), and urges him, "Absent thee from felicity awhile, / And in this harsh world draw thy breath in pain / To tell my story" (349–51). One reading of *Hamlet* is "as looking back over the tragic events of sixteenth-century English history and lamenting the sad passing of Catholic England."[16] But Hamlet's last words are support for a stable community under Fortinbras, and then "the rest is silence" (360). This is a quiet acceptance of mystery beyond political argument; "felicity" is in eternity, not in this world. This is an orthodox view; but Hamlet shows no joy, the spiritual quickening found in romance and more surely in Catholic than in Protestant theology. Part of the explanation is the absence of sacraments, images, liturgies, and devotions that enriched life both spiritually and imaginatively, not least by positive celebration rather than denial and obsession with sin in the severest terms of St. Augustine.

One example will serve as a summary comment on the complexity of change and continuity, and the persistence of a Catholic habit of mind. The large woodcut that introduces Edward VI's reign in Foxe's *Actes and Monumentes* shows changes in the Church of England that is a severe classical building which fills two thirds of the space (Figure 8). Above it is the "Ship of the Romish Church" into which recusants carry "trinkets" (church vessels) and the "Papists' Psalty," that were taken from "The Temple well purged," and not consigned to a large bonfire for "Burning of Images." A man pulls at a rope to bring down an image of the Virgin in an outside niche. Two thirds of the picture, the center, show the present temple: on the left a royal figure presents BIBLIA to kneeling men on his right, while courtiers stand on the left. In the largest part of the temple sit a closely gathered group who look up to a preacher in a pulpit; they include a woman holding a book and another entering the door with a child. Above the congregation in a large space with slender columns and round windows is "The Com[m]union Table," which is bare but for a plain cup and bread, and under the side arch is a baptismal fount with a group standing round. The iconography is clear: exile or destruction for Catholic items, royal sanction for the Reformed Church with emphasis upon reading the Bible and sermons, with women visible participants, and only two sacraments. There is an obvious irony in the reliance upon images in Foxe's *Actes and Monumentes*: Reformers who destroyed the old images of Catholicism replaced them with alternative ones to promote their new religion. This is especially bizarre for the Ship of the Church, a familiar image to show the spread of Catholicism in the early Middle Ages. The presence of women in the woodcut supports a frequent argument that women's situation became stronger with Protestantism.[17] But this is to ignore substantial evidence for the place of women in the Middle Ages, as indicated by the image of the Virgin Mary in the woodcut, the icon to be toppled. Devotion to Mary, and to many female saints whose legends, like those associated with the Miracles of the Virgin, were a source of inspiration, and the pragmatic experience of nuns who had significant autonomy within their religious communities—these support the view of medieval women's influence. A corollary is the prominence of women in romance, which they both inspired and gave patronage; such narratives are Shakespeare's inheritance.

The Romance Tradition

Penitence is crucial in the Pilgrimage of Life, the seeking that is both a metaphor and the reason for journeys to shrines, which means psychologically a way of coming to new understanding by altering one's situation. Few dynamics are more thoroughly explored by Shakespeare, one of whose most frequently employed devices is to remove his characters from the solidity and reassurance of their usual situations. Medieval romances are structured by settings forth into unknown domains, often forests fraught with danger, as knights embark on quests. This is the traditional role of the male, but there are a number of medieval romances that tell of young women who undertake comparable adventures to secure their identity. Shakespeare's plays contain similar journeys into forests or countryside (*The Merchant of Venice, As You Like It, The Winter's Tale*— to name a few) that lead to the kind of reassessment that comes with Confession and also a return to live a better life, after undergoing hardships and self-sacrifice.

The popularity of stories of questing knights, warrior kings, and chivalric companions has somewhat obscured the part that women play in medieval narratives, where they are often thought to be either devoted (or disdainful) ladies to serve or provocative forth-putting Saracens who are attracted to Christian Crusaders, whom they help to escape and wed after religious conversion. But there are strong precedents for the complexity of Shakespearean women who are resilient and resourceful, overcoming difficulties, including parental authority, to marry the men of their choice. A splendid example is Caxton's *Paris and Vienne* (1485), perhaps his best translation, a romance that anticipates many of the situations just discussed in *Romeo and Juliet* and *Measure for Measure* and that are more completely explored in the romances. Vienne's father deems Paris an unworthy choice for husband, and there are at least ten years of separation before the couple wed joyously and with approval in the community. *Paris and Vienne* is a composite of traditional romance themes and situations—obligations of filial piety, loyalty of lovers, rival suitors, chastity, elopement, coping with suicidal wishes, disguise, a religious acting as intermediary, journeys and separations, knightly prowess, and so on. But it is the character of Vienne that is most engaging. Like so many of Shakespeare's heroines, she dresses as a boy to ease her escape, she balances the claims of father and husband, and of a man's worth in relation to social position. Vienne is competent, witty, ingenious, brave, passionate, loyal, and quite attractive. The narrative is exciting, but Caxton's religious interests color it so that ideas of pilgrimage and penance hold its diversity together. The young lovers have many physical adventures but also spiritual development, for although they are always charming they learn through hardship and denial to become even more appealing. Caxton increased the moral orthodoxy of his source, adding positive religious references as well as chivalric details in his translation. *Paris and Vienne* is a typical combination of romance and religion, which seems to have assured success. The morally engaged life was a compelling topic.

The most popular Middle English poem, if one judges by the number of manuscripts, is *The Prick of Conscience;* it survives in 114 manuscripts, more than *Piers Plowman* or *The Canterbury Tales.* Immediately before the Reformation the medieval mystics were also much read: Theodoric Root printed Richard Rolle's *Explanation of Job* at Oxford in 1483, and Wynkyn de Worde published three other Rolle texts early in the sixteenth century. De Worde also printed Walter Hilton's *Scale of Perfection* (1490 and 1521), as did Julian Notary and Pepwell. Pynson printed Thomas à Kempis's *Imitation of Christ* in 1503 and de Worde in 1517. *Dives and Pauper*, a dialogue formed about the Ten Commandments with many lively episodes and examples, was printed by Pynson (1493), de Worde (1496), and Thomas Berthelet (1536). Catholic laity had a variety of religious texts to choose among, and they formed a habit of mind that combined piety and a medieval familiarity with the sacred that allowed the ordinary.

Chaucer was, of course, the acknowledged great English poet; his poems were issued several times by early printers Caxton, Pynson, and de Worde. During Shakespeare's lifetime there were two major new editions of Chaucer's *Works*, William Thynne's in 1532, dedicated to Henry VIII, and Thomas Speght's in 1598 and 1602. Chaucer's religious romances and saints' legends reflect medieval idealization of women, which also includes the determination that underlies Shakespeare's heroines. Characters like patient Griselda in the "Clerk's Tale" and Constance in the "Man of Law's Tale" are too often dismissed as flat, mere allegorical figures and victims. Yet their surmounting of oppression, both personal and political, models the independent heroine. They are touched with humanity, as are his virgin saints of pagan Rome—Virginia in the "Physician's Tale" and Cecilia in the "Second Nun's Tale," who are precedents for Marina's miraculous powers in *Pericles*. Saints are honored on their feast days, in carvings, paintings, and illuminations in *Horae*, and in collections of legends. These narratives are often very similar to romances, with extraordinary adventurous journeys and bizarre encounters, suffering, and miraculous triumphs. Such stories illustrate and encourage the Catholic belief in mystery. Lives of the saints were a staple of reading; for example, in the Middle English *South English Legendary*, Osbern Bokenham's *Legends of Holy Women*, separate lives of Saints Dorothy, Katherine, Bridget, and plays like the Digby *Mary Magdalene*. Caxton's *The Golden Legend* (1483), Englished from the original of Jacobus de Voraigne (c.1275), began a tradition of printed versions that expanded knowledge for the liturgical feasts of the year. Recusant saints' lives of the sixteenth century alter the medieval combination of adventure and hagiography by eliminating romance elements to record recent Catholic martyrdoms as examples of fortitude. But the tradition of romance, especially of the nature of women, is a model for silent patience and acceptance that repeat Christ's meekness at the Crucifixion—the ultimate heroism, albeit not the usual male gesture and speech of self definition—and the Virgin Mary's Magnificat. Images, plays, legends, romances—the heritage of medieval Christendom was drastically changed in the sixteenth century; but, to use a distinction of scholastic philosophy between accidents and substance, the surface and the essence were not the same, and much lingered as the habit of mind.

2
REFORMATION CHANGES AND LINGERING IMAGES

The pervasiveness of piety, particularly expressed in lay participation in the church, the richness and effectiveness of rituals to define life, the beauty and variety of ecclesiastical art, all argue the strength and popularity of Catholicism as expressed by late-medieval Christendom. The Church was a vital and growing social institution, but the reality of the English Protestant Reformation, although it is no longer accepted as rapidly achieved by popular enthusiasm, is also undeniable. In short, the process of change was both longer and more complex than that defined by historians who assume progress and follow the story John Foxe told in *The Actes and Monumentes; or, Book of Martyrs*, in 1563. Greater knowledge of late fifteenth-and early sixteenth-century religious experiences changes the view of Catholicism to make clear that the English break with Rome led to the decline of Catholicism and not the other way around. The impulses were more political, economic, and personal than religious. This revisionist understanding of the Protestant Reformation is crucial to an argument about Shakespeare and Catholicism. His discreet reliance upon the older traditions is credible when we identify the salient feature of the Reformation as struggle, a long period of uncertainty with impositions, resistance, and ignoring of laws in a deeply divided country in which ordinary people kept an essentially Catholic view of life and salvation while adapting to constant alterations—rather as post-Vatican II Catholics have in the twentieth century. The attitudes and efforts to enforce Protestantism vary greatly; they were much stronger in London, Essex, and Kent, and the universities, particularly Cambridge, than in the country, especially in Lancashire and the North. There the Pilgrimage of Grace (five northern risings in the autumn and winter of 1536–37, with the major one in October 1536) was an early manifestation of opposition to Henry VIII's policies and to attacks on the Church. This continued: in

1571 an intense search for recusants in Lancashire found fifty-four lay recusants (including forty gentry) and thirty-eight recusant priests; in 1600 the Jesuit Richard Cowling reported that there were so many Catholics in Lancashire that priests were able to move about freely and easily and that lay people knelt openly before them to receive a blessing.

Between Elizabeth's accession in 1558 and her death in 1603 there were many controversies, as there were into the seventeenth century. The scale and characteristics of disputation are evident in the printed sources, of which at least 630 survive. The commonplace use of the Marprelate Controversy—Puritan complaints against Anglican orthodoxy, the pamphlet exchanges of the 1580s, especially between Gabriel Harvey and Thomas Nashe—by literary historians has obscured the more numerous and theologically oppositional writings between Catholics and Protestants that are less frequently cited. This is a typical illustration of a selective emphasis to which revisionist historians of the Reformation offer a counter argument.

As studies of data increased, Christopher Haigh in 1987 identified several key areas for reconsideration and evaluation:

> The existence of long-term religious discontents can be disputed, the significance of Protestantism as a progressive ideological movement can be doubted, the continuing popularity and prestige of the Catholic Church can be stressed, and the political Reformation can be explained as the outcome of factional competition for office and influence. In fact, the revising of the English Reformation is only in small part a consequence of the deliberate use of revisionist approaches. It is much more the result of the exploitation of neglected evidence and the execution of regional studies. (2–3) . . . The long-term causes of the Reformation—the corruption of the Church and the hostility of the laity—appear to have been historical illusions.   (*English Reformation Revised*, 6).

Published historical data, read and selected in contradictory ways, is monumental. My brief survey gives only enough information to indicate the kinds of available materials, with full references in the Bibliographical Note, and to show evidence for reevaluation.

The usual case against priests centers on sexual misconduct and neglect of duties, but data do not support it. M. Bowker tallies incidents in Lincolnshire, the diocese that included 21.5 percent of all parishes in England. From 1514 to 1521 there were only twenty-five reports of misconduct with women in over one thousand parishes. Other areas have similar findings: in the arch deaconry of Winchester, only eleven cases in 230 parishes in 1527–28; in 200 Norwich parishes, only eight priests were charged in 1538. Complaints against negligence in Lincolnshire were similarly limited. Such figures report charges; there may have been suppressions of failures. However, if anti-clericalism was widespread, as today's endless scandals of priestly misconduct suggest, this seems unlikely; a sense of it comes from the famous scandals at high level. Cardinal Wolsley was the impetus for many attacks, notably the literary satires of writers such as John Skelton, Jerome Barlow, James Fish, and William Tyndale—the last three were active Lutheran propagandists, and Skelton wrote for the Howards, who opposed Wolsley. Anxiety about the cardinal's power dominated the passage of three anti-church parliamentary statutes in 1529, but this "Anticlerical Commons" passed twenty-three other bills not about ecclesiastical issues. Responses to Wolsey were mixed. Shakespeare's subtle and paradoxical treatment in *Henry VIII* reflects an enmity against abuses, but also a sympathetic treatment of Wolsey's remorse after his fall from favor.

In 1532 the Commons Supplication against the Ordinaries passed by a narrow margin. Probably the work of Thomas Cromwell, who needed to strengthen his political position as progress for Henry's divorce faltered, this broad attack on church courts is now generally judged unfounded. Another possible explanation was the Commons' anxiety because of burnings for heresy in 1531–32, when the Church acted against educated clergy and Londoners, leaders of Protestant reform. Whatever its origin, the impact of the Supplication was a movement away from church courts to strengthen the circumstances of common lawyers, who were more numerous than the cases available, by increasing their jurisdiction. It seems likely that self-interests, not religious attitudes, were the motivation for change.

The number of trial scenes in Shakespeare's plays indicates a preoccupation with law and justice; words like *law*, *just*, *judge*, *judgment*, and *trial* occur frequently.[1] There are alternative terms, but *lawyers* appears less than a dozen times in Spevack's *Harvard Concordance* of Shakespeare's works; this paucity suggests some possibilities. The most specific allusion to ties between religion and lawyers is in *As You Like It*: Jaques calls the lawyer's melancholy "politic," which means calculated (IV.i.13). Earlier, Rosalind initiates and sustains her first meeting with Orlando in the forest by quick and witty comments about how Time moves in divers ways with divers persons. It gallops for a thief to the gallows, but stays with "lawyers in the vacation; for they sleep between term and term, and then they perceive not how Time moves" (III.ii.325–27). The quip precedes Rosalind's statement that Time "ambles . . . with a priest that lacks Latin" (312–13). This is provocative and but one image of the old church in the play. A less specific reference is also embedded in apparent raillery. And Lear's Fool equates "nothing" with the lawyer's counsel: "Then 'tis like the breath of an unfee'd lawyer; you / gave me nothing for't. Can you make no use of nothing, nuncle?" (I.iv.127–29).

Most notoriously Dick the butcher, a follower of Jack Cade, the posturing rebel peasant leader, advises: "The first thing we do, let's kill all the lawyers" (*2 Henry VI*, IV.ii.74). The First Messenger reports Cade's actions to King Henry VI and his Queen: "All scholars, lawyers, courtiers, gentlemen, / They call false caterpillars and intend their death" (IV.iv.36–37). Later Dick is more selective, when he wants from Cade, "Only that the laws of England may come out of your mouth" (IV.vii.5). Cade's rebellion is one of Shakespeare's fullest treatments of the commons. The play, which conflates events of 1450 and the Peasants' Revolt of 1381, resonates with religious events of the sixteenth century. Interpretations stress Shakespeare's indebtedness to Hall's *Chronicle*, especially the spectacle of the horror of civil unrest, and an unsympathetic presentation of the mob, albeit Cade is encouraged by the aristocratic York, who is plotting for his own advantage (IV.ix.30). There is much anti-intellectual action, perhaps a gloss on Protestant insistence upon the individual's faith known through reading and sermons and Catholic reliance upon the sacraments and support of the community of saints, living and dead. A dialogue with the clerk turns on the dangers of reading, and Cade orders him hanged "with his pen and inkhorn about his neck" (IV.ii.106). Later Cade judges anyone who can speak French a traitor (161–62), and Lord Saye's speaking Latin elicits the same sentence (IV.vii.54). Saye's apologia—which includes his use of knowledge, "seeing ignorance is the curse of God / Knowledge the wing wherewith we fly to heaven" (54–75)—evokes momentary remorse in Cade (101); but he quickly decides that Saye "shall die, an it be but for pleading so well for his life" (102–3). The rebel's outrageous demands to be king, aristocratic posturing, violent destructiveness and killings, mitigate even valid claims for social justice. Yet Cade respects the achievements of Henry V, an anticipation of the way Clifford and Buckingham win the commons back to King Henry VI (IV.viii.33). Cade finds himself alone, and after five days hiding in the woods without food, Alexander Iden, "an esquire of Kent" discovers him and does not want to fight "a poor famished man" (IV.10.42–43). But Cade persists and falls (74). When Iden identifies him, he curses and damns the wretch, and then brings his head to the King (V.i), who makes Iden a knight and gives him a thousand marks. The Cade scenes are primarily about rebellion, but they also raise issues of law and varieties of justice.

Three other references to lawyers come as parts of comparisons, and all are unsavory. In *Timon of Athens* the Fool talks of usurers and bawds; a whore-master is a spirit said to take many guises: "sometimes 't appears like a lord, sometimes like a lawyer, sometimes like a philosopher, . . . often like a knight" (II.ii.111–15). One of Timon's exhortations is: "Crack the lawyer's voice, / That he may never more false title plead, / Nor sound his quillets shrilly" (IV.iii.155–

57). Timon gives gold, but with a punning curse that suggests the Four Last Things: "Do you damn others, and let this damn you, / And ditches grave you all!'' (167–68). These images and lawyers recur in the gravediggers' scene of *Hamlet*. Hamlet queries when he tosses up another skull: "Why may that not be the skull of a lawyer? Where be his quidities now, his quillities, his cases, his tenures, and his tricks? Why does he suffer this mad knave now to knock him about the sconce with a dirty shovel, and will not tell him of his action of battery?'' (V.i. 98–101). Shakespeare echoes both a medieval *memento mori*, a showing that death comes to all, and the cries of *ubi sunt*, the rhetorical asking *where are* the past concerns and achievements of life. Hamlet's view of the lawyer's process becomes a hyperbolic comparison in *The Winter's Tale* for the archetypal conman. Among the servant's claims for Autolycus, are "points more than all the lawyers in Bohemia can learnedly handle'' (IV.iv.205–06), identified as among his "unbraided wares'' (not used or damaged 203); but the point (heading of the argument) remains unscrupulous self-aggrandizement. Similarly, Cloten uses imagery of gold, bribery, and a lawyer when he seeks help with his suit of Imogen, who resists him (*Cymbeline*, II.iii.75–77).

The immediate consequence of the shift to common lawyers in the mid-1530s was a decline in litigation, followed by a resumption of plaintiff use of church courts to resolve disputes, when there was no further legislation against them. Accessible church courts handled a mass of litigation to the 1590s, with relatively low costs and efficiency. Figures from the dioceses show little resistance to the paying of tithes: three suits from 339 parishes in Winchester in 1529, four from 650 parishes in Lichfield in 1530, and four from 250 parishes in Canterbury in 1531. Predictably the record for London is higher, but even there from 1521 to 1546 tithe suits were brought in only one third of the parishes. And this is reduced because 70 percent of the wills included payments for "forgotten tithes.'' A strong modern tradition of the separation of church and state necessitates an adjustment to recognize that before the Reformation ecclesiastical courts were performing capably, or so the paucity of protests against their judgments implies.

Another index of attitudes toward the priesthood is the number of ordinations. Figures indicate that the attractiveness and possibilities for parish priests were highest in the 1510s and 1520s, when the population was about the same as in the 1420s. From 1504 to 1529 about twice as many priests were ordained each year (and in some years three times) in the Lichfield diocese as had been between 1364–1384. In York figures for the 1520s are almost twice those for the late fourteenth and mid-fifteenth century. This may still reflect the need consequent on the Black Death, but such substantial increases argue strong confidence in the clergy. The rates vary with the areas; the south is significantly smaller than the north and midlands, and explanations are not simple. A major change in ordinations comes after 1529 and is directly tied to the dissolution of the monasteries that meant a loss of places and more competition for benefices. Between 1536 and 1539, 900 monasteries, with one fourth of the agricultural land, were closed. The changes were momentous and included the disruption of the economy and social shifts, especially land speculation and the creation of a new Tudor aristocracy.

Protestants were virulent in attacking monasticism and asceticism (and its abuse) that was associated with Catholicism. But Shakespeare shows approval of contemplation and withdrawal, in *As You Like It* and in the good offices of the abbey in *The Comedy of Errors* (V.i). In *King John* he conspicuously omits the scene of looting the abbey that is central to his source *The Troublesome Raigne of John*, an aggressively anti-Catholic play. This is part of Shakespeare's revision to a more sympathetic view of the old faith in his only work that directly deals with the central religious question of the relation between the Papacy and the English monarch, since John is shown as a precursor to Henry VIII and a usurper. The dissolution still resonates in Shakespeare's image of "Bare ruined choirs where late the sweet birds sang" (Sonnet 73), and in a lyric lamenting the destruction of Walsingham, England's place of greatest veneration of Mary Queen of Heaven: "Owls do shriek where the sweetest hymns / Lately were sung."[2]

Henrician reforms inspired less violent reactions than might be expected with such drastic changes in authority within the church, inquisitorial royal supremacy, and the dissolution of the monasteries. In the 1530s quiet acquiescence seems to have been typical. Politics, not theology, governed the executions, according to the Treasons Act, of those who denied that Henry VIII was head of the Church. In the summer of 1535 these included six Carthusians, a vicar, a learned monk of Syon, and notables John Fisher, Bishop of Rochester, and Sir Thomas More, who both refused to sign the succession that discredited Katherine to recognize Anne Boleyn and any of her children. The friend of Erasmus, author of *Utopia* and a life of Richard III used by Shakespeare, the first layman to be Lord Chancellor of England—More was all of these, but he was martyred in 1535 because his first loyalty was to Catholicism and Tudor politics did not allow this. There are few such examples of pre-Marian martyrdom for Foxe to memorialize in *Actes and Monumentes*. A notable exception is the three men who objected to claims of miracles, took down and burned the Rood at Dovercourt, and were hanged in 1532. The illustrative woodcut is vivid and unusual; the image of the Crucifix is large, and the hanging figures contrast with the frequent scenes of burning that mark Foxe's book (Figure 9).

Although there had been clerical marriages by some Protestant clergy in Suffolk as early as 1536–37, they became legal in February 1549, and this was a major change. Again statistics of occurrence indicate both regional variety in

Within the illustration:

Actes and thinges done in the Reigne of King EDWARD the fixt.

The Ship of the Romifh Church.

Burning of Images.

¶ Ship ouer your trinkets & be packing you Papiftes.

The Temple well purged.

The Papiftes packing away theyr Paltry.

The comunion Table

8. The Romish Church reformed, Edward VI, John Foxe's *Actes and Monumentes* (1583)

¶ Robert King, Robert Debnam, and Nicholas Marſhe hanged for taking downe the Roode of Douercourt.

9. Hanging for Taking Down the Rood of Dovercourt, John Foxe's *Actes and Monumentes* (1583)

A liuely picture defcribing the weight and fubftaunce of Gods moft bleſſed word agaynſt the doctrines and vanities of mans traditions.

AT LONDON.
Printed by Iohn Daye, dwelling ouer
Alderſgate beneath Sainct Martins.

Anno. 1583.

Cum gratia & Priuilegio Regiæ Maieſtatis.

10. God's Word against man's traditions, John Foxe's *Actes and Monumentes* (1583)

Here folovveth the second Volume
AND THE VII. BOOKE, BEGINNING
WITH THE REIGNE OF KING HENRY E
THE EIGHT.

11. Henry VIII supreme above the Pope, John Foxe's *Actes and Monumentes* (1583)

response and a general conservatism under Henry VIII. Between 1549 and 1553, when Mary became queen and deprived clergy who had married, the highest incidence was in London with nearly a third of parish priests marrying; for Essex, Suffolk, and Norfolk, the rate was at least a quarter; for Cambridgeshire, it was one in five. In contrast, the rate was only one in ten in Lincolnshire and the diocese of York; in Lancashire—most pertinent for Shakespeare, if one accepts that he found patronage there—it was one in twenty. These figures, of Palliser, are part of the profile of a Catholic and conservative North.

Reactions against reforms became public in the Pilgrimage of Grace. Not all historians view the motivations as exclusively religious or to be largely a popular movement; some see the events as influenced by local nobles, gentry, and clergy who were unhappy with current changes.[3] The visible signs were certainly religious: the rebels' banner bore the device of the five wounds of Christ (a focus of late medieval piety). But the places of rebellion show variations of political influences. Contemporary accounts by John Hales and Robert Parkyn claimed that the protests were a reaction against the religious policies of the Crown, particularly action against the monasteries; in the north, of fifty-five suppressed religious houses, at least sixteen were restored. Participation in York may have been more a peasants' revolt than a religious defense of the old church, but in Lancashire the pilgrimage was undeniably a religious protest. This county is the textbook case for Catholic continuity, since the Church's vitality was greater than in more sophisticated regions where it was enervated by humanism and more highly educated clergy less at ease with the mystery of religion. Biographies of Shakespeare increasingly accept a probability that his "lost years" were in Lancashire.

Studies of literacy in Tudor England recognize that 70 percent of men and 90 percent of women could not read.[4] Protestant adherents were thus more likely to be men, and the evidence of Marian martyrs suggests this: of 280, just over fifty were women. Even in London, of 190 lay people persecuted for heresy in 1540, only 26 were women, and 17 of them were with their husbands. In Mary's reign 800 people fled to the continent, not all for religious reasons: 472 were men, 125 women, 146 children. The level of literacy meant not so much independence gained from individual reading of the Bible but a shift in dependency, from priests presiding at rituals to those reading and preaching for the illiterate. The Injunctions of 1538 required each parish to buy a Bible; by 1540 most had not done so, and those that complied were mostly in London and diocesan capitals, not the countryside. The real impact was the compliance with other Injunctions: to extinguish lights everywhere except on the altar, and thus end the custom of burning candles in the rood loft and before the Easter Sepulchre; to remove images that had attracted pilgrimages and offerings, and to be ready for later removal of images that remained but were to be regarded only as memorials; to end the veneration of relics—which few parishes had. Hutton's survey of ninety-one parishes showed that only nineteen purchased the *Book of Homilies*, published with government sponsorship in 1547, during the reign of Edward VI. These texts were those needed by less skilled rural priests newly expected to preach effectively. The English translation of Erasmus's *Paraphrases* had wider acceptance: forty-one bought it before the end of 1548 and by the end of Edward's reign a further twelve to make a total of fifty-three— or more than half of the parishes. The role of images seems to have been minimized; there are no records for removals, but only one new image was erected after 1538; and there was a decline in the importance of guilds, fraternities often associated with an image of a patron saint and civic performances. Two woodcuts in Foxe's *Book of Martyrs* show the hoped for change to reliance upon the Word and the fall of Romish customs and clergy (Figures 10 and 11). But the ordered purchase of parish Bibles—the replacement way to faith—did not happen.

Following Henry's death in 1547, Edwardian Injunctions became more aggressive. Major Catholic religious ceremonies were forbidden—the blessing of candles on Candelmas, of ashes on Ash Wednesday, and of palms on Palm Sunday, and the Adoration of the Cross on Good Friday. Then all images were ordered removed from churches. Next communicants were obliged to take communion in both kinds. Finally, since it was decreed that there was no Purgatory, endowments for chantries, religious guilds, and perpetual obits were seized by the government. This "stripping of the altars" was much more relentless, and a major text accompanied it. The parliamentary Act of Uniformity of 1549 prescribed the first *Book of Common Prayer*. Written in Cranmer's memorable and exquisite English prose style, this text became a foundation for the reformed church. The parishes in Hutton's sample had all bought it by the required date of Whit Sunday 1549. There were at first complaints that many priests were not using it, but orders for the destruction of old service books, which "should be a let to the using of the said *Book of Common Prayer*," meant that for most it was the order of service by 1550. Shakespeare's plays show familiarity with it; he also frequently echoes the Elizabethan *Homilies*, a part of every Sunday's reading at Holy Trinity Parish Church, attended by schoolboys in a body.

The tenor of sixteenth-century religious conviction was heard in the fluent styles of many throughout the century. A sample from Cranmer's *Homily of Good Works* illustrates the power of language and feeling and enumerates rejected Catholic practices:

> And briefly to pass over the ungodly and counterfeit religions, let us rehearse some other kinds of papistical superstitions and abuses, as of beads, of lady psalters, and rosaries, of fifteen oes, of St. Bernard's verses, of St.

Agathe's letters, of purgatory, of masses satisfactory, of stations and ju-
bilees, of feigned relics, of hallowed beads, bells, bread, water, psalms,
candles, fire, and such other; of superstitious fastings, fraternities or broth-
erhoods, of pardons, with such like merchandize, which were so esteemed
and abused to the great prejudice of God's glory and commandments. . . .
Thus was the people through ignorance so blinded with the goodly show
and appearance of those things, that they thought the keeping of them to
be a more holiness, a more perfect service and honouring of God, and
more pleasing to God, than the keeping of God's commandments.

This sermon was published in 1547, the same year as the intensely Protestant
Injunctions that set the pattern for stronger Protestantism and less tolerance of
alternatives. Injunction thirty-two, which decreed that parish clergy would use
the *Book of Homilies* every Sunday, assured widespread preaching of Cranmer's
message, but his use of the past tense is wishful thinking, when many of the
listed practices remained.

In fact, Henry VIII liked the old ceremonies, in spite of his enmity to the
papacy and desire for the divorce; this explains a relative moderation of Henrician reforms, and significant pullings back from more extreme changes. The
Reformer Latimer could not prevent traditionalist survival in The Ten Articles
of 1536, the first official doctrinal formulary for the Church of England. Thus
though the sacraments were limited to three—baptism, penance, Eucharist—and
justification by faith included, so were veneration of images and saints, and
intercessions for the dead, but not the name of Purgatory and indulgences. Retained ceremonies were now described as didactic and symbolic rather than
significant in themselves, and the many holy days that marked the ritual year
were no longer honored. The mode was compromise, albeit not entirely pleasing
to anyone, and there were ongoing shifts in policy. The second royal Injunctions
of 1538 proclaimed against the saints. Henry had drafted modifications for a
more traditional proclamation, but in the final version the Reformers decreed
that England's great saint Thomas Becket, whose shrine at Canterbury attracted
pilgrims from all of Christendom, was not a saint and that all images and references were to be removed to keep people from idolatry. Henry's drafted proclamation, strongly inspired by a concern about reading the English Bible, was
not published, but the Act of Six Articles in 1539 slowed the more radical
proponents of Protestantism, and Latimer resigned rather than enforce a conservative return. Although Cromwell did not assist them, he soon fell from favor
himself. Differences of allegiance raised new leaders—Cranmer and Ridley,
who urged sharper Protestant actions. But in 1543 the *King's Book* was a conservative replacement for the *Bishops' Book*, and the *Rationale of Ceremonial*
defended much Catholic practice that attracted greater attention than doctrinal

matters. Education was a key issue, and the *King's Primer* of 1545 judiciously followed the pattern of successful Catholic primers and included prayers by continental Catholic humanists like Erasmus and Vives. There were crucial shifts in the reliance upon English and in doctrinal emphases: no prayers to the Virgin and saints, and to the Blessed Sacrament, but prayers to focus on the Passion and everyday problems, and numerous translations of the Scriptures. Lady Anne seems to reflect upon the changed view of saints when she calls upon the "holy king," Henry VI, to whom devotion had grown rapidly. Beside the bier she prays: "Be it lawful that I invocate thy ghost / To hear the lamentations of poor Anne" (*Richard III*, I.ii.8–9). The cumulative effect of the Reformers was to mitigate the piety of medieval Christendom by replacing its affective quality with something much colder and more cerebral; a division between Catholics and Protestants, with a tradition of ongoing confrontation, was set.

Restoration and Reform under Queen Mary Tudor

When Mary Tudor became queen in 1553, every effort was made to restore Catholic rituals and church decorations. Parliament repealed the statutes passed under Edward: altars were now ordered to be built and a cross put in place, ashes blessed on Ash Wednesday, palms on Palm Sunday, water on Holy Saturday. There was some initial restraint, as Mary tolerated both creeds. But soon the enforcement machinery of Inventories and Visitations established by her predecessors was used to speed the return to former Catholicism. The process was swift—the high altar and mass from December 1553; roof lofts and the Rood, with Mary and John, by 1555; images of patron saints by 1556—but most parishes returned more than was required. Loyal priests could quickly restore Catholic rituals because many parishes had kept their vessels and vestments so that Mass could be celebrated in former style. But for others, the return of valuable physical objects was more complicated; some had been sold off, others were easily returned by loyal parishioners, but some needed repair. The costs to re-create what had been destroyed were high. Another huge expense was the paying of pensions to ex-religious displaced by the dissolution, an obligation that became the Church's when the crown divested itself of income from tenths, tithes, and so on. Expenditure under Edward in 1550–51 had been £44,861, and the authorities postponed payment in 1552. Getting proper accounts was a major difficulty, and Pole's greater concern was recovering from the schism and reforming discipline according to the Council of Trent.

Organized Christianity is an oxymoron. Christ's kingdom is not Caesar's, the Beatitudes begin "Blessed are the poor," and the rich do not easily fare well. But the Christian is enjoined to bring the Good News, and this does not just happen; it is the work of the clergy, leading the laity and supported by them, and this requires money. The Church's loss of material wealth because of the schism in England was enormous. Henry VIII received £160,000 each year, before proceeds from the chantries were added under Edward VI. The lands of former religious houses provided about three-fourths of this sum, and the other fourth came from benefices formerly held by monasteries. The value of seized church plate and ornaments was staggering, at least £1,000,000, perhaps even £1,500,000. The first-fruits taxes that had gone to Rome became a one-tenth levy imposed by Henry, with a value estimated as high as £40,000 to as low as £25,000. Inflation, a significant reason for Henry's seizure of Church resources, and for subsequent Elizabethan exploration, was a major problem in the sixteenth century when to retain the standards of one's parents required twice as much money. In this threatening economic climate Queen Mary and Archbishop Pole had to sort the finances in England, and render an account to Pope Paul IV, who had limited understanding of what had happened in the Church in England and who also wanted an appropriate restoration of income for the papacy, which involved another level of assessment of property for which there were not always full accounts from the previous decade. The problems were beyond solving, and efforts to regain the Church's wealth impeded many necessary changes.

As earlier noted, had Mary lived as did her half-sister Elizabeth, Edwardine reforms would have been an aberration, for England would have been Catholic, but not without incorporating features of Reformation introduced under Henry VIII and Edward VI. Greater centrality and uniformity are the general shift from medieval Christendom's variety and local characteristics. There was more emphasis upon the Word. The Marian church did not oppose an English Bible, only a Protestant English Bible. A new English translation of the New Testament was projected at Pole's synod in late 1555, although he favored the Catholic preference of experiencing faith and holiness through the liturgy and objected to the debates that emerged from diverse lay reading of Scripture. The key distinction from Protestantism, whatever the objections to Catholic excesses that Erasmus described in *Colloquy X: The Godly Feast*, is that text was not to be placed above sign, or symbolic and ritual gesture. Edmund Bonner, the Bishop of London, ordered longer quarterly sermons to explain the Church's ceremonies: ''that the people may perceive what is meant and signified by the same, and also know and understand how and in what manner they ought to use and accept them for their own edifying.'' An example is the carrying of the pax on Sundays to remind people of the peace left to the disciples by Christ, ''but also of that peace, that Christ by his death purchased for the people.''[5]

Bardolph's stealing of the pax and Henry V's consequent sentencing him to death (*Henry V*, III.vi.39–45) have, then, strong religious import. A *pax* is a metal disc that the priest kisses during Mass. Prior to the Reformation, paxes carried different designs like the Crucifix or Lamb of God. When they were replaced in the Counter-Reformation, throughout Europe, the embossed image was always the Crucifix, a sign of focus upon the Passion and redemption. There is a close verbal relation of *pax* to *pyx*. Raphael Holinshed's *Chronicle* (1587) includes an incident with a *pyx*, the vessel that contains the consecrated host. Holinshed depends upon Edward Hall's *The Union of the Two Noble and Illustre Families of Lancaster and York* (1542), which is intensely Protestant, the work of a man who was against civil war and writing to support Henry VIII. Shakespeare used both chronicles, and other texts, in writing his history plays. Both pax and pyx are among the Church vessels stripped from the altars; those that were misused were forbidden in the first years of the Reformation, restored in the Marian years, and then ordered destroyed in Elizabeth's visitations of 1559. Pistol protests Exeter's "doom of death" for "pax of little price," and his sought-after intercessor Fluellen disconcerts when he replies, "I do partly understand your meaning" but quickly agrees with the execution, "for discipline ought to be used" (III.vi.50, 56). Pistol is "an arrant counterfeit rascal" in the words of Gower, who denounces the opportunism of the coward soldier. To the king, Fluellen identifies Exeter's one casualty Bardolph, "like to be executed for robbing a church" (III.vi.101), and his physical description includes images of the fires of hell. An allusion to the dissolution of the monasteries and to the enforcement of state injunctions is unavoidable, albeit amidst other resonances.

Among these are attitudes about religious objects like the pyx; and a copy of Edward Hall's *The Union*, annotated in the sixteenth century, is relevant. A marginal note in a provincial secretary cursive hand, one that is not yet settled, comments about the theft of the pyx: " '*A cryme committyd & if this boke had one author it would not have been noted / nam oportet mendacem esse memorem*' ('For it behoves a liar to be mindful.')"[6] The suggestion seems to be that so anti-Catholic a man as Hall would not have recorded the display of Henry V's piety. Alan Keen presents evidence to identify Shakespeare as the annotator, who had "a strong Roman Catholic, even clerical bias." Notes like "here he begynneth to rayle," "Always lying," and "Note that when he speaketh of the Pope he sheweth himself of the englisshe schisme a favorer," put Catholicism before English patriotism (12–13). Keen has a strong wish to claim such extraordinary material as Shakespeare's, particularly to read it as his early effort as a seventeen-year-old; although this dating is sustainable, the case cannot be proved. More certain is the profile of whoever marked the text: "he shows himself to be studious, intelligent, and a persistent annotator, one surmises that this was his first reading in the subject" (9). Several points emerge: close analysis of a text, anxiety about civil discord, English patriotism, acute awareness of Protestant bias and concomitant argument of the Catholic position—a brave confronting of the reality of severe religious differences with sustained Catholic belief and an enthusiasm for intense Tudor patriotism.

The annotator avoids absolutism and acknowledges good in the other in ways that mirror the stances taken by some clerical figures during the opening years of the Reformation when changes occurred so frequently. Immediately upon Mary's accession printers rushed to issue the Sarum primer that Henry's version replaced and the subsequently very Protestant Edwardine issue of 1553. The restoration of popular Catholic prayers—the Hours of the Virgin, the Office for the Dead, the Commendations and the Psalms of the Passion—began eagerly; and in June 1553 John Wayland, who had continued to work in London and had government connections, published an official Marian primer. Like Catholic primers of the 1540s, it was printed in Latin and English, with the main text in English, and contained the traditional items. Wayland added the Form of Confession that had not been included for twenty years, and some sixty new prayers, printed only in English, from various sources, including even a prayer to Christ that is a Protestant rewriting of "Salve Regina." Missing are many items favored in pre-Reformation primers: indulgence rubrics; miraculous legends; many prayers to the Virgin, saints, and Blessed Sacrament; and the affective prayers of Christ's Passion. In their place were morning prayers for each day and a general morning prayer focused on the Passion as the means of redemption. This first major text for Marian reform demonstrates the Church's capacity for growth, acceptance of changes, and a flexibility in combining old and new to restore the ancient pieties of Catholicism and concurrently to provide prayers that suited contemporary daily circumstances. Some revisionist historians have examined such documents to balance the negative accounts of "Bloody Mary" and "Bloody Bonner" that Foxe, and many modern historians, did not acknowledge.

Another example of assimilation is that Bonner followed Cranmer in providing homilies for the clergy who lacked skill, and he issued a restatement of the faith. *A profytable and necessary doctryne, with certayne homilies adioyned . . . for the instruction and enformation of the people* (1555) follows the framework of the *King's Book* of 1543, the last most conservative statement of faith and thus attractive to traditionalists. *A profytable and necessary doctryne* provides a continuity with the reformers and acknowledges an increased need for catechesis, the instruction of the laity to understanding of the Church's ceremonies. It reestablishes the centrality of the Church with added explanations, especially those eliminated in the *King's Book*. The basic structure was the same, an exposition of the fundamentals of faith (unchanged), followed by specific sections dealing with key doctrines, with some crucial additions and emphases. Every section included long supporting quotations from the Gospels, St. Paul, and patristic fathers such as St. Cyprian, St. Ambrose, and St. Augustine. Generous and focused quotation from Scripture with correlated exegesis made the book very helpful for its intended audience of clergy and educated laity. At the start of 1556 Bonner followed it with *An honest godly instruction*, a catechism for children that schoolmasters could use.

A program for thoughtful and better-informed affirmation of Catholicism led to a strong recovery in many areas—and to tension and loss. Lack of money partially explains why images and the chantries associated with prayers for the souls in Purgatory were never restored to pre-Reformation status. The evidence of wills shows that the Edwardine practice of bequests to the poor prevailed, in spite of efforts to encourage a return to the old custom of bequests to the parishes that were much in need of money to restore all that had been lost. The Church has always been dedicated to helping the poor, but their numbers increased in the sixteenth century, so that medieval traditions of alms clearly were inadequate to handle pressing needs. Thus the Marian Church followed the Edwardine in encouraging testators to make bequests to alleviate the social problem of the poor, and inevitably this meant fewer bequests to the institutional church.

However, stern attitudes and statements accompanied such recognitions of the need for revised education, social justice, and reconciliation. As part of the plea for national unity Mary forbade religious disputation, both name-calling and the publication of satires and controversies, and in many places there was peaceful return. Even in London those first accused were generally cleared by defenses or repentance; of 470, only three became martyrs. The burning of heretics, even at a time in which public executions were commonplace, is not inherent in early showings of religious vigor. But Bonner subsequently became directly responsible for the burning of 113 men and women as heretics in the diocese of London, which had the highest number of excommunications. Bonner, Alexander argues, is pivotal in Foxe's *Book of Martyrs*, where he is an arch-villain. Protestants now had their martyrs, and a Protestant *Book of Saints*: the fierce woodcuts have terrifying and haunting images, and the ringing words of fervent devotion and defiance greatly strengthened the literary resources well established with the *Book of Common Prayer* and *Homilies*. But the issue of religious changes went beyond literary excellence to politically based enforcements for catechesis and restoration of forms.

The Visitation of 243 parishes in Kent in 1557 is the extreme example. Nicholas Harpsfield, Archdeacon of Canterbury, once Bonner's vicar general in London, was responsible for inspecting, recording, and implementing the return to Catholic altars. There is much evidence of prompt compliance, but also signs of heresy and resulting burnings, in which Harpsfield was involved. Such events, whether the results of sincere, albeit horribly misguided religious conviction, or of human enmity within the community, had occurred before, but not in such numbers. Bonner presided over the heresy trials in the consistory court. Foxe's record, based on the registers (now lost) and the personal accounts of the martyrs, indicates a procedure of questions and answers about acceptance of orthodox Catholicism. The choice was conformity or sentence as a heretic and corollary excommunication; those who did not submit were executed. Such a policy of repression, a continuation of state interference that began with Henry and Edward, was ill-advised and could not succeed. Foxe made Bonner a sadistic villain, crucial in the mythology of the persecution. But this is overstated; Bonner did not initiate the repression. However, extension of the precedents of religious persecution in an England that no longer adhered to a single Church was a disastrous intensification of political intervention. The consequence was to be heightened anxiety, objections, protests, and denunciations that led to yet greater stringency in Elizabeth's reign.

Elizabeth and Enforced Protestantism

Elizabeth, who had conformed under Mary but not without resentment, wanted to restore the Edwardine church, as the selection of her Protestant adviser William Cecil indicates. The close vote for the Act of Uniformity, which passed by only three, in April 1559, prefigured mixed reactions to the return to Protestantism and explains a shift to greater caution. Strong anti-Catholic actions of iconoclasm and the stopping of Catholic ceremonies in London contrasted with a last Corpus Christi procession in Canterbury that attracted three thousand people. Definitions of religion in England were not clear-cut, and the initial ease of Elizabeth's reign is illusory; the Injunctions of 1559 moved from evasive tolerance to a heightened Edwardine position. Now "all images," not just "misused images," were to be destroyed. Churchwardens of every parish had to produce inventories for royal visitations, and replies to the questions indicate there was no reconciliatory approach. Vessels and vestments were the "trifling tromperie for the sinful service of the popish priest," while sacred and honored texts were "feigned fables and peltering popish books." The authorities insisted that "monuments of superstition," sacred objects, be "put to profane use." Thus bells used in parish churches became part of the harnesses of horses, sheep and cows, or called farmers to work; holy water founts were animal troughs; and pyxes were used as balances for weighing spices and coins, after being split open.[7] Anyone who tried to save and protect images and books of the old faith faced a public demonstration of conformity. Destructions were widespread in the 1560s, but surviving churchwardens' accounts show that about half of the parishes, unwilling to conform, kept their mass utensils and vestments for another ten years.

The 1560s were the decade of formal separation. A committee of the Council of Trent had declared against English Catholics attending services of the Church of England, and in 1566 Pius V forbade it and sent Laurence Vaux to effect a change into recusancy by which English Catholics were received into a separate Church. This was especially successful in Lancashire, where there were seventy-five active recusant priests, and in Yorkshire, where there were over 150 "Marian priests," the largest known numbers, by the year of Shakespeare's birth, 1564. Areas in the north, such as Lichfield and Coventry, most resisted Elizabeth's enforcements. Inclusive records for Lincoln between 1559 and 1566 visitations show that of the 180 parishes only about a fourth complied promptly. But generally the records for detentions are slight, partially because there was still an Elizabethan attempt to avoid conservative resistance.

The previous shifts in definition of religious practice, Elizabeth's unmarried state, and the uncertainty of succession left a prospect of change. Part of the process of reform was clerical argument throughout the reign. At Paul's Cross on November 26, 1559, John Jewel, bishop elect of Salisbury, preached a "Challenge Sermon" to Roman Catholics; in twenty-seven articles he asked for a defense or justification of beliefs and practices. The basis of the controversy was Scripture and the Church Fathers of the first six centuries of Christianity. The deposed Dean of St. Paul's, Dr. Henry Cole, replied privately, but Jewel published the texts. His principal opposition was a former associate who had had retracted Protestantism under Mary. Thomas Harding published *An Answer to Maister Iuelles Chalange* (1564 and 1565); Thomas Stapleton, an eminent convert from Lutheranism to Catholicism, an exile to Louvain in Belgium, wrote one in Latin.

There was an extensive literature of religious controversy to expound the views of the Anglican church that everyone in England by law was obliged to attend and support, of Puritans who were radical in their wished for reforms, and of Catholics who stayed loyal to Rome and the old traditions. The role of Catholic recusant texts was crucial, since reading them became a way to conversion, as well as the alternative to attending Mass that was no longer regularly celebrated. There was also a pragmatic issue of authority and corollary charges of treason. The law required all to recognize the monarch, not the Pope, as supreme governor of the Church of England, and Pius V in 1570 issued a bull of excommunication of Queen Elizabeth. This meant that previously tolerated controversy now became treason: those who wrote, distributed, or possessed Catholic works were traitors. Counterattacks by Catholic conservatives were varied and protracted. The vicar of Whalley in Lancashire, for example, called the new Church of England "a defiled and spotted Church" in 1575. With the involvement of Spain that led to the Armada in 1588, the political ramifications became extreme. The 1581 Act stringently enforced earlier attempts at conformity to the Established Church; it made reconciliation, or any attempt to reconcile someone, to Rome an act of treason. The fine for not attending Anglican services increased from twelve pence to twenty pounds per month. In 1585 another Act declared that any Catholic priest not ordained under Mary was guilty of treason if he came to Britain. Among responses is William Allen's *An Admonition to the Nobility & People of England* (1587), to support the Spanish and the excommunication of Elizabeth.

The defeat of Philip II's Armada of 132 ships through a combination of bold seamanship and elements of nature gave Elizabethan England a brilliant victory and a sign that God did not want the country to return to Catholicism through the efforts of the austere monkish king who had been the husband of Queen Mary Tudor. But in the 1590s the number of Catholics in England had increased, and this led to further official persecutions. More exacting measures against Catholics, like the Royal Proclamation of October 18, 1591, which was directed at Jesuits, seminarians, and Philip of Spain, were inevitable. There were, of course, disaffected priests who opposed political involvement and concentrated on religious issues, a course of action begun when Henry VIII declared himself the head of the Church of England.

Some English Catholics chose exile on the Continent. One of the most distinguished was William Allen, born in Lancashire, a scholar who wrote extensively to defend basic Catholic doctrine. In 1568, Allen (later Cardinal) founded a college in Douai for other scholars in exile and to train the clergy whose return to England was necessary for the survival of English Catholicism. The seminary subsequently had to move to Rheims (1578–93). The first priests began returning to England from Douai in the 1570s—twenty in 1579, twenty-nine in 1580, and thirty-one in 1581. A known 460 worked in England between 1574 and 1603, and this quashed hopes that Catholicism would die out with the old priests. Probably most of the students at Douai came from Catholic families, and the available records show that throughout Elizabeth's reign about one sixth of the recruits were from Lancashire and another one sixth from Yorkshire. The Privy Council in 1574 identified Lancashire as ''the very sink of popery, where more unlawful acts have been committed and more unlawful persons holden secret than in any other part of the realm.'' There has been a suggestion that Shakespeare might briefly have been a seminarian in his youth.

Allen worked with Richard Bristow, whom he had earlier encouraged to publish a *Book of Motives*, under Gregory Martin, to produce a Catholic translation of Scripture. The New Testament was published in 1582, along with Martin's *A Discoverie of the Manifold Corruptions* in the Protestant translation. The two volumes of the Old Testament did not appear until 1609 and 1610 because of lack of funding. The so-called Rheims Testament was a serious threat, and several Protestants attacked, most notably Thomas Cartwright and William Fulke, who had already engaged in controversy with Bristow. Ironically, Fulke by publishing a refutation of *The Text of the New Testament . . . by the Papists* (1589) made it widely available because he legally printed the text and annotations as a parallel with the version of the Established Church. Allen's most significant writing was a *Defence of English Catholics* (1584) in which he argues that those executed were not traitors but martyrs for the Catholic faith. He sustained this point of view in *An Admonition to the Nobility & People of England* (1587).

Recusants in exile and their return to England have been part of the debate about the continuity of Catholicism through the Reformation, whether it is "survivalism" or "seminarism." Although there were still some older priests in England, the Jesuits, though largely recruited from English Catholic gentry, trained on the continent and came as "missionaries" during Elizabeth's reign. But in contrast to Jesuit missionaries in South America and Asia, Jesuits in England supported the Catholics who had been dispossessed and were forbidden to seek new converts among heretics. Their importance grew steadily, and they forged a view of Tudor Catholic history that was a crucial element in the propaganda of controversial pamphlets. The issue is really one of degree: historical evidence supports the strength of medieval Catholicism, which richly informs the artistic imagination, but Counter-Reformation Catholicism was also part of the theological and political ethos in which Shakespeare lived. His literary career coincides with the time of greatest Jesuit activity, from first arrival in 1580 to 1610, the death of Robert Persons. Shakespeare's plays show a knowledge of writings by leading Jesuits such as Robert Southwell, Edmund Campion, and Henry Garnet.

This strengthens the case for Shakespeare's affinity to Catholicism since a focus of anti-Catholic attack was the Jesuits, the militant order of the Counter-Reformation, founded by St. Ignatius of Loyola to be the army of the Pope. A mission to assist English Catholics began when the first Jesuits, Robert Persons—the papist of "the papist and his poet"—and Edmund Campion, got to England in the summer of 1580. Both were significant writers, whose impact was more literary and inspirational than parochial. There were at least eighty controversial books and pamphlets in the following five years, even though Persons returned to the Continent and Campion was martyred in December 1581. Two royal proclamations, probably the work of Burghley, were issued against Jesuits and seminary priests, specifically the English colleges at Rome and Rheims, in 1580 and 1581. These reinforced the Anglican position put by Thomas Bilson in *True Difference betweene Christian Subjection and Unchristian Rebellion* (1585) and John Stubbs's unpublished *Vindication of English Justice* that Burghley commissioned. His own pamphlet *The Execution of Justice* (1583) made the case clear. From the beginning, with Luther's *Theses*, printing was a crucial force in the advance of the Reformation.

Official regulation was part of the process. Mary's Charter incorporating the Stationers' Company on May 4, 1557, a response to increased publication that had already led to the 1534 Act to prohibit foreign and thus support native printers, gave authority over these workers. A characteristic of English printers was that most were in London; this led to a less academic concentration, made control of titles easier, and meant that publishing was located in the most Protestant part of England. Catholic printers, who produced at least 250 volumes between 1558 and 1603, also worked out of London. Books published on the continent were sent to London and distributed by the priests in lots of fifty or one hundred to all parts of the country. A few local Catholic printers attempted disguise with a fake continental place of publication. William Carter, who used Bruges or Antwerp, was executed after being charged with printing Gregory Martin's *The Treatise of Schisme* (1578). Stephen Brinkley in the early 1580s, in a period of ten months, was in three different locations, with false imprints. This underground press was a reaction against suppression. Elizabeth's awareness of the threat of controversial Catholic texts led to a decree in 1586 to prohibit all printing unless it was authorized by the Archbishop of Canterbury or the Bishops of London and allowed by the Queen's Injunctions. Control came through systematic searches, usually conducted on Sundays or feast days when Catholics were likely to be at services. A list of the books of the historian John Stow, made when his library was ransacked, showed several Catholic works, and this is not unusual. Inventories of books in Cambridge from 1580 and 1600 show a preponderance of theologians among the fifty most frequent authors. The Bible is first and Erasmus is second, then Cicero and Aristotle; Melanchton is fifth, followed by Patristic writers Chrysostom and Augustine. Calvin, at twenty-fourth, is far down the list; and Luther, at thirty-seven is still lower, while Aquinas is sixteenth and Peter Lombard thirteenth. Elizabethan and Jacobean books of religious controversy were numerous, and more ephemeral, and it is hard to establish readership.

An interesting dimension of licensing is that special caution was exercised for Spanish books, which included the romantic tales that were rivaling the old romances in popularity and treatises of chivalry like the *Myrrour of Knighthood* (1582). An ongoing success was the translation of Ortuñez de Calahorra; Margaret Tyler's *The First Part of the Mirrour of Princely Deeds and Knighthood* was in 1578, and subsequent parts continued until 1601. Between acquisition of a license and printing, many things happened. *Amadis of Gaul* was approved, although not yet translated, in 1589, but printed only in 1595, and by another printer. Anthony Munday followed the process of printing in parts, to make the costs manageable, for a *Palmerin* series. Thus in spite of interest in the classical Greek and Latin authors, the romance, with its newly popular Spanish stories, flourished as part of an increasing preference for literature of delight before literature of instruction. It was carefully made acceptable by an emphasis upon didactic and moral quality, as well as much practical detail, especially attractive to the Tudors, who continued to emulate medieval chivalric custom.

Robert Persons's *Reasons for Refusall* led to several confrontations, but— in addition to the Shakespeare association—he is best remembered for writing the most popular book of devotions among both Catholics and Protestants. *The First Book of the Christian Exercise*, published at Rouen in 1582, offered proofs for the existence of God and the truth of the Christian religion. This "Book of Resolution" transcended the usual prejudices, for it was an expansion of a work by an Italian Jesuit Gaspar Loarte, *The Exercise of a Christian Life*, earlier translated into English. A Protestant minister Edmund Burney deleted and revised to publish *Treatise tending to Pacification* (1584), and Persons issued a new edition as *The Christian Directory* (1585). Both versions saw subsequent editions, and echoes in the plays indicate that Shakespeare read it. Campion was the more public Jesuit, since he had been at court and many pamphlets gave the details of his martyrdom, brilliantly retold in Evelyn Waugh's *Edmund Campion Jesuit and Martyr* (1946). Campion sent a letter to the Privy Council to explain his apostolic journey to the provinces, and his *Rationes Decem* (ten reasons), was secretly printed in 1581 and distributed at St. Mary's, Oxford. This is a useful reminder of the affinity of a university that at least 100 fellows and senior members left in the first ten years after Queen Mary's death. The Vice-Chancellor received a letter from the Privy Council in 1581 that protested: "most of the seminary priests which at this time disturb the Church have been heretofore scholars of [your] university." There were many translations, including *Campion Englished* (1632).

Campion was on his way to Houghton Tower in Lancashire when he was captured in summer 1581. The Jesuit priest was arrested and sent to the Tower, where he was forced to listen to the preaching and denunciations of Protestants William Fulke and John Keltridge. Although Campion was allowed a chance for disputation, attendance at his trial was restricted and he was much weakened by torture on the rack. All of this is chronicled in the pamphlets, including an eyewitness account, Thomas Alfield's *A True reporte of the death & martyrdome of M. Campion Iesuite and preiste* (1582). The case of Campion was followed by executions of other Jesuits in 1582. Just as Foxe's *Book of Martyrs* captured the imagination, so many controversial pamphlets fostered the sense of persecution of Catholics that grew to become an analog of the Roman Empire against the Christians. Robert Persons's *A Treatise of Three Conversions of England* (1603–04) explicitly replies to Foxe by pointing out the limitations of the accounts of the Protestant martyrs; even the printing echoes because of the comparison with parallel calendars. Accounts of martyrdom led to a literature of consolation, like Persons's *A Brief Discours* (1580) and the memorable works of poet and martyr Robert Southwell, *Epistle of Comfort* (1588) and *Humble Supplication to Her Maiestie* (1600, but written early 1590s). There were many losses for which consolation was needed, since tensions, advocacies, and allegiances shifted constantly.

Puritans

The Puritans made a counterpoint to Protestants and Catholics. While early reformers like Matthew Parker could still focus on a practical issue such as wearing vestments in 1566, greater sympathy to Puritan ideas in the 1570s marked a change in emphasis. With Edmund Grindal as Archbishop of Canterbury there was less repression of Puritans, and doctrinal as well as liturgical issues grew in significance. The mid-1580s saw a plethora of Puritan publications, like the Marprelate tracts; there were also complaints and petitions in Parliament to threaten the Anglican position. A high point was the Lambeth Articles of 1595 that gave force to Calvin's teachings, like predestination by God, but there was not a long-term acceptance. Elizabeth's politics did not impose abstract theology. Moreover, although Catholicism provided some conservative tenets for Anglican apologists, it remained the principal opposition in the 1590s. One example illustrates the hold of the old religion. A preacher in Kent, Josias Nichols, defended Puritans in *Plea of the Innocent* (1602), which also records the ignorance of those with whom he worked. In one parish of 400 communicants he found that only 10 percent had a basic understanding of doctrine and that only 1 percent believed that salvation came from faith rather than good works.

If Puritan theology did not capture the consent of simple parishioners, it did generate a great deal of intellectual interest, especially in the theater. Shakespeare introduces Puritans several times. In *Twelfth Night* (1600–1602) Maria's first description of Malvolio is "sometimes he is a kind of a puritan" (II.iii.139), and Sir Andrew deems this a justification for beating him. Elements of Malvolio's behavior, absolutism and severity, are those associated with Puritans, but as Maria notes, he is not constant (146–47). The clown Lavatch in *All's Well That Ends Well* (c.1601–5) contrasts stereotypes, "young Charbon the puritan and old Poysan the papist"; then in the best tradition of fools he offers a characterization that is accurate contemporary observation: "Howso'er their hearts are severed in religion, their heads are both one—they may jowl horns together like any deer i' the herd" (I.iii.52–55). Under professedly centrist Elizabeth, Puritans and Papists were extremes of left and right, and the animal imagery is of a cuckold's horns and knocking together as futile. Later Lavatch returns to the stereotype to declare, "Though honesty be no Puritan, yet it will do no hurt; it will wear the surplice of humility over the black gown of a big heart" (92–94). Here the allusion is to accommodations made by Puritans to escape the authority of the legally established Church of England. *All's Well* provides Shakespeare's only use of the word *papist*.

He refers specifically to Puritans in two other plays, both late romances, where the stereotype changes. In *The Winter's Tale* (c.1609–11) the Clown,

Perdita's foster brother, reviews her shopping list for the sheep-shearing; it includes an item of singers who are mostly tenors and basses, "but one Puritan amongst them, and he sings psalms to hornpipes" (IV.iii.43–44). The dogged determination remains, but this time expressed in an indiscriminate singing of psalms, which often made Puritans into objects of ridicule. In *Pericles* (1606–8) the point is sexual purity. An indignant Bawd explains that Marina, who has been brought to serve in the brothel, is having an effect exactly opposite to that intended and expected: "When she should do for clients her fitment and do me the kindness of our profession, she has me her quirks, her reasons, her master reasons, her prayers, her knees, that she would make a puritan of the devil if he should cheapen a kiss of her" (IV.vi.5–10). Marina's purity is maintained by prayer, and she calls to mind virgin saints of the early Church. The salient Puritan trait of severity in judgment of others, and its human corollary of hypocrisy, though not specifically identified, also appear in Angelo in *Measure for Measure* (1603–4). Both are present but to a lesser degree, and that not sustained, in Isabella. Again the issue is sexuality and purity. Shakespeare's giving of the name *Mariana* to the legal wife rejected by Angelo suggests an affinity with *Marina* in *Pericles* and with the "woman at sea" in romance and legend. More challenging is to find Puritan elements in Falstaff, who originally bore the name of Sir John Oldcastle, a Lollard represented as a forerunner of Protestantism. Falstaff's comic genius and virtuoso wit belie a serious concern with sin and salvation, but the account of his death in *Henry V* (II.iii) focuses on religious issues: whether Falstaff is in heaven or in hell, his dying like one newly christened, apparently praying the Twenty-third Psalm, and crying out "God, God, God!" The Hostess reports that he "talked of the Whore of Babylon" (37), a common abusive allusion to the Church of Rome, but what he said is not told. The most provocative identification is in *The Merchant of Venice* (c.1596–97), where Shylock is seen not as a Jew but as a Puritan, a reading that I will discuss later.

The best documented influence of Puritanism is in *King Lear* (1605–6). Shakespeare bases details of Edgar's feigned madness on the heath on controversial religious pamphlets that argued the question of possession or dispossession of devils. The immediate occasion was the claim of a Puritan preacher John Darrell of successful exorcism in *A Breife Narration* (1598). Samuel Harsnett, chaplain of the Protestant Bishop of London, replied in *A Discovery of the Fraudulent Practices of Iohn Darrell* (1599) with the orthodox Anglican position that "miracles are ceased." Darrell's rejoinder was *A True Narration*, and there were further books against him. Harsnett expanded the argument in his *Declaration of Egregious Popish Impostures* (1603) by focusing his attack on earlier papist exorcisms, notably those of a Jesuit priest William Weston and several seminarians, including Robert Debdale, who had been at school in Stratford with Shakespeare before going with their recusant schoolmaster Simon Hunt to the seminary at Douai. There were no Catholic pamphlets in the exorcism controversy, probably because James I, who became king in 1603, intensified Elizabethan constraints, and exorcism was usually associated with Catholic priests. Edgar's mad words come from Harsnett's account of Catholic claims and are evidence of Shakespeare's reading pamphlets of religious controversy. The plays often employ the supernatural, a familiar dimension of sixteenth-century imagination and experience, perhaps because ghosts, witches, and fairies were a way of giving the lie to an assertion that miracles had ceased without the risk of the specificity of exorcism. Regulations governing the theater imposed constraints, and *King Lear* reflects the 1606 order of Parliament that banned references to ''God'' as blasphemous; it has a poor Tom o' Bedlam, ''Whom the foul fiend hath led through fire and through flame'' (III.iv.50–51). However, this mere verbal regulation was nothing compared to the earlier, sweeping suppression of community performances under Elizabeth that matched her father's dissolution of the monasteries.

Mysteries' End

Since late medieval Catholicism was so all-encompassing of the community, the laws that stripped the altars were paralleled by attacks on the Corpus Christi plays. This political action of suppression indicates how significant drama was to a knowledge of Catholicism. There is a poignant story from Yorkshire in the 1640s, when John Shaw observed that people in Furness were ''exceedingly ignorant and blind to religion.'' An old man recalled one memory of Christ: ''I think I heard of that man you spoke of once in a play at Kendal called Corpus Christi play, where there was a man on a tree and blood ran down.''[8] The memory of the Crucifixion demonstrates the power of the concentration on the Passion both in affective piety and in the plays; its vividness came at least partially from the medieval mindset of elaboration and telling the stories of Scripture in contemporary terms. Figures like Pilate, a Roman judge in early Christian imagery, became a medieval judge in paintings and plays. (Such adapting and transforming continues with Shakespeare, who rarely uses contemporary events but tells old stories with current resonances; his plays were usually performed in Elizabethan dress, as seen in woodcuts of the witches who greet Macbeth in Holinshed's *Chronicle.*)

The prevalence of midland and northern locations for cycle plays is significant because these areas remained strongly Catholic through the Tudor reigns, and there is abundant evidence of Shakespeare's connection with the regions. As a youth he could have seen the plays at Coventry, and most scholars assume that he did. Some Corpus Christi plays were still being performed through the 1570s, but a series of laws led to what Harold Gardiner so movingly termed ''Mysteries' End.'' A wariness about gatherings of people and the concomitant threat of uprisings in the reign of Henry VIII and Cranmer's increased favoring of Protestant plays under Edward VI prepared a way for Elizabeth's suppression of the old religious plays. A masque performed for the first Twelfth Night of her reign consisted of a mummery ''of crows in the habits of Cardinals, of asses habited as Bishops, and of wolves representing Abbots.'' An Act of 1559 that forbade performance of all unlicensed interludes favored Protestant plays such as *Lusty Juventus* (1560) and *Appius and Virginia* (1567–68), as well as those of propagandist John Bale.

The Privy Council controlled the statement of policy, but implementation was a different process. The report on justices of the peace required of bishops in 1564 showed that only 431 of 851 justices, in twenty-one dioceses, favored government policy in matters of religion, and in the North they moved slowly. A letter from the Diocesan Court of High Commission to Wakefield, May 27, 1576, sets limits:

> in the said playe no pageant be used or set furthe wherein the Ma¹ye of God the Father, God the Sonne, or God the Holie Ghoste or the admin- istration of either the Sacramentes of baptisme or of the Lordes Supper be counterfeyted or represented, or anythinge plaied which tende to the maintenaunce of superstition and idolatrie or which be contrarie to the lawes of God [and] or of the realme.   (78)

In the last line *and* has been struck through and *or* added to indicate a distinction between laws of God and of the state. There was a clear religious objection to drama: Luther opposed Passion plays because the spectators wept, and this was not right because Christ was innocent. Catholic affective piety was antithetical to emerging Protestant sensibility that relied upon direct personal encounter with God. The cycles were preeminently a community experience, and thus at vari- ance with the new individualism.

Nevertheless, survivalism was more extensive than might seem likely with such precise laws and Elizabethan coercive methods of enforcement. The pres- ence of Catholic players, Cholmeley's Men, performing at the houses of recusant Catholics in the North Riding in 1609–10, and at least as late as 1616, and perhaps from 1595, is startling; it is also predictable, given the region's religious sympathies. Moreover, these recusant players make a cogent argument for Shakespeare's tie to Catholicism. Their performances were varied, including miracle plays, ridicules of Puritans—and *Pericles* and *King Lear*. Thus were sustained the popular and esteemed dramatic traditions of York.

An amusing juxtaposition in theatrical history is with King Richard III (Richard of York), who was keen about plays. The city of York on September 7, 1483, celebrated his coronation and the investiture of the prince of Wales with a performance of the "Creed play," a favorite of the Corpus Christi cycle, before the king and queen in the municipal hall, the day before the ceremony in the Minster and a state procession through the streets. The Tudors came into power when Richmond (King Henry VII) defeated Richard at Bosworth in 1485. Shakespeare's *Richard III* owes more to morality plays than to cycle plays with which they first coexisted but subsequently supplanted as reassuringly not tied to scripture and theology. Richard's declaration, "Thus, like the formal Vice, Iniquity, / I moralize two meanings in one word" (III.i.82–83), overtly shows indebtedness to the morality play where the Vice tempted to evil. Shakespeare also attributes to the medieval Richard the most sophisticated skills of political scheming; in *Henry VI, Part III*, Gloucester explains that he can "set the murderous Machiavel to school" (III.ii.193). This is a far cry from the titular hero of the play. Henry VI, dressed as a pilgrim and unshaven, attracted many devotees, especially to his shrine for healing at Windsor—as attested by surviving pilgrims' badges (more than for St. Thomas Becket, though the cult had only fifty years to last before the Reformation)—and for protection against plague sought by observing the Tuesday fast in his honor. All is recorded in *The Miracles of Henry VI*, which described the king as a saint. Especially attractive were his gentleness and charity, qualities lacking in religious controversies and political strivings. Shakespeare's choice of King Henry VI as the subject for his earliest history plays might suggest a Catholic interest evident in Lady Anne's invocation of him as holy. Pilgrims seeking healing powers of the uncanonized but revered Henry visited his tomb at Chertsey and his shrine at Windsor.

Like Richard III, Falstaff is called "that reverend Vice, that gray Iniquity," by Prince Hal in *Henry IV, Part I* (IV.ii.448). Both Richard and Falstaff are, on one level, great comic characters and great tempters, like the Vices in morality plays. From the sixth-century work of Prudentius, *Psychomachia*, Vices appear as competitors against Virtues in many visual arts, not least primers, like that of Simon Vostre where woodcuts make them very contemporary. Richard III and Falstaff are also vehicles for some of Shakespeare's more penetrating and overt consideration of religious questions. Both Catholics and Protestants used the form of the morality play, and its thematic structure of debate matches the religious controversies of Elizabeth's reign. It also had a tradition of overt political commentary, as in John Skelton's *Magnificence* (1515–18), which is about a generic king but also alludes to Henry VIII.

The revival of modern interest in medieval plays began with the production of plays from the York cycle as part of the Festival of Britain in 1951, and subsequently repeated every three years. I saw the performance in 1957 and found it extraordinary, unlike any previous experience: four hours with no interval, and at the end (*Doomsday*) the audience left in hushed silence, moved by the religious intensity of the cycle. As a sign of changing theological emphasis in the twentieth century, later productions concluded with the *Resurrection*, showing how a contemporary performance can vary the images designed to teach and fixed by artisans in so many medieval representations of Doomsday. The change simply extends the modern suppression of medieval Christendom's Four Last Things (Death, Judgment, Hell, and Heaven—derived from the parable of the sheep and goats in Matthew 25), which fell from general notice in the early seventeenth century, although brooding about death did not cease. The obvious example of a literary figure is the self-designed funeral effigy of John Donne, in his shroud, in St. Paul's Cathedral. The gravediggers' scene in *Hamlet* is a witty and subtler deployment of *memento mori*. Present-day uneasiness with such material was obvious in Tony Harrison's *The Mysteries* (1985), first staged in London at the National Theatre in 1977 and then moved to the Lyceum. This three-part version (*The Nativity, The Passion, Doomsday*) told the full story, with modern updating which included lively music, dancing, and technology that was most relentlessly employed for Doomsday, with a great twirling metal sphere and cacophonous music. The audience was moved—many to indignation, anger, and fear with little evidence of the reassurance of faith and piety.

The Romance Tradition

A similar continuity in spite of sixteenth-century antipathy and polemic characterized the vogue of romance. England's first printer, William Caxton, built his success upon an understanding of the tastes of his audience and business acumen; a simple motto for his list of books is ''Religion and Romance.'' His work was initially directed toward the upper classes, but gradually as literacy expanded the same kinds of books continued to be successful. To Caxton is owed the greatest debt for understanding and fostering late-medieval concerns and tastes; his translations were a means of expressing his own religious and moral sensibility, often explicitly stated in his prefaces. As previously noted, the first printers were religiously conservative. Caxton's successor Wynkyn de Worde shows his achievement by both adding romances to the list and introducing less pretentious printings to serve an expanding audience. Caxton is a key figure in the furthering of English, and old romances were significant items. In the sixteenth century special attention went to Spanish books; this was complex since many popular tales, rivals to the old romances, came from this intensely Catholic country. There were fewer problems with books of instruction, and a large trade developed.

Richard Mulcaster's *First Part of the Elementarie* (1582) cited a need for English and recognized that this was not automatically acquired in the grammar schools that taught Latin. The expanding audience available for Shakespeare is neatly summed up in Edward (Edmund) Coote's *The English Scholemaister* (1596), a guide for instructors and a textbook for pupils that was frequently issued up to 1704. The Master of Bury St. Edmund's identifies his readers as: ''the unskillful, which desire to make use of it for their own private benefit; and to such men and women of trade as Taylors, Weavers, Shoppe-keepers, Seamsters, and such others as have undertaken the teaching of others.'' A rather different approach to expanding literacy governed a collection of instructional songs, John Rhodes's *The Countrie Man's Comfort; or, Religious Recreatione, Fitte for All Well Disposed Persons* (1588, rpt. 1637), that is, both ''the Scholler of pettie Schooles'' and poor countrymen and their families to pass ''the long winter nights.''

Such books are a gloss for the endeavors of Autolycus to sell ballads and songs in *The Winter's Tale*, and for the village schoolmaster Holofernes in *Love's Labour's Lost* (c.1588–89). Shakespeare's early comedy has an interesting relation to romance; Holofernes and the Spaniard Don Armado lead the rustics in performing for the nobles, and they present the Nine Worthies. The concept of the Worthies probably originated in the fourteenth century with Jacques du Longuyon, and many romances recount their exploits. The identification of three sets of three heroes from the three principal periods of western history (Biblical: Joshua, David, Judas Macchabeus; pagan: Hector, Alexander, Julius Caesar; and Christian: Arthur, Charlemagne, Godfrey of Bouillon) had several literary consequences. Caxton seems to have chosen romances to print by following the list of Worthies, and thus he extended their popularity. A very curious work by Richard Lloyd, *A brief discourse of the most renowned actes and right valiant conquests of those puisant Princes, called the Nine Worthies* . . . (1584) makes a complex comment on attitudes toward romance heroes in Elizabeth's England. Lloyd's dedicatory Epistle, to Thomas Bromley, Lord Chauncellour of England, begins: ''To God giue honour due, feare him aboue all things: . . . Eschue ech vice, and loue ech vertue euermore'' (ii). Here both honor and fear are associated with God, and the human is seen as a theater for the conflict between Vices and Virtues that recurs in primers and morality plays. Lloyd recognizes that God performed miracles for the Jews who feared him, while the pagans fell through ambition, pride, and avarice. The virtue of the Old Testament worthies reflects a Reformation enthusiasm for the Bible, and the failures of classical heroes the costs of living without it. The fates of the Christians are a blend; Charlemagne was a Godly man who died well, but Arthur was plagued by lasciviousness—as he is in Ascham's view. To strengthen the Christians, Lloyd substitutes a renowned English champion for Godfrey of Bouillon, the French hero of the Crusades. This is Guy of Warwick, the most popular hero of romance and one well known to Shakespeare, who twice alludes to his exploits in *Henry VIII*, and to Michael Drayton, who celebrates him in *Poly-Olbion* (1598/1613). Shakespeare and Drayton were both Warwickshire men.

The influence of country origins may be seen in the sympathetic treatment of the rustics in *Love's Labour's Lost*. There is much laughter at their expense, but the behavior of the aristocrats is no less wanting in sense. The plan of Ferdinand, King of Navarre, to found an Academy, with severe restrictions upon behavior—particularly forswearing food and women—is a humanist experiment that in conception, and almost immediately in execution, has little correspondence to the reality of human behavior. All their clever repartee, a hallmark of humanism, is inadequate to deal with life and death, however amusing it is in academic situations. Don Armado is a Spanish braggart, but he follows his natural instincts to pursue the dairymaid Jacquenetta, and the exposure of his failure to keep Ferdinand's laws only just precedes similar revelations of how the courtiers have also foregone their promises by following their sexual instincts. As Hector in the pageant of the Nine Worthies, Don Armado prepares for the play's resolution. He protests the rude, albeit amusing, teasing that ignores his well intended efforts and the character of the Worthy: "The sweet warman is dead and rotten. Sweet chucks, beat not the bones of the buried. When he breathed, he was a man" (V.ii.659–61). This is a reminder of enforced Protestant attitudes that relentlessly stopped many prayers for the dead and denied Purgatory. The Princess is conciliatory, showing something of the quality that is fully displayed when a messenger brings news of the death of her father. Seriousness is an appropriate response to the Nine Worthies, heroes of romance whose feats and deaths are dishonored only at some peril. Shakespeare's early warning of the failure of humanism, when it derides the mystery and inspiration of romance, is part of a counterargument that grew steadily through his plays and parallels the printings of romances that had a substantial market, not least in popular chapbooks that brought the old heroes to the barely literate in the seventeenth century.

Caxton did not involve himself with the new Humanism, and the objections to romance by leading humanists indicate an incompatibility of taste. For Erasmus, a bold critic of abuses in the Church, stories of Lancelot and Arthur were "fablae stultae et aniles," unacceptably distracting students from proper concern with history and classical poetry. Juan Luis Vives, writing in a treatise for women, *De institutione feminae christianae* (1523), included a list of forbidden romances. Richard Hyrde's first translation in 1540 added English examples, and the book was printed in various editions as late as 1592. Thomas Paynell's translation of 1546 well explains the antipathy to stories "written in the vulgar tonge . . . by suche as were ydle & knewe nothinge. These books do hurte both man and woman, for they make theym wylye & craftye, they kyndle and styr up covetousnes, inflame angre, & all beastly and filthy desyre." The lack of Latin and the flexibility of mind derived from imaginative literature rank with the three most obviously pertinent deadly sins.

Such moral condemnation of the romance tradition found in Roger Ascham, a strong Protestant and tutor to then-Princess Elizabeth, its most influential voice, sounded in his two famous books. *Toxophilus* (1545) is a treatise on archery that includes not just technical information but also pronouncements about moral character.

> In our fathers tyme nothing was red, but books of fayned chivalrie, wherein a man by redinge, shuld be led to none other ends, but only to manslaughter and baudrye. Yf any man suppose they were good ynough to passe the time with al, he is deceyved. For surelye vayne woordes doo worke no smal thinge in vayne, ignoraunt, and younge mindes, specially yf they be gyven any thynge therunto of theyr owne nature. These bokes (as I have heard say) were made the moste parte in Abbayes, and Monasteries, a very lickely and fit fruite of suche an ydle and blynde kinde of lyvying.   (19)[9]

Ascham revised this passage in his best-known book, *The Scholemaster* (1570):

> In our forefathers tyme, whan Papistrie, as a standyng poole, couuered and ouerflowed all England, fewe bookes were read in our tong, sauying certaine bookes Cheualrie, as they sayd, for pastime and pleasure, which, as some say, were made in Monasteries, by idle Monkes or wanton Chanons: as one for example, *Morte Arthure*: the whole pleasure of which booke standeth in two speciall poyntes, in open mans slaughter, and bold bawdrye.   (80)

The infusion of Reformation is as heavy in this condemnation of the romance as it is in Elizabethan pamphlets of religious controversy. Several points need noting. First, Ascham expresses the humanist's concern about vernacular literature, an awareness of its potential for a broader audience and greater influence, especially on youth. Second, there is a severe objection to "pastime and pleasure," a phrase that resonates of the feasts and community events that marked the festivals of medieval Christendom. Third, there is a vast simplification of the nature of romance, which includes much more than manslaughter and bawdy; Ascham conveniently ignores the Holy Grail, a spirituality toward which

Malory points all the disparate parts in *Morte Arthure*. The reading indicates a lack of scholarly exactness in this great humanist that is best explained by the final and main point of his attack on the romance: its association with Catholicism. Romances are evil because they were written by monks in abbeys and monasteries: since Henry VIII dissolved these religious houses there must have been evil, and sexual indulgence and idleness are the charges—not supported by the evidence of cases noted above, but because of such passages part of the mythology of Reformation in England. Particularly compelling as a difference between the two passages is the specific identification of "Papistrie" and the evocative imagery of a standing pool that covered all England. What a difference twenty-five years makes in the phrasing of the arguments, from "our fathers tyme" to "our forefathers tyme," a revision that signals the passing of a generation. In *Toxophilus* there is still an anxiety that some might accept the old romances "as good enough," and Ascham identifies this as being "deceived." In *The Scholemaster* that time is passed, and he need only record a bad history that is finished. One final point is that Ascham's denunciation of the romance concludes with a poignantly patriotic judgment: as bad as *Morte Arthure* is, it is ten times less so than a translation of a book in Italy. The persuasion of pleasure remains a threat, since "Mo Papistes be made, by your mer[r]ly bookes of *Italie*, than by your earnest bookes of *Louvain*" (79).

An anti-Arthur stance is curiously unpatriotic. Henry VII chose to name his first son Arthur, an evocation both of Celtic (Welsh) origins and of a new era of greatness, albeit Prince Arthur died and Henry VIII succeeded to the throne. Tudor roses were made the centerpiece of the fourteenth-century round table that can still be seen at Winchester. Edmund Spenser exploited national pride by making Arthur the sum of all virtues, Magnificence, in *The Faerie Queene* (1596), and romance is an essential literary form in his creation of a Renaissance/Reformation epic for Protestant Elizabeth. But the plight of the sixteenth-century King Arthur is generally summed up in the title of Thomas Hughes's play, *The Misfortunes of Arthur* (1587).

The Puritans objected to romance in their religious writings. A clergyman, Edward Dering in a *Bryfe and Necessary Catechisme or Instruction* (1572), laments the present taste in books that are "full of synne and abominations." Romances are principal offenders, alike in "wickedness" with the reading of forefathers who "had their spiritual enchantments, in which they were bewytched, Bevis of Hampton, Guy of Warwicke, Arthur of the round table, Huon of Burdeaux, Oliver of the Castle, the four sonnes of Amond, and a great many other such childish follye." Very significant is the phrase "spiritual enchantments," which declared the relation between romance and religion in Catholicism. These examples, across a spectrum of time and from authors of varied sophistication and religious conviction, indicate that established affinity.

Some humanists condemn the romance tradition without identifying a religious dimension; their moral indignation is merely against a worldview fostered by romance. Montaigne's first book of *Essays* (1580) uses some of the same titles as Puritan Dering, but he admits that his judgment is based on hearsay since he has not read the romances:

> For of King *Arthur*, of *Lancelot du Lake*, of *Amadis*, of *Huon of Burdeux* and such idle time consuming, and wit-be-sotting trash of bookes wherin youth doth commonly amuse it self, I was not so much as acquainted with their names, and to this day know not their bodies, nor what they contain: So exact was my discipline.

The translation is that of John Florio, one of several intellectual and literary men suggested as the inspiration for Don Armado, in *Love's Labour's Lost*. Florio added Arthur to the list, another example of fascination with this hero. Montaigne, whose religious attitudes are enigmatic, assumes a superiority to romance because it distracts from serious work. Even Ben Jonson faulted his loved rival for frivolity and old-fashioned taste. He refers to a "Shipwrack in Bohemia, wher ther is no Sea neer by some 100 Miles" (Chambers II, 207) and "another time makes Athyns in Bohemia" (II, 248). Jonson resented the success of Shakespeare's romances and denigrates: "a mouldy Tale, / Like *Pericles* stale / As the shrive's crust, and nasty as his fish" ["On *The New Inn*: Ode. To Himself" (1629)], and glances at *The Winter's Tale* again in *Bartholomew Fair*.

Perhaps inevitably time was on the side of a Protestant Church of England, and the power of Elizabethan language eased its ascendancy. Cranmer's magnificent prose in the *Book of Common Prayer* and *Homilies* brought the Word as the outlawed centuries-old forms of worship receded. Puritan claims, rival competitors to Catholicism's threat in the 1580s, were similarly mitigated by Richard Hooker's answer to claims of Presbyterian discipline in the *Laws of Ecclesiastical Politie* (1593–97), which made the case both for justification by faith and the possibility of the Church of Rome as part of the Church of Christ through which members might find salvation. With the removal of the physical signs of medieval Christendom, a steady reiteration of its evils, and a gradual supplanting with new forms, even the memory of Catholicism dimmed.

There were certainly limitations and abuses in the Catholic church, but current evidence indicates that prejudicial interests, of both contemporary Protestants and subsequent historians and literary critics, greatly exaggerated these. Two assumptions, supported by reliance upon Protestant propagandists and literary sources, have governed Reformation historiography: that Catholicism was no longer respected in the late Middle Ages and therefore the laity were open to a new religion, and that evangelical Protestantism, as a religion of the Word, greatly appealed. In short, as Christopher Haigh summarized in "The Recent

Historiography of the English Reformation'' (1987), for such ''whig'' historians the Reformation was

> an inexorable process, a necessary sequence unfolding easily in a prede-termined conclusion: the medieval Church was in decline, the laity was anti-clerical, Lutheran ideas were readily accepted, a centralising state espoused reform, superstition was attacked and, after a brief Marian fiasco, a finally Protestant England was recognized in the legislation of 1559, the date at which many Reformation textbooks stop. (30–31)

Recently expanded evidence includes substantial records from the country-side—accounts of churchwardens, records of benefices, clerical marriages and pensions, wills, gifts for building additions and church furniture, especially in parish churches, concealments and removals of images, resistances and enforce-ments of policy, and a broader view of printed theological controversies. More-over, both the greater focus on political rather than religious ideas that typifies the end of the twentieth century and an alternative historiography, to the old 'whiggish' one, indicate that in Shakespeare's world much remained Catholic. The published data are extensive; I have offered only representative evidence and conclusions from the work of historians to give some sense of religious circumstances in which Shakespeare lived, beginning with the Henrician reforms that initiated the process of Reformation in England and continuing with its enforcement in Elizabeth's long reign. This greater stringency stemmed at least in part from more volatile and insistent expressions of religious convictions by Protestants, Puritans, and Catholics. In the end there was a single orthodoxy, which meant no provisions for variety; Elizabethan Protestantism was very aus-tere indeed when compared with the Catholic Church of medieval Christendom. Bible-reading, moralizing sermons, and severe services supplanted rich church ornament, images of the Crucifixion, the Virgin Mary, and countless saints, elaborate vestments and altar vessels, civic and religious celebrations of feasts and festivals throughout the year that marked the rhythms of nature, and rituals that communicated mystery and wonder. The specific biographical details of the Shakespeare family in fact show many affinities with that rich Catholic tradition.

3
THE SHAKESPEARES OF STRATFORD

In contrast to popular belief, biographical information about William Shakespeare is unusually extensive for a person of his class. There are about a hundred legal documents in parish registers and municipal archives, and a few references to theatrical business and legal documents about property. Contemporary references in literary works number about fifty. But these leave gaps for speculation and critical interpretation, which scholars and critics have filled with many arguments. Not least is a view of the poet-playwright as a discreet Catholic in Elizabeth's England. But, as earlier noted, this has only recently been seriously considered. By definition religious conviction and loyalty required caution, since avowed Catholics were constrained to seek exile on the continent or often subject to prosecution in Reformation England. There is not adequate evidence to prove Shakespeare's formal religious conviction, but a cluster of details demonstrates a probability. Even those not traditionally attracted to the idea of Shakespeare as Catholic, admit that he was not anti-Catholic, as were so many of his contemporaries. This can be viewed as a sign of the compassion and tolerance of his mind and personality or as a deep conviction muted by discretion in a society where alternative religious belief was illegal. In fact, the two are not incompatible, although this is hard to acknowledge when confronted by the mass of polemical writings by Protestants, Puritans, and Catholics. Here I want only to review the key points and some of the arguments for an affinity of Shakespeare to Catholicism, an experience of reality that is rooted in mystery and rejoices in signs to figure what is beyond verbal statement. This is a paradox for a writer so much a master of language and living at the time when the Word was replacing images as the way to religious understanding. But as we have seen in Queen Mary's use of homilies, Catholics could deploy Reformation skills. The Council of Trent (1547–63) recognized this by identifying the Jesuits as propagandists for the faith. Cyprian Soarez, a Jesuit lecturer on rhetoric, wrote *De arte rhetorica* (1562), which became a textbook for schoolboys in Jesuit schools and colleges from the late 1570s. Like medieval rhetoricians, Soarez relies upon Quintilian and Cicero, with some use of Aristotle, Horace, and Virgil. Like Prudentius, who imitated Virgil, he sees rhetoric as a tool to glorify God, when eloquence is rid of vain error. In *Dismembered Rhetoric* (1995) Ceri Sullivan finds in Catholic recusant writing a sophisticated knowledge of effective ways to sway the audience, albeit with a simpler style than the ornate rhetoric of writers for the Protestant case. Shakespeare's use of romance, on the surface unusual storytelling and theatrical spectacle, is analogous in its combination of appearance and reality.

A simple contrast between Catholic images and Protestant words is inadequate for understanding the continuities and affinities that coexist with sharp differences. Just as the woodcuts in Foxe's *Book of Martyrs* show a continued reliance upon images, so the use of rhetorical techniques in recusant writing indicates Catholic acknowledgment of the power of language to influence an audience. Since most of the authors were university and Jesuit trained, this is not surprising. But there is a crucial difference because Catholic writers rely upon centuries of authorities and faith that is based not on human understanding but upon God Himself, although they follow arguments of reason and offer proofs. As Robert Persons summarizes in *A Treatise of Three Conversions of England* (1603–4): "the Maiestie of allmightie God, who will be beleeued at his woord, without being asked for proofe or reason for the same." The title page of the Douai/Rheims New Testament makes the point in a slightly different way: "a man must show himself meekminded, lest by stubborn contentions he become incapable and unpat to be taught." Christ embodies such meekness, frequently in women, but this feminization is not weakness but strength. Mary is the icon, both the Handmaid of the Lord and the Woman of Valor.[1] Just as the Crucifixion makes salvation possible, so obedience and humility—which are not passivity—open the possibility of activity.

A commonplace about religion is the likely continuance in the faith of one's family, and there is evidence of the Catholicism of both Shakespeare's parents and his favorite child. Born before an aggressive political establishment of Protestantism, his parents would have been Catholic, but theirs is more than automatic participation in the old church. Richard Shakespeare, probably his grandfather, was a farmer at Snitterfield and a tenant of Robert Arden of Wilmcote. Richard's son John Shakespeare married Mary Arden, thus improving his social and financial situation. He also increased his tie to Roman Catholicism, since the Ardens were strongly Catholic, remaining loyal to the old religion in spite of reforms. They were connected to the Catesbys. Mary's cousin Edward Arden of Park Hall was indicted for treason in 1583. He and his son-in-law John Somerville were executed, their heads set on London Bridge, and the family imprisoned, all part of the investigation of Sir Thomas Lucy, a local Puritan magistrate, about the Somerville plot to kill the Queen. The Shakespeare family has been traced to the area of Wroxhall Priory, north of Stratford. An Isabel Shakespeare (d.1504), as noted earlier, was prioress, and Shakespeare uses this name for his most significant nun, the novice of St. Clare who is the heroine in *Measure for Measure*. When Wroxhall closed as part of Henry VIII's dissolution of the monasteries, a Domina Jane Shakespeare, listed as sub-prioress in 1525, went to Hatton, where a register records on October 21, 1571, "Mortua et sepults erat Domina Jana aliquando una monicarum Wraxall." There was a theory of her being William's aunt, but a remoter kinship is more likely. Mary and John named their first child "Joan," and after her death their fifth child was "Joan." To have relatives who are nuns is a significant experience in a Catholic family. To have cousins who are executed and imprisoned for their religious beliefs is not likely to be unnoticed.

John and Mary Shakespeare moved to Stratford sometime before 1552, and John became a prominent figure, to whom there are many references in borough records. The first years were under Mary Tudor, who tried to restore Catholicism in England, 1553–58; Mary and John Shakespeare's first child was baptized in the Latin rite by Roger Dyos, who was later deprived of his post because he refused to change back to Protestantism under Elizabeth. William Shakespeare was born in April 1564; he was baptized on April 26, and the birthday is traditionally set as April 23, the feast of St. George, patron saint of England. Holy Trinity Church contained characteristic Catholic features of the late Middle Ages, a red and gold painted Rood loft with many carved images and a ceiling painted with St. George and the Dragon, the Last Judgment, and the History of the Holy Cross, the work of local craftsmen. The burgesses of Stratford did not act to destroy images, as ordered in 1547, until a Visitation of the Bishop of Worcester, coincidentally in 1564. Yet a Catholic sympathizer, William Butcher, formerly President of Corpus Christi College, Oxford, became the new vicar in 1564. He was replaced by Henry Haycraft, a Protestant, after the 1568 Rising of the Northern Earls. The parish church, as was typical, preserved more of its Catholic identity longer than the Guild of the Holy Cross, a house with four priests who cared for the poor and aged. There the Rood screen was pulled down, images broken, and the great wall painting of the Dance of Death—traces of which are now visible—was whitewashed.

The Birthplace in Henley Street, albeit now larger than in Shakespeare's youth, is the house of a prosperous businessman. As late as 1576 John Shakespeare, a glover or worker in leather, was enjoying success and applied to the Herald's office to be identified as a gentleman with a coat of arms. He was among those who moved from tradesman to esquire as part of Tudor economic development; his civic positions included election to the town council, serving as a magistrate, and a brief time as mayor when William was an infant. But there was an apparent sudden and mysterious decline in John's fortunes, and he did not attend Council meetings, although his name remained on the roster until 1586. The arms were granted much later, probably because of William's success and efforts. John Shakespeare's financial and legal difficulties coincide with the intensified suppression of Catholics that, as we have seen, reached a height in the 1580s. His name is the first on a March 1592 list of recusants who did not make the required once-a-month attendance at church, and Sir Thomas Lucy noted ''came not to church for fear of process of debt.'' The recusancy may be only a matter of economics, but it was a typical Roman Catholic subterfuge to evade paying the penalties for nonattendance at church, and John had sufficient funds as late as 1586–87 to stand surety for friends. Others on the 1592 list include: John Wheeler, who was Deputy to Bailiff John Shakespeare, and his son John Wheeler; and two names—Fluellen and Bardolph—found in *Henry V.*

Most intriguing is the discovery of a Catholic will hidden in the rafters of the Birthplace—possibly in the 1583 crisis of the Somervilles when the houses of all related to the Ardens were searched—and found in 1757.[2] The will can support an argument that John remained Catholic until his death in 1601. Edmund Malone, to whom the will was sent by John Jordan, a wheelwright and amateur antiquarian of Stratford, printed it in 1790. Although the original is strangely lost, few doubt the probity of the antiquarian who published a document described as four sheets of paper stitched together, written in an old-fashioned hand, and thus perhaps earlier than the Jesuit influx of printed testaments.[3] The Catholic character is obvious because it closely resembles the *Last Will of the Soul* written by St. Charles Borromeo, a Catholic archbishop of Milan from 1538–84 and an inspired leader of the Counter-Reformation who also drew up the revised Catechism designed to instruct parish priests. Modern discovery of Mexican (1661) and Italian versions and then an English translation, *The Testament of the Soul* that has survived in editions of 1636 and 1638, as well as other similar testaments, have authenticated the document. The Jesuit Persons, according to William Allen, the head of the English College in France, in 1581 wanted three to four thousand testaments for England. But it seems likely that Edmund Campion brought the first copy into England, since on their journey from Rome to England as the first Jesuit mission in 1580, Campion and Persons spent eight days in Milan in Cardinal Borromeo's palace, where Campion gave a daily discourse. It is probable that Campion got a copy of the Will to take to England and that he brought it to Warwickshire, where he stayed with Sir William Catesby of Ashby St. Leger, Lord Vaux of Harrowden, and Sir Thomas Tresham. Thus there is a connection between Campion and John Shakespeare. Malone never saw the opening sheet of the first two and a half articles and printed Jordan's transcription, which is generally thought to be a forgery, not least because of its Protestant character, but subsequent articles correspond very precisely to other versions. The conclusion of Article XIV, part of the original transcript, reads:

> I, John Shakespeare, have made this present writing of protestation, confession and charter in the presence of the Blessed Virgin Mary, my Angel Guardian, and all the Celestial Court, as witnesses hereunto: the which my meaning is, that it be of full value now, presently, and for ever, with the force and virtue of testament, codicil and donation in cause of death; confirming it anew, being in perfect health of soul and body, and signed with mine own hand; carrying also the same about me; and for the better declaration hereof, my will and intention is that it be finally buried with me after my death.
>
>   Pater noster, Ave Maria, Credo,
>   Jesu, Son of David, have mercy one me.
>   Amen.[4]

The preceding articles of the Will refer to: repentance, purgatory, avoidance of despair, acknowledgment of good works, pardoning of injuries received, reliance upon guardian angels, the Virgin Mary, saints—especially Winefride, favored by the mission of 1580—patient endurance, the sacrifice of the Mass, the last sacrament of Extreme Unction, and acceptance of death, "infinite thanks to His divine majesty for all the benefit of my creation, redemption, sanctification, conservation, and vocation to the holy knowledge of Him and His true Catholic faith, but above all, for His so great expectation of me to penance" (IX). This is a gloss on Shakespeare's previously noted emphasis on penance. The English version of 1638 emphasizes: "I will liue and dye obedient vnto the Catholike, Romaine, & Apostolicke Church, firmly belieuing all the twelue Articles of the Fayth taught by the holy Apostles, with the interpretation, & declaration made theron by the same holy church, as taught, defined & declared by her" (I, Schoenbaum 44). The Council of Trent (1545–63) was slow in being convened and slower in implementation, but Borromeo's Testament reflects historical circumstances of Reformation and Counter-Reformation. The substance of each article is unchanged, although there are variations of language. Shakespeare's mother Mary Arden did not die until 1608. There was, then, a long period for an influence of parents noted as Catholic recusants.

The continuity of a Catholic family shows in Shakespeare's favorite daughter Susanna, who was twenty-eight years old when her name appeared as one of twenty-two on the recusants' list for 1606 as one who did not receive the sacrament at Easter. One summons was ignored, and then it was dismissed. Greater stringency followed the Gunpowder Plot of

November 5, 1605, a foiled attempt to blow up Parliament that still lingers, in annual celebration of Guy Fawkes's Day, as the most notorious Catholic action against the government. Susanna married Dr. John Hall, a Cambridge graduate with both Catholic and Protestant patients; he was buried next to Shakespeare in 1635. Susanna died in 1649, and a commendatory poem suggests an interplay of family and religion:

> Witty above her sex, but that's not all
> Wise to salvation was good Mistress Hall
> Something of Shakespeare was in that, but this
> Wholly of him with whom she's now in bliss
> (Chambers II, 12)

Peter Whelan's recent play *The Herbal Garden* (1996), speculates about Shakespeare and Susanna, but not about her devotion to her father. Shakespeare's will makes her chief beneficiary and with her husband "executors of this my last will and testament," perhaps a reminder of the Established Church's abolition of many Catholic ways of dying. Shakespeare's parents and favorite child were overtly charged with Catholic sympathy.

Much lies in the interpretation of events. A pointed example is the Gunpowder Plot, which shocked both Catholics and Protestants, but roused great anti-Catholic sentiment that echoes through the centuries. A revisionist view of the Reformation argues that the plot may have been Sir Robert Cecil's, a calculated and controlled action—the last-minute discovery of not very subtle movements—designed to inspire anti-Catholic feeling and squash any optimism associated with King James as the son of Catholic Mary Queen of Scots, and to ensnare Henry Garnet, the Jesuit superior in England. Pamphlets about Cecil's duplicity appeared almost immediately. There are fascinating connections to *Macbeth*, which was probably completed after the conspiracy and resulting trials. Shakespeare's much commented upon Porter's scene combines medieval Hell's Mouth, drunkenness—a noted court response to the Gunpowder Plot was excessive drinking—and several references to *equivocation*, a Jesuit technique. Garnet was directly accused as the ringleader, though actually he served as confessor to the conspirators and thus, under the inviolable seal of the confessional, "equivocated" to protect them. A specific reference to Garnet seems likely in "farmer" (II.iii.4), since Farmer was his alias. The Porter suggests: "Faith, here's an equivocator, that could swear in both the scales against either scale, who committed treason enough for God's sake, yet could not equivocate to heaven. O, come in, equivocator" (8–11). He repeats the idea to Macduff, when he describes drink to be an equivocator with lechery (29–35) and deploys sophisticated theological argumentation in the comic physical analogs. The maxim that fools and children speak truth seems to be completed when Ross reports Macduff's death, in the dialogue between Lady Macduff and her son (IV.ii). Finally at Birnam, Macbeth begins "To doubt the equivocation of the fiend / That lies like truth" (V.v.43–44). The only use of the word *equivocation* other than this cluster in *Macbeth* is in the gravediggers' scene when Hamlet exclaims: "How absolute the knave is! We must speak by the card, or equivocation will undo us" (V.i.137–38).

The political and religious dangers are great, and the play suggests more about contemporary practices by Walsingham and Burghley in England than circumstances in medieval Scotland (or Denmark). Macbeth employs spies on all, and Malcolm is understandably mistrustful. Claudius uses the shadowy figures of Rosencrantz and Gildenstern to spy on Hamlet, when he and Polonius are not themselves spying. Lady Macbeth has been read as a comment upon Elizabeth, who was anxious and repentant soon after the execution of Mary, Queen of Scots in 1587, and tormented by nightmares at her own long death. Waugh begins his biography of Campion with a moving account of Elizabeth's anguished dying and suggests that her haunted memories included the brilliant Oxford scholar who refused noble patronage to become a Catholic priest and martyr. An association with regicide dates from at least 1588, when William Allen's *An Admonition to the Nobility and People of England* compared Elizabeth to Jezebel (1 Kings 21). Even in death Elizabeth dominated her rivals: Her splendid white marble tomb was placed, as ordered, above that of her Catholic sister Queen Mary Tudor, who has no monument. Amidst an effusion of tributes for Elizabeth after her death, there is none from Shakespeare, as Henry Chettle noted at the time. There is Cranmer's speech about the "promise" of the "royal infant" at the end of *Henry VIII*; but this rhetoric seems inconsistent in a play that celebrates the Catholic Queen Katherine, and usually includes among the hearers Elizabeth's mother Queen Anne Boleyn, who was subsequently beheaded. Ambiguity, the uncertainty about seeming lies that yet are true because of a different meaning in the mind of the speaker, is seldom more evident than here.

What is certain is that Warwickshire was a Catholic stronghold and home to many of the conspirators of the Gunpowder Plot. Most notable is Robert Catesby, the son of William Catesby who earlier supported the earl of Essex, to whom Shakespeare was closely tied because the Lord Chamberlain's Men performed *Richard II* on the eve of the abortive rebellion in 1601; Essex (friend of Shakespeare's patron, Southampton, of a powerful Catholic family) was executed in grisly fashion. The Catesby family seat was at Lapworth, near Stratford; there or at Bushwood, the family sheltered Campion. The conspirators met at Clopton House, another Catholic home, and at Coughton Court, the home of the Catholic Throckmortons. They also met at the Mermaid Tavern in London, where Shakespeare often went with friends such as Ben Jonson, who was at the time a Roman Catholic. (While in Newgate prison for killing Gabriel Spencer in a duel, Jonson was converted by a priest.) Another connection between Shakespeare and prominent Catholics in Warwickshire are the Underhills of Idlicote; he bought New Place on May 4, 1597, from William Underhill, who had been imprisoned as a recusant. There were also the Grants of Northbrooke, Snitterfield, and the Smiths, lords of the manor of Shottery, and the Reynolds family in Stratford. Inevitably with the flux of religious affiliation Shakespeare would know both Catholics and Protestants, but the number of contacts with influential Catholics suggests more than accident.

Shakespeare's attendance at King Edward's New School is assumed, though there are no surviving records. This new foundation followed upon the seizure of lands of the medieval free school, under auspices of the Church at least from the thirteenth century. Much has been made of the excellence of its curriculum and teachers, particularly their being university graduates. Most interesting is Simon Hunt, who went to Stratford in 1571, having graduated from Oxford in 1568, and taught Latin. The earl of Warwick nominated Hunt as master of the Stratford school. In 1573 Hunt's sympathies turned to persecuted Catholics, and he stayed only four years before going to Douai, accompanied by Robert Debdale, a pupil from Shottery, the son of a Catholic farmer. Shakespeare encountered his fellow student again through his interest in exorcism, already expressed in *The Comedy of Errors* (c.1589–94). Debdale was one of the seminary priests who returned to England and with William Weston (alias Edmonds) conducted exorcisms. Debdale's letter and religious tokens were brought to his family by Thomas Cottom, younger brother of a Stratford schoolmaster, from Rheims in June 1580; the letter survived because Cottom was arrested, as was Debdale himself shortly afterward. Cottom was released at about the time of Shakespeare's marriage, but arrested again four years later and soon executed. A tie to his schoolmate is Shakespeare's use of Harsnett's pamphlet about exorcism in *King Lear*. This connection is certain, as is Hunt's being a Stratford schoolmaster when Shakespeare was a boy; however, whether William, like Robert Debdale, went to Douai is speculation. Hunt was important to the Jesuit mission; he replaced Persons at St. Peter's and thus Persons accompanied Campion to England.

Another schoolmaster at Stratford was Thomas Jenkins, from 1575–79, when Shakespeare was ten to fifteen years old. Jenkins taught Latin—rhetoricians Cicero and Quintilian, prose historians Caesar and Sallust, and the poet Ovid. Again there is evidence for a Catholic background. Jenkins was the son of Sir Thomas White, who had founded St. John's College, Oxford, where he took a B.A. in 1566 and M.A. in 1570, and was a fellow. Campion, the first and most celebrated of the more than 200 Jesuits executed between 1580 and 1603, was also a fellow of St. John's. John Cottom, the elder brother of Thomas

Cottom, Debdale's associate who was executed, followed Jenkins as school-master for a time. Then he resigned, declared his Catholicism overtly, and became a landowner in Lancashire. Thus the school retained something of its Catholic quality after its Reformation redefinition, and there is a direct tie between Stratford and Lancashire. In Elizabeth's reign twenty-one Catholic school-masters were executed; nine were Lancastrians. Shakespeare may have been a schoolmaster; this is one tradition for the "missing" or "lost years" that cannot be proved or dismissed. Honigman has shown that John Cottom could be the link, the schoolmaster who recommended Shakespeare as a schoolmaster to the Catholic Alexander Houghton, whose will made a bequest to "William Shakeshafte." The tradition began before the discovery of the will with John Aubrey's record of a conversation with William Beeston, an authority about the theater, son of an actor in Shakespeare's company and thus probably personally acquainted. Aubrey noted: "He understood Latin pretty well, for he had been in his younger years a schoolmaster."

The expectation would be of a record of Shakespeare's early marriage to Anne Hathaway in Holy Trinity Church, Stratford. But the only record is the Bishop of Worcester's license, dated November 27, 1582, for the wedding to take place without the usual triple announcing of banns on successive Sundays. And a bond of sureties—a guarantee of £40 if an impediment were to be charged—from the Bishop's registry, dated November 23, 1582. Shakespeare's youth and his bride's comparative old age—he was eighteen and she was twenty-six—and the birth of their first child Susanna on May 26, 1583, six months later, are the points most biographies stress. A license was customary only to speed a marriage when banns were suspended for Advent or Lent, the penitential periods before the great feasts of Christmas and Easter. Since Anne was pregnant, there were reasons to avoid delay. There is much speculation about a relationship that involved disparity of age, haste, and subsequent separations, though Shakespeare made frequent journeys to Stratford and retired there at a comparatively young age. The marriage probably took place at Temple Grafton, since Anne's father was dead and she had relatives there, but the parish records have not survived. The priest at this time was John Frith, who is described as "an old priest and unsound in religion, he can neither preach nor read well"—that is, he was probably Roman Catholic and considered too insignificant to remove. Again religious preference is a possible explanation for the circumstances of Shakespeare's marriage. The other children, the twins Hamnet and Judith, were baptized in the Stratford Church on February 2, 1585. Their names are those of a baker and his wife, Hamnet and Judith Sadler, friends of Shakespeare and neighbors. Hamnet Sadler's name is on the recusancy list for 1606.

Much light has been cast upon "the dark or lost years" that come between Shakespeare's marriage and his being noted in London. Again there are cases for several Catholic connections. The possibility of his being in Lancashire is of long standing, and it has been suggested that he briefly went on to Douai. Most likely is the argument of association with the Houghton family, a great Catholic house in the North, believed by some to have been the center of the English Counter-Reformation. The will of Alexander Houghton of Lea Hall, near Preston in Lancashire, leaves instruments and clothes to Sir Thomas Hesketh to keep the players "ffoke Gyllome and William Shakeshafte." Sixteenth-century spelling was not consistent, even for surnames, and "Shakeshafte" was his grandfather's variant. Several scholars have amassed much evidence to show that Shakespeare spent part of his youth at a great house in Lancashire, thus learning much about courtly manners and beginning to perform. The easy commerce with the Continent in the early plays corresponds to the flow of English Catholics to and from exile. One suggestion is that John Shakespeare, himself at risk because of his religion, might have sent his son to a trusted, strongly Catholic family to assure his education; an alternative motive was to avoid a teenager's entanglement with Anne Hathaway; another urges that he was recruited by Catholic schoolmasters for preliminary study as a seminarian at Douai; another that he went to the continent, but chose to be a player rather than a priest, and alternatively that he went underground as a player in the troubles of the early 1580s.

The Houghtons were deeply committed to the Catholic cause. Thomas Houghton, elder brother of Alexander, helped Allen, who had been a guest at Houghton Tower in the mid-1560s, to found the college at Douai that later moved to Rheims. Shakespeare refers to the institution in *The Taming of the Shrew*; Lucentio is presented as a "young scholar that hath been long studying at Rheims, as cunning in Greek, Latin, and other languages," (II.i.79–82)— necessary for the New Testament translation. Thomas Houghton became an exile to Antwerp in 1569/70 because he could not accede to the religious demands of Elizabeth's reign. He was outlawed and his estates taken, and he never returned to England in spite of a trip to Antwerp by his half-brother Richard, who attempted to persuade him to submit to Elizabeth, who had authorized this effort. His son, also a Thomas Houghton, was in exile, studied at Douai, was ordained, returned to Lancashire, and was imprisoned at Salford; there are no references after 1582.

Alexander Houghton's will was written in August 1581, a crucial moment because Campion was then being tortured on the rack. He had been captured, when celebrating Mass in Berkshire, while on his way to Houghton, where a library could provide the theological and philosophical resources needed to make good his "brag" or "challenge" that he would justify the Catholic faith. This letter to the Privy Council explained his apostolic mission to the provinces in nine points or articles that subsequently were secretly printed in *Rationes*

Decem. Burghley's efforts were to discover Campion's Catholic contacts, the places he stayed, and religious conversations and acts. The Houghtons were among those raided. Houghton's wife Elizabeth was reported for harboring at Lea ''an obstinant Papist well acquainted with seminaries, and he was teaching the children to sing and plaie upon the virginalls.'' A priest hole can be seen today, and there is a family tradition of players' costumes kept until modern time.

The effect of Alexander Houghton's transfer of ''William Shakeshafte'' to Sir Thomas Hesketh for patronage was to spur his (if indeed this is William Shakespeare) way to the theater, and to sustain an affinity with Catholic adherents. Ties between the Elizabethan theater and the Catholic tradition, as noted in considerations of medieval drama, were very close. Puritan attacks partially stem from opposition to Catholicism. William Prynne in *Histriomastix: A Scourge for Stage Players* (1633), for example, observed: ''most of our present English *actors* (as I am credibly informed) being professed *Papists*, as is the founder of the late erected playhouse.'' The latter was Richard Gunnell (fl.1614–30), a Catholic actor and dramatist who built the Salisbury Court Theatre. Many of the great personages of the theater were Catholic. The famous clown Richard Tarleton, a member of the first troupe that Shakespeare worked with, was denounced as a Catholic sometime between 1585–88. Thomas Lodge (1558–1625) became a Catholic in middle life, fled to the continent about 1603 when his conversion became known, and returned in 1610. James Shirley (1596–1666) also became a Catholic in middle life. A similar conversion of Ben Jonson (1573–1637) has already been noted. Philip Massinger (1583–1640) was a Catholic from his student days, and it is worth noting that he is buried next to Shakespeare's brother Edmund in Southwark Cathedral. Moreover, the composer William Byrd (1540–1623) of the Chapel Royal, was denounced as a recusant and even excommunicated from the Anglican Church in 1598, while the architect and stage designer Inigo Jones (1573–1618) was an avowed and loyal Catholic. This list indicates an extraordinarily rich Catholic environment for the stage in London where Shakespeare worked for twenty-five years. Shakespeare's most detailed account of performance is in the players' scene in *Hamlet*; it reflects a tradition of players traveling to perform at great houses, especially in times of plague when the theaters closed in London. It also recalls the role of companies performing for the great Catholic households in the North, a tradition well established in Shakespeare's youth that continued at least until 1610 and included two of his own late works.

The way to those plays was long and complex. With Robert Greene's allusion in a *Groat's Worth of Wit Bought with a Million of Repentance* (1592) the trail of specific references, missing from the time of the twins' baptism in 1585, resumes. Greene's diatribe, written as he was dying at the end of an erratic career that included diverse writing of plays, pamphlets, and romantic fiction, warns his fellow university wits—Christopher Marlowe, Thomas Nashe, and George Peele—against writing plays because favor is going to another:

> . . . there is an vpstart Crow, beautified with our feathers, that with his Tyger's hart wrapt in a Player's hyde supposes he is as well able to bombast out a blanke verse as the best of you: and beeing an absolute *Iohannes fac totum*, is in his owne conceit the onely Shake-scene in a countrey.
>
> (Chambers II, 188)

The obvious point is that Shakespeare is sufficiently successful to be regarded as a rival, and the "Tiger's heart" reference is to *3 Henry VI* (I.iv.137). It was performed by Lord Strange's men and brought in large receipts: £30 in fourteen entries during a three months' period of 1591. The *Henry VI* plays are of particular interest because the titular subject is a saintly figure, in Catholic terms, well known through the *Miracles of King Henry VI* and focus of a cult just before the Reformation. The enhancement of the historical Stanley favors a prominent Catholic family. Henry Stanley's Catholic marriage at a brilliant ceremony in Whitehall was attended by Queen Mary and Philip of Spain. Shakespeare's achievement is offensive to Greene because he is competing with accomplished playwrights who are university educated—an anxiety that recurs through the centuries and partially explains the variety of theories about alternative authorship. *Iohannes Fac totum* means a jack-of-all-trades, and it refers to the many roles in the theater: actor, playwright, poet, and stage worker in productions.

The concept of the first tetralogy, the three *Henry VI* plays and *Richard III*, is a very complex one for a beginning playwright.[5] The spectacle and patriotism of the Henry plays continue to appeal to today's audiences who are unfamiliar with the complexities of history leading to the establishment of the Tudor dynasty. They were interesting enough for an Elizabethan audience to assure the success of Shakespeare's three distinct plays, as well as a morality play called *The Seven Deadly Sins* that has Lydgate as chorus and features Henry VI and elements of *Gorboduc*. The conclusion of *Richard III* with the crowning of Richmond, who becomes Henry VII, the first of the Tudor dynasty, explains one attraction—along with the archetypal fascination of villainous Richard, exploited in several film versions. Much open to speculation is a connection of the plays with patronage for a youthful man of the theater. Shakespeare enhances, and changes, the historical account of Thomas Stanley, Earl of Derby, by heightening his role: Stanley seeks out Henry Richmond to offer support at Bosworth, finds the crown, and physically puts it on his head. Such praise of the Stanley family perhaps reflects a patron's interest. The descendant at Elizabeth's court was Ferdinando Stanley, Lord Strange, later Earl of Derby (1559–94), patron of a company of players. His mother was a granddaughter of Henry VII, and thus he was a potential claimant to the throne for which Elizabeth had produced no heir. Ferdinando was a talented young man; he participated in the Accession day tilts and showed other signs of chivalry in his devotion to hunting, especially at Lathom, the family's Lancashire seat. He was educated at St. John's College, Oxford, as had been one of Shakespeare's schoolmasters with Catholic affinities. A cousin, Sir William Stanley was at Zutphen with the Earl of Leicester; he returned Deventer, and two-thirds of his force of 900 remained on the Spanish Roman Catholic side. These family experiences indicate Catholic commitment that could have been shared by Ferdinando. But he was dreadfully caught in religious and political conflict when Richard Hesketh brought a letter asking him to lead the Roman Catholics in exile and seek the throne. Ferdinando showed it to Elizabeth, and Hesketh was executed in 1593. His decision may have come from allegiance to the Queen or from uncertainty about whether he was being set a trap. He died in April 1594; poisoning has been suggested—whether because of his religion or his younger brother's ambition is unknown. Shakespeare's unexpected use of the name ''Ferdinand'' for the Henri IV figure in *Love's Labour's Lost* may reflect this oscillation of faith, since the French king changed sides more than once.

It seems likely that Shakespeare was part of Lord Strange's Men that had joined with the Admiral's Men, who included the famous actor Edward Alleyn, who left the theatrical records known as *Henslowe's Diary* to Dulwich College. Among the company list for touring the provinces in 1593 were Will Kemp, John Heminges, and others who were later in the Lord Chamberlain's Men with Shakespeare, but his name does not appear. An alternative association was the earl of Pembroke's Men; there are records of their performing four early plays. With the death of the earl of Derby there was no patron, and new theatrical companies had to be formed. Shakespeare and the leading actor Richard Burbage are in the Lord Chamberlain's Company in 1594.

The patron whom Shakespeare praised in print is Henry Wriotheley, earl of Southampton, and baron of Titchfield, to whom he dedicated *Venus and Adonis*, ''the first heir of my invention,'' printed in 1593, and *The Rape of Lucrece*, printed in 1594. The cautious hope of pleasing ''so noble a godfather'' of the first is followed by ''the love I dedicate to your lordship is without end'' in the second. And the confidence of a favorable response leads to a further declaration: ''What I have done is yours; what I have to do is yours; being part in all I have, devoted yours. Were my worth greater, my duty would show greater.'' The last sentence recalls Chaucer's modesty topos in the Retraction to *The Canterbury Tales*, suggesting also a medieval religious tradition much older than the seeking of favor from a Renaissance patron.

Southampton's education was complex. Lord Burghley had charge of the royal ward and hoped he would marry the Lady Alice de Vere, his granddaughter, the child of his favorite daughter, which would have been a prestigious marriage and a way to further the young man's alliance to Protestantism. His father, the second earl of Southampton, was one of those implicated in the 1569 Catholic Rebellion of the Northern earls and imprisoned; he died in 1581. His widow the Dowager Countess Mary remained strongly Catholic. One of her son's tutors was captured at Mass, tried, and executed in 1591, and she was known to hide priests. In 1594 she married the elderly Sir Thomas Heneage, and theirs is one of several noble weddings suggested as the occasion of *A Midsummer Night's Dream*, in which the mature lovers receive most compliment, but there is not adequate evidence to prove this.

The Stationers' Register shows both *Venus and Adonis* and *The Rape of Lucrece* were licensed for Richard Field, a native of Stratford and an apprentice printer. Again Shakespeare worked with previous associates, and there is ambiguity: Field was cited for nonattendance at church in 1592, though his wife Mary was a Protestant Huguenot. From a lawsuit we know that in 1604 Shakespeare was a lodger with a Huguenot family (Mountjoys) in London. *The Sonnets* are dedicated to ''Mr. W. H.'' by Thomas Thorpe. The title page reads: ''SHAKE-SPEARES SONNETS. Neuer before Imprinted. AT LONDON. By *G. Eld* for *T. T.* and are to be solde by *Iohn Wright*, dwelling at Christ Church gate. 1609.'' An alternate seller of the edition was William Aspley. In contrast to *Venus and Adonis* and *The Rape of Lucrece*, which bear Shakespeare's dedication to Southampton and were carefully seen through printing, *The Sonnets* were not formally authorized by him. There is a link in the phrase ''All Happiness,'' the last in the dedication to *The Rape of Lucrece* and first in the dedication to *The Sonnets*. External evidence indicates a much earlier date of composition: the Elizabethan sonnet vogue was in the 1590s; Francis Meres's *Palladis Tamia* (1598) refers to Shakespeare's ''sugared sonnets among his private friends''; *The Passionate Pilgrim* (1599) included Sonnets 138 and 144.

Few works carry more vexing uncertainties, beginning with the identity of ''Mr. W. H.'' A likely candidate is again the earl of Southampton; this requires a reversal of the initials for Henry Wriotheley. Alternatively, the initials could be for Sir William Harvey, third husband of the Dowager Countess Mary. Since most of the opening 126 sonnets seem to urge a handsome, aristocratic young man to marry and beget an heir, they fit the circumstances of Southampton's unwillingness to follow Burghley's proposed marriage and a Catholic mother's dissatisfaction with it. Incomplete records allow possibilities. Because the theaters were closed from June 1592 to May 1594, Shakespeare was not daily involved in the writing and production of plays, and the non-dramatic poems are clustered in this period. One elaborate argument is that Shakespeare was at

Titchfield, the Southampton country estate, a household at least partially Catholic in sympathy. John Florio, translator of Montaigne and a possible original for the pedant in *Love's Labour's Lost*, was Southampton's Italian tutor and a reporter to Lord Burghley. In Elizabeth's England many prudently exercised the subterfuges of characters in thrillers, but Shakespeare was definitely associated with Southampton, who had Catholic ties. Thus his patrons, like his parents and daughter, and many friends and associates in the theater, link him to Catholicism.

Other friends and acquaintances also had Catholic affinities. John Fletcher (1579–1625), with whom Shakespeare collaborated on *Two Noble Kinsmen*, was the son of an Anglican clergyman who became Bishop of London. Fletcher, who was buried next to Massinger and Edmund Shakespeare, was an Anglican. Fletcher's closest collaborator was Francis Beaumont (1584–1616), whose brother married Elizabeth Fortescue, the only one of London Catholic John Fortescue's twelve daughters who did not become a nun. The son of the marriage was Francis, who became a Jesuit priest. The Fortescues lived at Blackfriars Gatehouse, a well known center for Catholics, later purchased by Shakespeare. Michael Drayton, a Warwickshire friend and fellow poet, had Catholic sympathies, as is evident in *Poly-Olbion* (written 1598, published 1613). This poem praises Henry VI as a saintly monarch and judges Henry VIII's "polygamy" and destruction of the monasteries harshly; it also celebrates old heroes of romance like Guy of Warwick and Bevis of Hampton. Mutschmann and Wentersdorf's survey of thirty-three friends and acquaintances found no information about the religion of seven, leaving twenty-six, of which eleven were Anglicans, one an extreme Protestant (the Huguenot Mountjoy).[6] Fourteen (a majority) were Catholics or Catholic sympathizers.

Once Shakespeare was established successfully in London, most of the biographical documents deal with economic matters—ownership in the theater and purchasing of property, largely in Stratford-upon-Avon. The exception is one of the Gatehouses at Blackfriars in March 1613, for which Shakespeare paid £140. The property had been owned by John Fortescue, a nephew and namesake of Elizabeth's master of the Royal Wardrobe, who married a daughter of Sir Edward Stanley, a cousin of Ferdinando and a supporter of the Catholic cause. Fortescue's wife was Ellen Henslowe, daughter of a recusant and relative of the earls of Southampton (Chambers II, 154–57). The priest-seeker Topcliffe watched the building in the 1590s; there was a major raid in 1598, but escape through secret passages, perhaps to the water, meant no arrests. Richard Frith had told the authorities of "sundry back-dores and bye-waye, and many secret vaults and corners." The Gunpowder plotter John Gerard asked for the use of a secret room at the Gatehouse, and this was enough to implicate the Fortescues, who subsequently went to St. Omer in France (Chambers II, 168). The deed for the Gatehouse property excludes Anne Shakespeare from any rights because there were three named co-purchasers, who did not contribute to the cost. Such facts give rise to speculation. Shakespeare's only property in London, apart from shares in the Globe, had notoriously Catholic associations, and he did not involve his family in the purchase. With the accidental burning of the Globe on June 29, 1613, and no evidence for subsequent shares held by Shakespeare, the Gatehouse was his only London property.

In 1608 the King's Men, Shakespeare's company, had signed a twenty-one-year lease for Blackfriars, a former Dominican house where the Burbages constructed an indoor playhouse. This is a sure sign of their success, partially increased by James I's decision, very soon after he came to the throne, to abolish all the players except three royal companies, renamed for himself and his family; and they were frequently employed. Letters patent were issued May 19, 1603. In the Christmas period, December 26 to January 6, are recorded six plays at Hampton Court and two at Whitehall with payments of £53 for performances and an additional £30 "free gift"—a more frequent use of the players and greater reward than under Elizabeth.

The final major document is Shakespeare's will, dated March 25, 1616, that is, a month before his death on April 23, 1616. The differences in the three signatures suggest that the three pages were not written at the same time and that his physical strength was changing, possibly because of a stroke or at least the emotional stress caused by changing the will to leave only £150 to his younger daughter Judith. She married Thomas Quiney on February 10, 1616. Quiney was a man of dubious character: Margaret Wheeler, pregnant by him, died in childbirth; Quiney was tried at Holy Trinity Church and given a public penance, subsequently changed to a fine. The will identifies the legacy as a "marriage porcion." The elder daughter Susanna is the principal beneficiary and executor, with her husband John Hall, as previously noted. The only specific naming of Anne is: "It[e]m I gyve vnto my wief my seciond best bed wth the furniture." This was a substantial extra bequest, perhaps sentimental and personal, since existing law provided automatically for the widow, but the lack of any overt affectionate reference is curious. There are specially designated small bequests, including items for known recusants William Reynolds, Thomas Russell, and Thomas Combe II, who was given the most personal item "my Sword." Money to buy mourning rings was left to Shakespeare's "fellowes Iohn Hemynges Richard Burbage & Henry Cundell."

Shakespeare's will has the preamble used in the early seventeenth century by both Catholics and Protestants: "ffirst I Comend my Soule into the handes of god my Creator hoping & assuredlie beleeving through thonelie merittes of Iesus Christe my Saviour to be made partaker of lyfe everlastinge. And my bodye to the Earth whereof yt ys made" (Chambers II, 170). This leaves little doubt that Shakespeare was a believing Christian, whatever the particular articulation of his religion.[7] One special point about the will is that it does not contain items that generations who revere the playwright and poet are most concerned about. There is no mention of shares in the Globe Theatre, of books in his possession, or of his writings. The restriction of interest in the will to his rendering his soul to God and his worldly goods to family and friends, with a concomitant lack of concern with his reputation or the legacy of his work, is a far cry from Renaissance fame and Reformation focus on individual personality. But Shakespeare's whole career displays his modesty. This, along with the inscription on the gravestone, traditionally ascribed to Shakespeare, can be interpreted as a detachment from worldly concerns, or a prescient anticipation of the passionate curiosity of admirers.

The epitaph, which does not carry Shakespeare's name, is on a plain slab on the floor in Holy Trinity Church, near the altar; it reads:

> GOOD FREND FOR IESUS SAKE FORBEARE,
> TO DIGG THE DVST ENCLOASED HEARE;
> BLESTE BE Y^e MAN Y^t SPARES THES STONES,
> AND CVRST BE HE Y^t MOVES MY BONES.

This is not the usual request, and it has been interpreted as a wish that his bones remain in the church and not be moved to a charnel house, or as a safeguard against the disrepair and rearrangements in post-Reformation churches, especially an increasing late sixteenth and early seventeenth-century custom of erecting very large monuments that displaced earlier burials. But anonymous detachment was not the end of Shakespeare's memorials. Within a short time, before 1623, a monument with a contemporary likeness was placed on the wall next to the gravestone; Shakespeare is named, his wit praised, and his legacy of "living art." The stonecutting was the work of a Southwark firm, Gheerart Janssen, a Fleming, that was also responsible for the funeral monument of the second earl of Southampton, at St. Peter's, Titchfield in 1594.

Both funeral memorials have survived, in spite of apprehensions like that expressed by Leonard Digges when he noted the Stratford tomb and monument as more impermanent than the lines that Shakespeare wrote. The plays remain because his fellows John Heminge and Henry Condell published The First Folio in 1623, printed by Isaac Jaggard and Ed Blount. Heminge and Condell begin with an address "To the great Variety of Readers," who range "from the most able, to him that can but spell," to urge purchase and to explain that their collecting of the plays and printing were necessary because Shakespeare did not himself undertake the work of preserving. But the most moving statement urges readers "to praise him":

> And there we hope, to your diuers capacities, you will find enough, both to draw, and hold you: for his wit can no more lie hid, then it could

be lost. Reade him, therefore: and againe; and againe, and againe: And if then you doe not like him, surely you are in some manifest danger, not to vnderstand him. And so we leaue you to other of his Friends, whom if you need, can bee your guides: if you need them not, you can leade your selues, and others. And such Readers we wish him.

A glance at the bibliography of works about Shakespeare shows that the variety of his readers is legion; recently his place as the supreme writer in English has been challenged with current concerns of theorists, especially post-colonial and multicultural, who argue that his position owes more to British imperialism than to the intrinsic worth of the plays.[8] There is, as always, a concurrent alternative: the reconstructed Globe Theatre at Bankside, many successful films of the last decade, and the recent BBC poll that chose Shakespeare as ''the Briton of the Milennium.'' The author most fully explored by academics, the playwright most produced in 1990s America, is acclaimed today by readers/hearers as he was in his own day.

This variety seems to validate the view of England's first critic, John Dryden, for whom, in *An Essay of Dramatic Poesie* (1668), the purpose of criticism was to praise:

To begin then with Shakespeare; he was the man who of all Moderns, and perhaps Ancient Poets, had the largest and most comprehensive soul. All the Images of nature were still present to him, and he drew them not laboriously, but luckily: when he describes anything, you more than see it, you feel it too.

Dryden notes failures—''He is many times flat, insipid; his Comick wit degenerating into clenches, his serious swelling into Bombast.''—and acknowledges that fashion may lead to greater praise of others, not least because of greater refinement of the language. Thus as with his criticism of Chaucer, whose Middle English was mispronounced to seem rough—Dryden goes to an essence, a habit of mind, for the excellence of the earlier poet. Dryden's balancing of characteristics, like his own changing religious understanding and formal commitments to Anglicanism and Catholicism in the ongoing conflict between specific articulations of Christian faith in the seventeenth century, in the end settles as a Catholic. My review of Shakespeare and Catholicism suggests the same juxtapositions and conclusion to support the late seventeenth-century assertion of Richard Davies that Shakespeare ''dyed a papist.''

The linking of Shakespeare to the Roman faith is older than the first anti-Stratfordians of the eighteenth century, since it antedates Shakespeare's death. John Speed's pairing of Shakespeare with the Jesuit Robert Persons in 1611 is both contemptuous and vague; he is writing only in reaction against Persons's *Of Three Conversions of England* (1603) that described Sir John Oldcastle (Falstaff) as ''a ruffian knight, as all England knoweth, and commonly brought in by comedians on their stages.'' The Lord Chamberlain, William Brooke, Lord Cobham, objected to the mistreatment of his ancestor as ''a ruffian, a robber, and a rebel,'' and the name Oldcastle was changed. But it is worth remembering that the misguided Ford in *The Merry Wives of Windsor* takes the name ''Brook'' as his alias to thwart Falstaff in his final appearance, in the play traditionally written at the request of Elizabeth to see Falstaff in love. The historical Oldcastle is a key Lollard martyr in Foxe's *Actes and Monumentes,* and further defended by Protestant Anthony Munday in a play *Sir John Oldcastle* for the Admiral's Men. Speed specifically links Shakespeare and Persons:

> And his [Persons's] authority, taken from the stage players, is more befitting the pen of his slanderous report than the credit of the judicious, being only grounded from theis Papist [Persons] and his poet [Shakespeare], of like conscience for lies, the one ever feigning and the other ever falsifying the truth. (Wilson 228, citing Cotton MS Julius C III, f.280)

Much of the recovery of historical details to support this relationship has been the work of Jesuits, occasioning the extreme case that ''The Jesuits Wrote Shakespeare.''

The data for possible connections, and the analogous data for a revisionist view of Reformation history, support a case for a Catholic sensibility that is more than Jesuit apology or the critic's wishful thinking. Even those who urge that religion is the salient defining characteristic of the personality allow greater complexity in the plays. Until modern Western thought, spurred by horror at religious wars that led to denial and avoidance rather than affirmation and reconciliation, began to erode it, the interlacing of religion and art was easily accepted across centuries and cultures. Keats hints at this when he writes about the ''symbolic relation between an artist's *modus vivendi* and his artistic achievement'' and gives the example that ''Shakespeare lived a life of Allegory. His works are the comments on it.'' Shakespeare's final plays, since Dowden introduced the category in 1877, are conventionally identified as ''romances'' because they are markedly different from the preceding ''problem plays'' and tragedies. But an apt way of thinking is to recognize that the so-called romances are the culmination and richest expression of a habit of mind that is evident from the earliest plays that explore many of the same situations. There are differences from one play to the next, and from early to late periods, but to look across the canon is to recognize how constant and thorough is Shakespeare's consideration of the tradition of romance, both in plots and outcomes.

Part 2
THE TRADITION OF ROMANCE

4

THE ROMANCE MODE: MEDIEVAL ORIGINS AND SOME REWORKINGS

Studies of Shakespeare's romances often begin, rightly, with the immediate sources, but there is also a deeper intertextuality, the medieval origins of the romance mode that developed with Christendom and still informs Renaissance responses and adaptations. Although his indebtedness to medieval drama is always noted, Shakespeare's relation to medieval narrative is a less frequently explored tradition. A brief exception is Gillian Beer's summation that cites John Danby's *Poets on Fortune's Hill* (1952):

"Shakespeare is responding richly—and with almost lyrical excitement—to the inward theme of Romance."

It is the inwardness that is important: the externals alone would never explain either Shakespeare's excitement or the individuality of his accent even when he is handling material that might otherwise be dismissed as merely conventional or in the sources.

Shakespeare penetrates to the organic patterns celebrated in romances: the patterns of suffering and survival, of regeneration, of the pastoral, of the sensuous present eternally fleeting by, of wish-fulfillment which can create a new world in its own image, the intricate harmony of chance and time. In the romance nothing is ever abandoned past recovery; resurgence is always possible. Shakespeare gives full human form to the truths first expressed through the narrative patterns of medieval romance.[1]

The medieval romance, in my reading, is a favored literary form for Christendom, and many of Shakespeare's plays, not just the late romances, are of this mode. He overtly acknowledges both the high art of Chaucer and Gower—the English poets most esteemed in the sixteenth century—and the popular art of the anonymous writers of folk tales such as those of Robin Hood and Robin

Goodfellow. And he favors stories familiar in medieval collections of engaging narratives designed to reinforce didacticism.

In two very early plays, *The Comedy of Errors* (c.1589–94) and *Two Gentlemen of Verona* (c.1590–94), based most obviously upon the Roman comedy of Plautus and Renaissance pastoral and debates of courtesy, Shakespeare introduces elements of traditional medieval romance to resolve the conflicts. Gower's *Confessio Amantis* provides material for *The Comedy of Errors* that shows Shakespeare's interest in Greek or Byzantine romance, and his particular fascination with *Apollonius of Tyre*, which he uses more fully in *Pericles*, where Gower opens the play as Chrous, as I shall consider in a later chapter. He also relies upon St. Paul, who made the first Christian attempt to transform pagan thought in Greece. In *Two Gentlemen of Verona* Shakespeare introduces the popular outlaw tradition best known today in stories of Robin Hood, and he later relies heavily upon outlaws in *As You Like It*. The idea of exile and outlawry dominate Catholic experience in sixteenth-century England, and many saw the pastoral as a likely genre for subversion. Inclusion of such material resonates of Catholic concerns, which may explain why Shakespeare introduced it.

Shakespeare's selection from the rich variety of Chaucer's poetry suggests similar interests and choice of analogs. Although there are echoes from many other poems, he most completely reworked Chaucer's tales of Thebes and Troy in *A Midsummer Night's Dream*, *Two Noble Kinsmen*, and *Troilus and Cressida*. These plays complement the Roman history plays dependent upon Thomas North's translation of Plutarch's *Parallel Lives*. The hero of ''The Knight's Tale'' is Theseus, whose significant conversion from conqueror to beneficent ruler is part of Chaucer's argument. Shakespeare used this first *Canterbury Tale* early in his career for many ideas and details in *A Midsummer Night's Dream* and later more closely adapted the story in *Two Noble Kinsmen*, a collaboration with Fletcher at the end of his career. This argues an ongoing fascination with the material, and between these two plays comes *Troilus and Cressida*. *Troilus and Criseyde* is Chaucer's most finished poem, a thorough consideration of courtly romance with a querying Pandarus, whose more homely ideas and proverbial expressions are deeply English. Chaucer faces philosophical quandaries, not least the relation of pagan antiquity to Christendom, and finds resolution only in a Christian perspective of eternity, but Shakespeare disallows this transcendence. His treatment of Troy is an aggressive anti-romance, a severe counter argument that precedes the fulfillment in the last plays where romance as his own habit of mind triumphs.

In *The Comedy of Errors* and *Two Gentlemen of Verona* an infusion of romance stopped the threat of state execution for alien identity. *A Midsummer Night's Dream* allowed many vagaries in a world of suffused magic with threats and dangers as the subtext in a triple leveled society of pre-Christian Thebes, Eastern fairies linked to native Puck, and contemporary English rustics. A corollary interest is a tradition of Theseus as tyrant; medieval enhancement of his virtues as a chivalric knight is a wish fulfillment of romance that many find in Chaucer's treatment and in Shakespeare's adaptation. For *The Merchant of Venice* Shakespeare chose a contemporary setting, albeit in Italy to maintain some distancing. Here he directly confronted social, economic, and religious questions; the trial scene, like the bond and pound of flesh story, makes explicit the very real penalties that could be exacted. But as in other early plays, Shakespeare finds a resolution in romance; he returns to Gower's *Confessio Amantis* and the *Gesta Romanorum* for the story of the three caskets, an archetypal tale both entertaining and didactic, as are these collections.

Just as Chaucer lived in a Catholic world and tried to understand pagan antiquity as an alternate culture, so Shakespeare tried to understand living in an Elizabethan world in which Catholic identity was challenged. Elizabethan concern with princely behavior is particularly central to the experience of Catholics. Public executions parallel those that Chaucer and Gower knew in the fourteenth century. Especially cogent are the public executions for treason, which were a vivid part of sixteenth-century life, and partially explain why the threat of execution is prominent in Shakespeare's plays. The stories of Protestant martyrs in Foxe's *Actes and Monumentes* gave emotional power to Reformation. But the deaths of Thomas More and Edmund Campion were also a part of public consciousness; both were the subject of immediately published accounts. Both men had enjoyed brilliant careers based in part upon favor from a Tudor monarch, but subsequently became martyrs for their Catholic faith because, although they insisted that they were not traitors, their loyalty to the sovereign stopped short of the required absolute submission that judged anyone whose first loyalty was to the Catholic faith guilty of treason. A major dimension of Catholic apology in Elizabethan religious controversial literature is that adherence to the old religion is not treason but a matter of personal faith. Law and justice are corollary concerns.

Shakespeare's interlace of fairy lore in *A Midsummer Night's Dream*, like the introduction of the outlaws in *Two Gentleman of Verona*, adds native English elements, familiar from folklore and medieval romance. The contemporary English rustics in *A Midsummer Night's Dream* point to the limitations of aristocratic attitudes and behavior and argue the inadequacy of other precedents. Without denying the use of classical and Renaissance texts and subjects in the early comedies, I want to emphasize that Shakespeare concurrently explores the romance mode of medieval Christendom; its subtle interlacing undermines the dominant, harsher comedy of pagan Rome.

The Comedy of Errors

Shakespeare lived and worked in Southwark, the place from which Chaucer's pilgrims set out for Canterbury, and where the tomb of his friend John Gower is the most impressive medieval monument in St. Mary Overeys Priory Church, now Southwark Cathedral. Shakespeare would have seen the effigy of Gower, his head resting on three books, including the *Confessio Amantis*, which Caxton first printed in 1483, and Berthelette reprinted with corrections in 1532 and 1554. *Apollonius of Tyre*, which begins as a Latin prose *Historia*, has a long record in England; a fragment of an Old English translation documents early interest, and its later inclusion in the *Gesta Romanorum* attests both its entertaining and its didactic appeals before Gower made it the climactic story in the *Confessio Amantis*. It is useful to understand this larger work.

As the title *Confessio Amantis* indicates, Gower chose Confession as the device for structuring his collection of stories that most resembles the *Consolation of Philosophy* in theme. Confession is a sacrament in the Catholic church; it is also remembering and self-discovery, today's psychoanalysis. Boethius (c.480–520) wrote his philosophical treatise while in prison awaiting death. This deeply personal work is the attempt of an honorable man to understand what is happening to him. Once famous and powerful, Boethius fell because he supported a senator accused without adequate evidence, and thus brought false charges against himself. The *Consolation*, a moral medication or remedy for illness, raises the eternal questions of ''Who am I?'' and ''Why do I suffer?'' The book was widely read as a poetical work that is accessible because it lacks the difficult vocabulary of philosophy and theology but addresses the same questions with compelling emotion. Its appeal in England is clear from the notables who translated it: Alfred the Great, Geoffrey Chaucer, Queen Elizabeth I. The topicality for sixteenth-century Roman Catholics, whose worship was illegal and whose priests were executed by the state, is obvious.

Moreover, Gower points the analogous quality and offers a paradigm that fits many of Shakespeare's plays. ''Prologus'' recognizes the need to hold an audience's attention, for wisdom alone ''dulleth ofte a mannes wit,'' and thus ''I wolde go the middel weie / And write a bok betwen the tweie, / Somwhat of lust, somwhat of lore'' (14, 17–19), and at the end he reiterates that he undertook to ''make a book / Which stant betwene ernest and game'' (VIII.3108–9).[2] Unlike Chaucer, Gower overtly addresses the contemporary situation: discord and hatred, lack of justice, schism in the church, restive people ready to rebel. Gower first says that Richard II suggested he write the *Confessio*, but he also praises Henry of Lancaster as ''Ful of knyhthode and alle grace'' (89), and he later wrote a dedication ''In Praise of Peace'' to Henry IV. Thynne included it in his edition of *Chaucer's Works*, so that it was well known to Elizabethans.

At the end of the fourteenth century Henry of Lancaster deposed Richard II. These political contexts would have been especially pertinent to Shakespeare, when he wrote the second tetralogy after *The Comedy of Errors*. Elizabeth objected to the deposition scene of *Richard II*, performed on the eve of Essex's rebellion; she declared, "Know you not that I am Richard." Prologus offers incisive analyses of temporal rulers, church, and commons—the three estates. Gower casts all against a nostalgia for a golden age, the days of old. Some of the finest passages in *Apollonius of Tyre* are descriptions of sea travel; the hero faces many tempests, and these accounts perhaps influenced the openings of *Twelfth Night* and *The Tempest*. In short, Gower's concern is not simply Amans, and in *The Comedy of Errors* Shakespeare is not writing only about sexual behavior and misidentifications. Gower makes the lover's seeking for ease analogous to England's need for peace and justice. Similarly, Shakespeare avoids writing only farce and uses romance to resolve the madness and to recall the plight of Catholics. He offsets the concentration of farce in Plautus to make the story of mistaken identity compatible with English conventions, and he elevates the story told by "moral Gower."

Apollonius of Tyre is Gower's key item; it is the longest narrative and positioned at the end as the catalyst for Amans's resolution. The Confessor and Amans have reviewed the Seven Deadly Sins through discussions that come after tales. In the Prologue Gower argues that sin is "moder of divisioun" (1030) and ties this to the political situation where division is "moder of confusioun" (852); and "there is defaulte non, / So most it stonde upon ousselve" (524–25). Gower's citing of "Croniques" as his source puts the *Confessio* into a realm of history, albeit this is often legendary. Book VIII begins, as do so many medieval texts, with a noting of the falls of Lucifer and of Adam and Eve. Then ensues a longer discussion of the "Laws of Marriage." Shakespeare, like Chaucer in the "Introduction of the Man of Law's Tale" (II.77–89), eliminates the incest of Antiochus and concentrates upon good prince Apollonius; however, as we shall see, in *Pericles* he includes the idea of incest.[3] He further selects the reunion of a separated husband and wife, which makes a happy ending in the context of Time, crucial in romance and so different from the farce of a day's misunderstandings and confusion. The story of Egeon and his long-lost wife Emilia, Lady Abbess at Ephesus, is the romance element of the play, and this is from Gower. The play begins with Egeon before the Duke: "Proceed, Solinus, to procure my fall, / And by my doom of death and woes end all" (I.i.1–2). The merchant of Syracuse, in an adverse town, accepts his fate and even welcomes the end of a woeful life, which he tells at some length. This long narrative both sustains the quality of storytelling and prepares for the happy ending, since separation in romance ends in reunion. Solinus must adhere to the law, but suggests a large ransom as an alternative—not unlike heavy penalties imposed after 1580 on Catholics for hearing Mass or refusing to attend Protestant services. This show of mercy gains a day of respite, and anticipation of further life. At the end of the day, and of the play, Egeon refers to "Time's deformèd hand" (V.i.299) and "Time's extremity" (308) that make him un-recognizable, though the fault lies in there being two Antipholus. The Lady Abbess of Ephesus resolves the quandary when she enters with the second master and servant, those from Syracuse. The action illustrates the message of St. Paul to the Ephesians, "walke circumspectly, not as fooles, but as wise, re-deeming the time: for the dayes are euil" (5.15–16).

There is also a significant echo of Gower, when the Duke says, "One of these men is genius to the other; / And so of these, which is the natural man, / And which the spirit?" (333–35). Amans's Confesor is Genius, keeper of both past and present; his questions lead to a redefinition that places man in natural and historical environments. The process is a remembering of what he is and forgetting what he is not; in short, what must happen to the principals in *The Comedy of Errors*. And the figure who clarifies is the Abbess, both the leader of a religious house and the mother of Egeon's lost twins. Apollonius's wife is Abbess of the temple of Diana, and their reunion is at Ephesim. Shakespeare, writing in Reformation England, replaces Gower's pagan references with Catholic experience. His choice of a romance, a story of understanding and restored order, and of a lost family, as the frame for a Roman farce is a very serious one.

There is a pointedness in the selection of Prince Apollonius's many com-plicated adventures; he is in exile because he recognized Antiochus's sin of in-cest and thus provoked plans to slay him: "Of treson that he deie scholde, / For he the king his sothe tolde" (447–48). The affinity with Henry VIII's divorce and the subsequent fate of Catholics is marked. Apollonius finds happiness in exile, after being shipwrecked at Pentapolim, where he excels in games and wins favor. The daughter of the king consoles him with the harp, and he responds, singing "as a voice celestial . . . As thogh he an Angel were" (780, 782). Apol-lonius becomes her teacher, and she falls in love with him. Like Shakespeare's independent heroines, the daughter of the king chooses her man, and they are happily wed. With the news of Antiochus's death, Apollonius can safely return to Tyre. On the voyage his wife gives birth to a daughter and seems to die. The mariners fear keeping a corpse on board, and the body is placed in a tight coffer and cast into the sea. Apollonius writes an accompanying letter; the identification is: "Hier lith a kinges doghter ded" (1126). This phrase resonates in several plays that explore the falsely accused queen that I will discuss more fully in Chapter 7. Katharine of Aragon, in Shakespeare's last history play *Henry VIII*, identifies herself to Wolsey: "We are a queen, or long have dreamed so, certain / The daughter of a king" (II.iv.69–70). Gower's heroine is never given a name, but after the reunion she returns as "the queen" (1896) with her husband Apollonius to Tyre. This conclusion of a return to queenship is a wish-fulfillment that Shakespeare deploys in *The Winter's Tale*, which in many ways is an alternate writing of *Henry VIII* as romance. *The Comedy of Errors* may be seen as a similar counter-argument to the kind of Protestantism so aggressively voiced by Spenser in *The Faerie Queene*, when he shows Roman Catholicism as the monster Error, doctrinal heresy, who vomits "bookes and papers," pamphlets of religious controversy, and is devoured by her progeny (I.i.14–26). Error was a major threat for the sixteenth century: Shakespeare considers "errors" in a pagan setting that was a place of Christian conversion and transcends error with his use of reconciliation from Gower's Christian adaptation of the Greek romance of Apollonius. This counters Spenser's adaptation of the questing knight of medieval romance for his allegory of Error overcome by Anglicanism.

For Shakespeare a main attraction of *Apollonius of Tyre* may have been such apt analogy. Gower even points to the typological way of reading and thinking that was common in the Middle Ages. In the Prologue is a long section about Empires of the World, which centers on Nebuchadnezzar's Dream and Daniel's interpretation and includes an update of medieval kingdoms. Gower follows this with a reference to "Thapostel" (881) and a paraphrase of St. Paul: "Now all these things came vnto them for ensamples, and were written to admonish vs" (1 Corinthians X.11).[4] This is a context for the setting of *The Comedy of Errors* in Ephesus.[5] Paul traveled to Ephesus, a pagan site of pilgrimage with worship of Diana, several of whose magnificent fecund statues are now in the Vatican Museum. The city was a commercial center, famous for strange happenings and devils, a place in need of exorcism, which is tied to sixteenth-century Catholicism. In Gower there is a miraculous recovery when Maister Cerymon, a "worthi clerc, a Surgien, / And eke a gret Phisicien" (VIII.1163–64) revives the body of Apollonius's wife with all his scientific skill. He then comforts her and reassures her, helping her as she recognizes that she will no longer belong to the public world. The queen thus becomes veiled, dresses in black clothes, and lives among women religious in a temple of Diana. Reunion with Apollonius comes after a vision from the "hihe god" bids him sail to Ephesim to offer sacrifice and learn of his wife and daughter, and a strong wind confirms the direction. He enters the temple of Diana, "Wher as with gret devocioun / Of holy contemplacioun / Withine his herte he made his schrifte" and offering (1837–40). Apollonius and the Abbess are happily reunited.

Shakespeare substitutes for Gower's combination of science and miracle a "conjuror"; he thus first expresses an abiding interest in exorcism and strengthens the scriptural texture in *The Comedy of Errors*. Paul's miracles in Ephesus are unusual, most notably the failure of the exorcists, who cease to practice magical arts as the Word of Jesus prevails (Acts 19.11–20). Antipholus of Syracuse, confronted with unintelligible confusions, thinks that Lapland sorcerers inhabit Ephesus (IV.iii.11). With Dromio he recalls the fall of Adam in Paradise and recognizes that ''here we wander in illusions. / Some blessèd power deliver us from hence!'' (41–42), and he identifies the Courtesan as devil and Satan. In an attempt to cure his madness the women bring Doctor Pinch, who calls out Satan to give up possession of Antipholous by ''my holy prayers'' and ''all the saints in heaven'' (IV.iv.54–57). The name echoes R. Phinch, author of *The Knowledge or Appearance of the Church* (1590), an anti-Papist tract that attacks false miracles.[6] Since the subject of the exorcism is Antipholus of Ephesus there is no devil to call forth, only further confusion. In the priory, where Antipholus finds ''sanctuary'' (V.i.94), the Abbess lectures Adriana about jealous women and urges patience (102) in a speech that recalls the wife's earlier reaction against Luciana. Adriana's response to her sister's urging ''be patient'' (II.i.9) was to decry ''helpless patience'' and ''fool-begged patience'' (39, 41) for ''a wretched soul, bruised with adversity'' (34). Sight of Antipholus of Ephesus makes the wife understand that her husband is ''past thought of human reason'' (189), and this awareness anticipates the unraveling of identities and restoration of all who have been lost. Luciana cites Paul (Ephesians 5) on marriage, but ''patience in adversity'' echoes medieval Chaucer and Gower. There are further scriptural references: ''rude fishermen of Corinth,'' a population at first notoriously impervious to Paul's message, deprived the Abbess of her child. More importantly, the Abbess identifies the time of her patience and waiting; now after ''thirty-three years'' (401) there is ''joy'' and ''such nativity'' (406–7). These allusions to Christ's age at the time of the Crucifixion and to birth, His and the baptized, occasion spiritual joy. Emilia and Egeon have their sons restored in a happy ending. The paradoxical nature of human experience is underscored in the date of the two recorded performances of *The Comedy of Errors* in Shakespeare's lifetime, the Feast of the Holy Innocents, December 28, in 1594 and 1604. The feast falls between Christmas and New Year and is a reminder of threat, loss of male heirs, in a world of tyrants and empire. The Innocents are an emblem of humility and submission to God's will in the face of great human error. The loss of children is a crucial theme that points the aptness of Northrop Frye's designation of romance as *The Secular Scripture*.

With a fuller acknowledgment of the many affinities between Gower's *Confessio Amantis*, Scripture, and Shakespeare's play, the significance of the romance of medieval Christendom is clearer. Of the early plays, *The Comedy of Errors* combines greatest dependence upon a Roman play with the most thoughtful introduction of romance. He returned to *Apollonius of Tyre* for unused elements, like the daughter Thaise and her extraordinary role in the brothel, in his late romance *Pericles*, which is a full deployment of *Apollonius of Tyre*. But long before the last plays, Shakespeare continued to combine the habit of mind developed in the romances of medieval Christendom with contemporary romantic pastoral.

Two Gentlemen of Verona

In *Two Gentlemen of Verona* the main interests are friendship and its testing by rivalry in love, themes recently explored in Thomas Elyot's *The Governour* (1531), in John Lyly's *Euphues* (1579) and several plays, and in pastoral fiction such as Jorge de Montemayor's *Diana Enamorada* (1559) and Sidney's *Arcadia* (1590)—in short "the world of Renaissance story" (Bullough I,211). Although not often acknowledged, this world owes much to medieval romance, as in the commonplace application of religious language to love. More significant is the conflict between brotherhood, a primitive concept of individual loyalty, and adherence to Christian virtue, both worthy claims, explored in romances like *Amis and Amiloun* and *Valentine and Orson*. Further concerns in *Two Gentlemen of Verona* are exile and outlaws, who sustain brotherhood and provide a space between the heroes' separation and reconciliation, and the exceptional forgiveness that pervades at the end. Modern readers often find Valentine's conduct in the climactic scene when he forgives Proteus—who has betrayed their friendship, slandered him to force his exile, and just been caught attempting to rape Valentine's love Sylvia—improbable or unlikely, the act of a nincompoop.[7] A counter-argument recognizes the essential Christian quality of forgiveness.[8] Many details suggest a Catholic experience. Shakespeare sets the play in Italy, a change from the obvious sources. He also puts repentance, a major issue in Elizabethan England, in the context of the Sacrament by introducing both Penance and friars, who are crucial in later plays such as *Romeo and Juliet* and *Measure for Measure*, and characterized by compassion and charity. Sylvia is to go to holy confession at Friar Patrick's cell (IV.iii.45–46), and Sir Eglamour meets her there (V.i). Moreover, "Friar Laurence met them both / As he in penance wandered through the forest" (V.ii.40–41). These details suggest the three elements of the Catholic sacrament—contrition, confession, and satisfaction—reconfirmed at the Council of Trent (1551). The setting in the forest heightens the idea of banishment and exile, well conveyed by the outlaws, who are explicitly tied to the English legend when the Third Outlaw exclaims, "By the bare scalp of Robin Hood's fat friar" (IV.i.36), and Speed urges Valentine that "It's an honorable kind of thievery" (40). In short, exile provides an alternative to the court; it has a greater spirituality and nobility, which is a central experience for sixteenth-century recusants. Shakespeare's choice of names reinforces this interpretation because the romance heroes explain the reconciliations that today puzzle many, but then epitomized a Catholic vision.

The name "Eglamour" comes from *Sir Eglamour*, a short medieval romance, rich in episodes.[9] A lovesick knight accomplishes three extraordinary feats; the heroine Christabelle is cast out to sea by her cruel father and separated from her newborn; fifteen years later this son wins her in a tournament, but the device on his armor reveals his identity and she resists marriage; Degrebelle persists and has to fight his father in another tournament to sustain his claim and thus is defeated; knight, lady, and child are reunited as a family when the knight father, also recognized by his armorial device, and lady marry. As in *Apollonius of Tyre*, the themes are exile, mistaken identity, seeking the lost ones, and restored family. "Sir Eglamour" is one of Julia's suitors, called a "knight well-spoken, neat, and fine" and rejected by Lucetta (I.ii.9–10). The old hero is usually identified as an object for laughter, as when Ben Jonson so names his "distract" *Sad Shepherd*. But there is another Eglamour in *Two Gentlemen*, the aptly named gentleman who helps Shakespeare's Sylvia, threatened by her father, to escape to the woods and then himself outruns the outlaws (V.iii.7), so that the lady is left to Proteus's threat and Valentine's rescue. Often ignored, this character is sometimes played as a coward, but he was not a jest to those who knew the romance. Eglamour called forth the chivalry of medieval Christendom; initially in the play he alone tries unselfishly to help the lady in distress.

Sir Eglamour was composed in the north or north midlands and is a miniversion of the composite romance, similar to *Guy of Warwick* in dramatic bold adventures but with less moral fervor. Its survival in several manuscripts and five sixteenth-century editions attests success. Quartos of such romances were cheap popular literature; an account book of about 1520 shows that an Oxford bookseller John Dorne sold *Sir Eglamour* and *Robert the Devil* for three pence. There were also dramatic versions; a London chronicle records a performance in 1442–43, and touring English troupes offered it on the continent in 1626 and later in the century. Sidney's *Defense of Poesie* (1580) centers an attack on popular plays with a satirical plot that is close to Sir Eglamour's story. The story as romance and ballad was a popular item for sale in the 1580s and recast by Samuel Rowlands in the early seventeenth century. Shakespeare could hardly avoid it; he shows an unexpected, protean, break in Eglamour's character.

Another name, even richer in association, is "Valentine." Henry Watson translated *Valentine and Orson* about 1502, and de Worde and Copland printed it.[10] This composite romance also enjoyed great popularity; it was presented as a pageant at the coronation of Edward VI in 1547, and was a source for many details in Spenser's *Faerie Queene* and in *The Seven Champions of Christendom*, Richard Johnson's popular new romance for a Renaissance audience. Shakespeare used *Valentine and Orson* for details of the murder and banquet in *Macbeth*, and the bear appears in *The Winter's Tale*. Cervantes and Bunyan show their indebtedness, and a reference by Scrooge in Charles Dickens's

Christmas Carol indicates the romance's long continuing popularity. Like *Sir Eglamour, Valentine and Orson* was widely read in the sixteenth century, and it contains themes of special interest in Shakespeare's early plays. Its compelling treatment of sworn brotherhood centers on twins whose separation at birth took place in a forest whence their banished mother Bellysaunt fled after being falsely accused of infidelity. One babe is carried off by a bear (Orson), and the other is found by the lady's brother King Pepin, who rears him at court with the name "Valentine." Breughel's *Combat of Carnival and Lent* (1559) shows the two young heroes. The wild man was a fascinating subject, inherited from paganism and rich medieval representation and often illustrated in tapestries, heraldry, and by artists like Dürer and Étienne Chevalier. A contrast between this figure and the cultivated knight led to a consideration of man's animal and spiritual natures, a more potent argument with twins. Predictably the two youths meet in the forest and begin a deadly fight that is stopped only when Valentine prays and offers his wild opponent Christianity (69). This is the model for Valentine's forgiveness and Proteus's change to human decency. Valentine early teaches his untutored brother to become a cultivated knight, and later Orson consoles Valentine after the unwitting patricide that leads to his self-knowledge and penitence, including a pilgrimage to Rome for the Pope's absolution. Roles are further reversed with his retreat to the woods and living a variant of Orson's original wild man. Twins are not easy to distinguish, and sworn brothers are interchangeable; all sin and need penitence.

With a clear view of good and evil the issue is choice, and this does not require sophisticated psychological analyses of slowly evolving attitudes. The quick pious conclusion is typically medieval and lies behind Valentine's declaration: "All that was mine in Sylvia I give thee" (V.iv.83). His decision follows Proteus's admission, "My shame and guilt confounds me" (73), and acknowledgment that penitence must satisfy the world as it appeases "th' Eternal's wrath" (81). Sylvia's final speech that protests Proteus's mistreatment of Julia anticipates penitence in its first review of his sins:

> For whose dear sake, thou didst then rend thy faith
> Into a thousand oaths, and all those oaths
> Descended into perjury, to love me.
> Thou hast no faith left now, unless thou'dst two,
> And that's far worse than none. Better have none
> Than plural faith, which is too much by one.
> Thou counterfeit to thy true friend!   (V.iv.47–54)

Using the same language for religion and love is a commonplace, but in an age of religious controversy with oaths and forswearing, disguises, trials and executions, so that some became atheists, the repetition of "faith" and decrying of pluralism make another point. Sylvia is closer to the heroines of medieval romance than is the independent Julia, whose pluck as page anticipates the qualities of Shakespeare's mature "breeches parts." Sylvia is beautiful, loyal, and patient (V.iii), a medieval ideal that is faithful and vulnerable, as when she swoons and is silent when made the victim of inconstancy. However, *Two Gentlemen of Verona*, like *The Comedy of Errors*, has a romance ending. Forgiveness for a fault inspires good behavior in the principal lovers, with a widening generosity reminiscent of the end of Chaucer's "Franklin's Tale," and the return of the outlaws is a wish fulfillment in the public domain. English Catholic exiles, both on the continent and legally constrained and punished at home, longed for a return. Valentine praises "These banished men . . . endued with worthy qualities" and asks the duke to "forgive them . . . And let them be recalled from their exile. / They are reformèd, civil, full of good, / And fit for great employment" (152–57). Of the happy ending, Valentine acknowledges, "That you will wonder what hath fortunèd" (169); since he has directed the conclusion, this is fitting. *The Golden Legend* gives the etymology of "Valentine": from *valorem tenes*, one who perseveres in holiness, or *valens tiro*, a strong warrior who fights for Christ.

Less explicitly used by Shakespeare in *Two Gentlemen*, *Amis and Amiloun* is one of the most popular medieval tales in many languages, the heroes are known as proverbial friends, and there are modernizations up to the present day. In the Middle Ages it is a romance of friendship and a hagiographic legend with didactic intent.[11] The tale was also a fourteenth-century miracle play of the Virgin in France and used as a dramatic disguising at Henry VIII's court. In *The Golden Legend*, Caxton describes the heroes as "two noble knights of Our Lord Jesus Christ, of whom be read marvellous actes, which fell and died at Mortaria whereas Charles overcame the Lombards" (Life of St. Pelagius). Many note a moral confusion in the extreme loyalty to friendship in the romance versions, and its secular values occasion most praise. Its didactic quality persists, I think, in a combination of the classical theme with Christian virtues of charity and humility. *Amis and Amiloun* stretches credulity with dramatic events—oaths, substitution in judicial combat, the Chastity Sword when in bed with the friend's wife, child sacrifice, leprosy, token-cups—that are resolved happily at the end. Supernatural voices speak to the protagonists, angels appear in dreams, marvels are accommodated, the imagery of the Crucifixion glosses sacrifice for one's brother, and prayers abound. These are not superficial trappings but outward signs of deep religious faith. The influence of *Amis and Amiloun* on *Two Gentlemen of Verona* is not in the details but the habit of mind. Personal friendship is only part of the individual's life; there is also charity, the basic and distinctive Christian virtue, one not exercised in the enforcement of a state religion at a time when theological definition and individual conscience were matters of life and death. As St. Paul tells us:

> Thogh I speake with the tongues of men and Angels, and haue not loue, I am as sounding brasse, or a tinkling cymbal . . .
>   Loue suffreth long: it is bountiful: loue enuieth not: loue doeth not boast it self: it is not puffed vp: It disdaineth not: it seketh not her owne thing: it is not prouoked to anger: it thinketh not euill: . . . It suffreth all things: it beleueth all things: it hopeth all things: it endureth all things. Loue doeth neuer fall away.   (1 Corinthians 1,4–5,7–8)

This higher love is more appealing and powerful than any human friendship or loyalty. St. Paul concludes: "And now abideth faith, hope & loue, even these thre: but the chiefest of these is loue" (13); the gloss of the Geneva Bible explains: "Because it serueth bothe here & in the life to come: but faith and hope apperteine onely to this life." Oppressed Catholics would especially need this consolation. In Chaucer's romances Shakespeare finds another use of the mode—to explore conflict between pagan and Catholic culture.

A Midsummer Night's Dream

Direct reliance upon Chaucer's "Knight's Tale" is obvious in several ways. *A Midsummer Night's Dream* begins with the Athenian conqueror Theseus and his captive queen Hippolyta, who frame the play; major emphasis is upon companions, the disturbance of young love, generational differences in responding to passion, elements of the supernatural, and native English experience. As is usually the case Shakespeare combines sources; he includes details from other *Canterbury Tales* and from English medieval romance, not least the structural device of doubling, and from folklore. More details about Theseus are in Chaucer's *Legend of Good Women* and *Anelida and Arcite* and in Plutarch's *Lives of the Noble Grecians and Romans*, translated by Thomas North in 1579. The idea of fairy monarchs is in the "Merchant's Tale," where Proserpyna and Pluto, rulers of the underworld, observe and influence human behavior and are responsible for the resolution of sexual misalliance. Like Theseus, Pluto won his wife by force, and there is lingering sadness, both seriousness and sorrow. But much about Oberon and the fairies comes from the later romance *Huon of Bordeaux*, a collection of adventures in exotic places, that was translated into English by Lord Berners and printed by Wynkyn de Worde (c.1534), with a third edition in 1601. Contemporary interest in the fairy king is evident in Spenser's *The Faerie Queene* (1596) and Robert Greene's *James IV* (c.1591), and

Henslowe's *Diary* lists three performances of a now lost *Huon* play in 1593–94. A concept of the transformation of human into bestial and Titania's name come from Ovid's *Metamorphoses* (III.173), as does the tale of *Pyramus and Thisbe*, another popular story found in Chaucer's *Legend of Good Women*, as well as several Elizabethan collections and satirical versions. Critics usually place *A Midsummer Night's Dream* between early more imitative and later mature festive comedy. The emphasis is upon mirth and merriment, metamorphosis, and marriage—all regarded through a spectrum of illusion and reality. By turning to Chaucer, "the noble Rethtor," "worthy to have the laurel of poetry," and also "a moralist," Shakespeare examines some interconnections of Classical and Gothic traditions and their divergent conclusions about human experience in the world.

Where Chaucer concentrates upon warrior prowess and the male companionship of Palamon and Arcite with its destruction in the wake of competitive passion for the love of Emily, Shakespeare does not show warriors in action but instead multiplies the lovers, the reconciliations, and the marriages. As in *Two Gentlemen of Verona*, he doubles the narrative line so that two disturbed youths woo two young women instead of one, a significant alteration that allows all to have a happy ending in marriage. Helena and Hermia illustrate single gender companionship, a parallel to Lysander and Demetrius, and the young women are more individualized than their male suitors. Chaucer's Theseus conquered "Femenye," his coinage for the land of the Amazons, a word that announces an interest in women. But the "Knight's Tale" maintains a concentration upon men that is typical in many courtly medieval romances that define women by their relation to men, albeit these women have influence. Plutarch identifies Hypolita as the peacemaker, describing the occasion of the wars against the Amazons as Theseus's refusal of Queen Antiopa to marry Phaedra. Much in the Greek legends about Theseus clashes with heroism in Christendom. Indeed Plutarch's summary comparison with Romulus stresses that "Theseus' faults touching women and ravishements, of the twaine, had the lesse shadowe and culler of honestie" (Bullough I,387–88). Chaucer goes far to transform this flawed Theseus into a mature chivalric knight who is the voice of order, best symbolized in marriage, a joining of the one and the other and a key subject for both Chaucer and Shakespeare, who expanded this alternative to worldly strife and loss.

Much of the complex plotting involves the four young lovers who, like characters in medieval romance, find resolution in a forest, after going from one adventure to another. As fairy tales tell us, to go "into the woods" is fraught with danger, and much in *A Midsummer Night's Dream* is frightening. Strange creatures and the dark offer both an immediate physical threat and the ongoing consequences that are psychological, emotional, and social. Knights like Tristram and Yvain flee to the forest as exiles when they can no longer cope; there they go mad, a medieval equivalent of a nervous breakdown, and then emerge with wits restored and greater spiritual strength, often inspired by a religious hermit. Chaucer's Palamon and Arcite meet and fight in the woods, where Theseus intervenes and prevents the death of companions. In the ''Knight's Tale'' Theseus's charity to the grieving ''compaignye of ladyes,'' the widows of his slain enemies who plead to bury the dead, anticipates this act of generosity that mitigates the ferocity of warriors. Chaucer places Theseus between the youthful intemperateness of the Theban youths and the wisdom of his father Egeus, who alone can comfort him with the recognition that the world is a thoroughfare of woe, on which all are pilgrims passing, until the inevitable coming of Death (I.2843–49). Theseus's consolation, spoken in the ''First Mover'' speech (I.2987–3074) that draws heavily on Boethius, admits human incapacity to understand the apparent vagaries of Fortune but proceeds pragmatically. Emily is to wed Palamon, a decision made ''With al th'avys heere of my parlement'' (3076). Resolution, a happy ending of romance, comes with an affirmation of the community best epitomized in marriage and with public approval. But this is explicitly set in a context of eternity. The other world in *A Midsummer Night's Dream* is that of the fairies, whose supernatural powers are circumscribed by human behavior, and Bottom enters it.

Shakespeare increases the number of marriages—Matrimony is the sacrament that he shows most frequently, one no longer identified by the Established Church of England—and shifts some tensions. In the opening scene Theseus and Hippolyta still show the conflict and conquest that underlie their marriage, when Egeus—a father but of a daughter, Hermia, not Theseus—asserts a patriarchal right to choose his daughter's husband. This is a familiar theme of romances and a reflection of aristocratic arranged marriages, and stories like *Floris and Blancheflour* and *Paris and Vienne* tell how the young rebel. Theseus supports Egeus (I.i.37, 47–51) and vividly describes the consequence of disobedience as death or life as a nun (65–78). A Reformation anti-monastic view introduces the description of life in a cloister as hard and barren, but Theseus qualifies ''Thrice blessèd they that master so their blood / To undergo such maiden pilgrimage'' (74–75), a very Catholic sentiment consistent with Shakespeare's positive view of monastic life, albeit now only a nostalgic memory. Hermia adapts the ideas of Chaucer's Emily, who prays to Diana that she would prefer a virgin's life but that not being possible, asks to wed the companion who loves her most. Hermia echoes sentiments of the ''Knight's Tale'' when she acknowledges ''destiny'' and advocates a Chaucerian response, ''Then let us teach our trial patience, / Because it is a customary cross'' (I.i.151–53). A way of ''patience in adversity'' is, of course, salient in medieval Christendom and appears frequently in Chaucer's poetry. But Hermia is more aggressive in asserting her rights and following her romantic passion of the moment, and her companion Helena is similarly independent, for all that she fawns like a spaniel before Demetrius (II.i.202–10). The rivalry of male companions is repeated in these female companions, who also quarrel with each other and even aim physical blows (III.ii). Interestingly, Hermia and Helena find themselves alone in the woods, and without the protective covering of male attire that Shakespeare provides in many later plays. The effect is to portray uniform willfulness and danger, youth driven by passion to ignore restraints, and to justify Puck's observation: "Lord, what fools these mortals be" (III.ii.115). The racing about that Puck frenetically directs has a nightmarish quality, an essential subtext in *A Midsummer Night's Dream*, which Henry Fuseli's several paintings of this play brilliantly evoke in a style that finds its boldest expression in his *Nightmare*, the painting that art historians now most frequently praise and identify as an epitome of Romanticism, the early-nineteenth-century reworking of the Gothic.

The young lovers are the occasion for much of the action, but the fairies are the distinctive feature of the play. Shakespeare transformed the conception of fairies as small people into diminutive creatures and thus inspired subsequent poets and painters.[12] Pluto is "kyng of Fayere" (IV.2227) in Chaucer's "Merchant's Tale" and with his wife Proserpyna suggests the already married Oberon and Titania, but not their ongoing quarrel and competitiveness or their alliance with Puck, the Robin Good-fellow of English native tradition. This combination of courtly and ordinary plays out in Puck's selection of Bottom as Titania's love. Middle English romances like *Melusine* and *Partenay* tell of the union of an immortal with a mortal of the noble house of Lusignan, but closer in spirit is *Thomas of Ersyldoune and the Quene of Elf-Land*, a fourteenth-century metrical romance that describes the Scottish minstrel's love of a queen of fairy and journey with her to the otherworld.[13] Thomas Rymour's prophecies, for which the poem is famous, were honored through the mid–eighteenth century in various collections; notable is the *Whole Prophecie of Scotland*, printed in 1603 in Edinburgh. Shakespeare's awareness of the prophecies is evident in his parody of such obscure sayings in *King Lear*.[14] What is unusual about *Thomas of Ersyldoune* is that the author of the prophecies, the poet Thomas Rymour of Erceldoune, thought to be the author of *Sir Tristrem*, becomes the hero of a romance. Moreover, when he pursues the elf-queen, who is a prototype for Titania, he combines the roles of "the lunatic, the lover, and the poet" that Theseus identifies with imagination.

Many details of the romance have implications for the religious situation in the sixteenth century. The opening lines include prayers to Jesus Christ for "Ynglysche mene" (14, 24), and the setting is a wood on "a mery mornynge of Maye" (Fyrst Fytt 3). Thomas's view of the lady is a useful gloss upon Bottom's encounter with Titania, which, I believe, is central to Shakespeare's vision. Thomas first thinks that she is Mary the Mother of Jesus and rushes across the mountain to meet her at Eildone tree, near Melrose; and he kneels ''Vndir-nethe that grenwode spraye'' (54), a phrase that suggests Robin Hood. The lady immediately says that she is of another country; Thomas asks her love and plights his troth, whether in hell or heaven (75–76). But this tale of the otherworld is not simple escapism. The lady evokes a Christian vision: she recognizes sin in the relationship that will destroy her beauty, and she fears discovery by her husband; she warns Thomas against temptation—nicely heightened as many fruits, not just an apple—and she shows him the roads to heaven, paradise, purgatory, and hell. At the castle Thomas, enjoined to speak only to her, spends what he thinks is three days (archetypal and the time between Good Friday and Easter), but the lady says it is three years. Like Bottom, Thomas, the human male, enjoys himself but lacks full knowledge. The elf queen takes Thomas back to earth to prevent the foul fiend of hell from taking him as a fee (255–58), and he finds himself at Eildone tree under the greenwood spray. The Second Fytt is her farewell to ''Thomas, with-owttyn gyle'' (13), a characterization that describes Bottom, and her agreement to give him ''ferlys,'' prophecies. These are of fourteenth-century battles and political contests between Scotland and England. Similar conflicts in the sixteenth century centered upon the Catholic Mary Queen of Scots and Protestant Elizabeth of England, and the fate of the north country, as contemporary prophecies record.[15] In the Third Fytt, which is the most confused, the elf queen sounds like Chaucer's Egeus: ''This worlde, Thomas, sothely to telle, / Es noghte bot wandrethe and woghe!'' (5–6). There is no simple happy ending but many prophecies, and a habit of romance that is a prophecy to be made. Shakespeare offers one.

Enmity between the rulers of fairyland and Robin Good-fellow is partially a sign of rival sophisticated and popular traditions. It is also part of an anxiety about creatures from the otherworld, well exemplified in Reginald Scott's negative view of Robin in *The Discoverie of Witchcraft* (1584), which makes much of his cousinship with Incubus and sexual lusts, while reassuring that there is current safety from Robin's ''illusion and knaverie,'' although ''it hath not pleased the translators of the Bible, to call spirits by the name of Robin good-fellow, as they have termes divinors, soothsaiers, poisoners, and couseners by the name of witches'' (Bullough I,394–96). Scot includes the popular story of a man with an ass's head through enchantment, recorded in Apuleius's *The Golden Ass* and analogous to the ass's ears of Midas in Ovid's *Metamorphosis*.

The fairies are not simply engagingly curious as the other and catalysts for erratic human actions in the forest; they also force a thoughtful response. In the opening scene Hippolyta—older, humbled, and wiser—speaks briefly and only of time; she is silent while Theseus and Egeus display power to determine the fates of youths. But the last act begins with Hippolyta's '' 'Tis strange,'' a recognition that there are transforming powers, and thus she provokes Theseus's most famous speech (V.i.2–22). He begins with a rational assertion, separating true from strange, and asserts that "I never may believe / These antique fables nor these fairy toys." Theseus's response to "the forms of things unknown" is usually read as a comment upon the imagination, found in "the lunatic, the lover, and the poet," but there is another level. As a wife Hippolyta has a voice, and she counters this eloquence with a further statement replete with theological import, when she argues "More witnesseth than fancy's images." The lovers' "minds transfigured," more than "fancy's images" grow to "something of greater constancy." And to "strange" she adds "admirable" as her judgment (24–27). Theseus has no reply but turns to plan worldly entertainment. He justifies his selection of the "tedious brief scene of young Pyramus / And his love Thisbe; very tragical mirth" (56–57) with a belief in the ordinary good will of citizens: "For never anything can be amiss / When simpleness and duty tender it" (83–84). This is a thoroughly idealistic view that typifies romance. But Hippolyta still does not trust Theseus's rationality, and she pleads with him to exercise charity: "I love not to see wretchedness o'ercharged" (V.i.85). She is reacting against Philostrate, a supercilious male critic of the popular players who would celebrate the royal nuptials. Theseus now offers his apologia, which seems to be pragmatism as witty paradox, "The kinder we, to give them thanks for nothing" (89) and yet echoes the Beatitudes of the Sermon on the Mount (Matthew 5.3–11): "Love . . . and tongue-tied simplicity / In least speak most" (104–5). Hippolita, reconciled to her role as a married queen, is now accommodating, even adding a tease as she hears the play in company with all. The chosen harmony of the couple echoes that of Pluto and Proserpyna in the "Merchant's Tale," where their decision not to press differences is set against the self-canceling arguments of Justinus and Placebo, the two male friends of January whose names indicate the extreme sides in a debate over whether the sixty-year-old should wed. With fallible human beings neither extreme is adequate, and relinquishment of self is an advantage, since "Mariage is a ful gret sacrement" (IV.1319).[16] When Theseus ends the celebration at midnight so that all can go to bed, he acknowledges that " 'tis almost fairy time" (359), and indeed the three principal fairies and their train conclude the play with their otherworldly celebration. The "shadows" and the "dream"—an alternate co-existing world—have been a more powerful reality than the human lovers. This is most fully understood by Bottom.

Just as Puck, the Robin Good-fellow of English folklore, is the catalyst of what happens in the woods, so Bottom, the English weaver, is the respondent who understands what has really happened. In weaving a *bottom* is the object around which thread is woven, and this is but one way in which the name signifies and indicates his role in the play. Bottom's verve and apparently outrageous behavior mark him as a great comic character, and in performance his effectiveness often determines the success or failure of a production. While elegant court figures preside, the man in homespun, who has an ass's head during much of the action, is the real center of the play. Bottom's folk qualities, an ordinariness, is a part of English reaction against court sophistication much more characteristic of the continent and of French, Italian, and Spanish literary texts that Shakespeare uses. The prose that the menials speak makes this obvious, and there are many resonances of Chaucer's language, and something of a reenactment of the medieval poet's struggle to find an appropriate English voice.

A concentration upon performance, as in *Hamlet*, glosses Shakespeare's life in the theater. But the production of *Pyramus and Thisbe* is not that of a London theater, but of a provincial interlude. The weavers at Coventry, where Shakespeare is most likely to have seen medieval religious drama, contributed significantly to guild pageants that lasted as late as 1579; a 1580 earthquake precipitated their cancellation, already ordered as a Protestant rejection of the old religion. The records also show that Coventry weavers had exuberant celebrations of "Mydsomer even," at which unruliness was often noted.[17] Much of the city's medieval prosperity was founded upon its clothmaking, but by the mid–sixteenth century this had vanished before competition and the taxation of Henry VIII. The names of Shakespeare's characters are all indicative of their crafts; as in Chaucer's "General Prologue," identity comes from the work one does. There is nostalgia in the creation of Peter Quince's company, the "hempen homespuns" (III.i.72) who provoke laughter and ridicule from those who think themselves superior.[18]

The struggle with attitudes and definition in *Pyramus and Thisbe* is provocative, since the play within the play is a parody of the vagaries of young love and its tragic consequences, not least Shakespeare's concurrent writing of *Romeo and Juliet* (1594–95), also containing suicides. Quince calls the workers' play "The most lamentable comedy and most cruel death of Pyramus and Thisbe" (I.ii.11–12), and this becomes "very tragical mirth" as presented to Theseus (V.i.57). Such contradictions suggest confusion about genre, but they also point up differences between a classical pagan and a medieval Christian ethos, the latter rejecting a tragical end because of the paradox of the Crucifixion and Resurrection. Bottom as Pyramus neatly illustrates the conjunction when he calls upon Greek goddesses who determined the thread of human life to urge medieval weaving practices to include both warp and loose end: "Approach, ye Furies fell! / O Fates, come, come, / Cut thread and thrum" (280–82), and as Bottom he rises from the dead, unlike the corpses at the end of tragedies. Bottom conceives of two possibilities for the role of Pyramus, lover or tyrant, a polarization evident in Theseus. He may have a "chief *humor for a tyrant" (whim 24), but his native enthusiasm leads him to want to play all of the parts, not privileging any, and his concern about audience reaction, not wanting to offend or frighten, is a mark of charity. Such flexibility and generosity explain why Bottom is the recipient of "a most rare vision," and he is outwardly signed with an ass's head. Quince says that he is "translated" (transformed III.i.113), and all run away. Bottom thinks this is "to make an ass of me" (114). According to *The Oxford English Dictionary*, this is the earliest use of the phrase, even though "ass" is an Old English word that was always used in Scripture, as in the Lindisfarne Gospels. But medieval popular tradition—not Matthew (2.1–18) and Luke (2.1–20)—gives an ass a place of honor at the Birth of Jesus and for the Flight into Egypt. Both familiar episodes in cycle plays, sculpture, and illuminations include an ass. The nativity episodes parallel the account of Jesus' entry of Jerusalem, riding an ass according to Matthew (21.2,7) and John (12.14). This sign of humility in Christ refutes the tradition of Greek fables that associate the ass with stupidity, ignorance, and clumsiness and a medieval concretizing of the story. Shakespeare's phrase thus suggests two opposite meanings.

Bottom's speech upon waking supports a theological interpretation:

> I have had a most rare vision. I have had a dream, past the wit of man to say what dream it was. Man is but an ass if he go about to expound this dream. Methought I was—there is no man can tell what. Methought I was—and methought I had—but man is but a patched fool if he will offer to say what methought I had. The eye of man hath not heard, the ear of man hath not seen, man's hand is not able to taste, his tongue to conceive, nor his heart to report, what my dream was   (IV.ii.203–14).

There are three main points: the rarity of the vision, which is of the supernatural; the inadequacy of man to put this experience into words; and the Scriptural passage that Bottom uses as an apt response to his experience. Editors always note that he "garbles" the line from St. Paul (1 Corinthians 2.9), and some specify the confusion of the senses. A further look at St. Paul supplies a context. Chapter 2 explains that Paul "came not with excellencie of wordes, or of wisdome" (1) to preach, but was with the Corinthians "in weakenes, and in feare, & in muche trembling" (3)—the condition of the artisans. Paul discounts the wisdom of men and of eloquence, urging instead the demonstration of the Spirit and the power of God as the basis of faith (5). He makes the crucial distinction between the human wisdom of the sensual man and that "which the holie Gost teacheth, comparing spiritual things with spiritual things" (13). This context indicates that Bottom is less garbled than many suppose; however inadequate his analysis or language, he recognizes the Spirit. St. Paul is himself quoting, but not exactly. "For since the beginning of the worlde they haue not heard nor vnderstand with the eare, nether hathe the eye sene, *another* God, beside thee, which doeth *so* to him that waiteth for him'' (Isaias 64.4) becomes: ''But as it is written, The things which eye hathe not sene, nether eare hathe heard, nether came into m[en]ns heart, *are*, which God hathe prepared for them that loue him'' (9). In the context of discounting the senses to acknowledge the power of God, the shifting of specific physical senses is less significant than their general irrelevance. But there is a distinctive addition of ''man's hand is not able to taste, his tongue to conceive,'' followed by ''nor his heart to report.'' It is not fanciful to find here an allusion to the Catholic belief in Transubstantiation in the Eucharist, a change known by the spirit but not the senses. Catholics in the sixteenth century received the Host on the tongue, Protestants in the hand. The allusion is reinforced by a ballad, '' 'Bottom's Dream,' because it hath no bottom'' (is unfathomable 213–14). This reiterates the incomprehensible nature of the divine that is, nevertheless, available in humble form—Christ as man, the Eucharist as bread and wine. Bottom's last point is to place the ballad within the community: ''to make it more gracious, I shall sing it at her death'' (216–17). The word ''gracious'' often means courtesy, but there is also a resonance of ''grace'' as the gift of God, and this seems likely in a concern to honor the dead. As we have seen, Protestant reformers decried the late medieval Catholic practices of praying for the dead, especially Masses. The precision of Shakespeare's references is again remarkable. The guilds, supporters of plays and celebrations, also devoted themselves to the afterlife of their brothers and sisters. Guilds presented prayers and chantries, and a member's name remained on the register after death, or could be added posthumously. The record of the Guild of the Holy Cross in Stratford-on-Avon shows admission in 1535 of the soul of Thomas, a fool in the family of Lady Anne Graye. The tradition of guilds was strong until the 1540s; it is a part of the Shakespeare family and of Bottom. The deaths of medieval heroes like Roland, Lancelot, and Guy of Warwick are foretold by angels, who take them to heaven. Thomas and Bottom return to the mundane, but tied to the supernatural through the dream in which they were transformed. The minstrel poet seeks foreknowledge, and the simple weaver resumes his place in the world.

In several other worldly ways there are signs of medieval Christendom. The play has a Classical subject and Bottom imitates a ranting Senecan Ercles (I.ii.24–35), but there is an English center, Wall and Moon (V.i.131ff.). From ''Alas, thow wikkede wal!'' (756) in *The Legend of Good Women* comes much play with ''O wall, O sweet, O lovely wall'' (Bullough I,374). Details of construction, the precise interest of building trades, are echoed: Chaucer's ''lym'' and ''stoon'' (765) become ''Thy stones with lime and hair knit up in thee'' (190), and ''that o syde of the wal . . . on that other side'' (750–51) becomes the cranny ''right and sinister'' (162). Bottom reiterates this materialism in rehearsal, when he proposes costuming Wall with plaster, loam, roughcast, and held-up fingers for the cranny (III.i.63–67). Chaucer's Thisbe sees "by the mone" (812), and Piramus sees well because "the mone shon" (825). Shakespeare gives a substantial part to Moon, a character who is himself the man in the moon. The courtly lovers relentlessly jest at Moon but cannot inhibit his straightforward statement of identity (V.i.253–55). Simplicity and humility triumph over cleverness and corollary mean spirits. That is essential medieval Christendom, demonstrated by *Piers Plowman*, a fourteenth-century text with a workman hero, by local hero Guy of Warwick, who best triumphs when not using his name and fame, and by the church and guilds that formed Shakespeare's family.

The poetry of Chaucer and Gower were another dimension of the English tradition; amidst condemnations of secular literature, especially romances, they were set apart. This begins with Henry VIII's "An Act for thaduauncement of true Religion and for thabolisshment of the contrarie" (1542–43). This Statute of the Realm controls forbidden publications but also excepted those printed before 1540 and specific items:

> translacions of the Pater noster, the Aue Maria and the Crede, the psalters, prymers prayer statues and lawes of the Realme, Cronycles Canterburye tales, Chaucer's bokes and Gowers bokes and stories of mennes lieues, shall not be comprehended in the prohibition of this acte.[19]

The list sustains the medieval combination of religious works with secular texts, and this persists as a view of Chaucer as a moral author. Ascham, who condemned romances in *The Scholemaster*, praises Chaucer, albeit he cites the "Parson's Tale"—incorrectly. Similarly, John Foxe favored Chaucer in *Actes and Monumentes* (1570), by placing him in "the descent of the Church." He first claims Chaucer's Protestant virtue in a wrongly attributed treatise of a ploughman. Foxe becomes polemical when he marvels at the achievement of a layman, so much greater than that in "the idle lyfe of yᵉ priestes and clergy men of that tyme," and he cites the Bishops' exemption:

> did yet authorise the woorkes of Chaucer to remayne still & to be occupied: Who (no doubt) saw in Religion as much almost, as euen we do now, and vttereth in hys workes no lesse, and semeth to bee a right Wicleuian, or els was throughly aduised, will testifie (albeit it bee done in myrth, & couertly).   (Brewer 108)

The issues of reader response and finding evidence for a theory are illustrated when Foxe again identifies Chaucer as an anticipatory Protestant. In *The Testament of Love*, Book III:

> purely he toucheth the highest matter, that is the Communion. Wherin, except a man be altogether blynde, he may espye him at the full. Al-

thoughe in the same booke (as in all other he vseth to do) vnder shadowes couertly, as vnde a visoure, he suborneth truth, in such sorte, as both priuely she may profite the godly minded, and yet not be espyed of the crafyte aduersarie: And therefore the Byshops, belike, takyng hys workes but for iestes and toyes, in condemnyng other bookes, yet permitted his bookes to be read. So it pleased God to blinde then the eyes of them, for the more commoditie of his people, to the entent that through the readyng of his treatises, some fruite might redounde therof to his Churche, as no doubt, it did to many: As also I am partlye informed of certeine, whiche knewe the parties, which to them reported, that by readyng of Chausers workes, they were brought to the true knowledge of Religion.

(Brewer, 108–9)

Shakespeare's interest was more comprehensive than Sidney's favorable references to the courtly "Knight's Tale" and *Troilus* in *An Apologie for Poetrie* (1581). He persisted in trying to find in Chaucer the Catholic habit of mind that characterizes medieval romances. *Troilus and Criseyde* was the primary source for *Troilus and Cressida* (c.1601–02), Shakespeare's earliest "problem play," where genre is unclear. And he returns to the "Knight's Tale" in *Two Noble Kinsmen* (1613–14), a collaboration with John Fletcher, that raises even more questions. But before those returns to Chaucer's romances and his fascination with women's roles, Shakespeare considered many other medieval romances to create his dynamic women, many with "breeches parts." The way begins with Portia.

The Merchant of Venice

Since World War II, the post-Holocaust era, Shakespeare's play about a Jew has ceased to be a favored school text, with Portia's "The quality of mercy" speech popular for elocution. There has been much controversy about anti-Semitism in both text and productions.[20] Critical and political emphasis upon the marginalized finds in Shylock a rallying point; thus this character dominates many readings, although he appears in only five scenes. Edward I officially banished Jews from England in 1290 so that the Jew was more imagined than known, a stereotype. There was a burst of anti-Semitism in 1594 with the hanging, for an alleged plot against Queen Elizabeth, of her Portuguese physician Roderigo Lopez, who was probably known to Burbage, and perhaps to Shakespeare, when he was attached to the household of the earl of Leicester. Revival of Marlowe's *The Jew of Malta* fanned interest, and Shakespeare's play, which echoes and changes this text, was part of the response. With the breaks from Rome came a struggle to redefine what it means to be a Christian, and consideration of a group neither Catholic nor Protestant is illuminating, and especially cogent since Shakespeare adds the conversion of Shylock that is not in the sources. Shylock's naming Portia ''a Daniel,'' and the redeployment of this type as she wins the case, gain from an awareness that Elizabethans read the prophet Daniel, along with Revelation (Apocalypse), as authority for the conversion of the Jews, and there were many accounts of such conversions.[21]

The complex definition of who is a Jew and the role of Jews in England's history, James Shapiro argues, show ''strong continuities in thinking about the Jews from the 1570s well into the 1650s'' (12). Thus ''fantasy'' and ''history'' interlace as modern issues of religion, race, and nation developed with an increasing insistence upon Anglo-Saxon origins. Religious controversial writing pitted Catholic against Protestant, and included conversion tracts that demonstrate an Elizabethan desire and efforts to convert Jews as a way to reground the Christian faith, to make the Protestant church legitimate as the victor over the papal Anti-Christ, or alternatively to confirm the one true Catholic church. An obvious sympathy between Protestant and Jew is shared aversion to Catholic images and ceremony, and respective conversion narratives stress sermon over Roman spectacle. A prime example is a sermon of John Foxe, author of *Actes and Monuments*, to mark the conversion of the Jew Yehuda Menda in London on April 1, 1577. Foxe uses St. Paul's expectation of the ''blessed and joyful return of the Jews,'' and he also attacks contemporary arguments and acts that stray from the simple faith. Francis Walsingham, a Puritan member of the Privy Council, thought the sermon important; unable to be present because of illness, he had Foxe repeat it for him. For Shapiro, the Jew in Shakespeare's time was of great significance. Christians, whose faith the Reformation had undermined so that they were in desperate need to recover from the exposure of ''how unstable Christian religious identity could be'' (139), could play out ''the fantasy of Jews rejecting their own beliefs in favor of Christian ones'' (153), although tales of apostasy also appeared.

An alternative interpretation to this Jewish focus is the Catholic reading of Peter Milward, who finds ''a topical allegory'' for religious controversy and argues that Shylock is more Puritan than Jew.[22] Severity, especially of ''sober house'' and ''thrifty mind,'' distinguished Puritans, who were called ''Christian Jews,'' noted for their taking of Hebrew names, and ''pure Pharisees,'' who refused to associate with others, as Shylock stays apart from Christians. Usury, a root of antipathy in the play, was practiced by Puritans like Thomas Cartwright, who was formally charged. The famous lines ''The devil can cite Scripture for his purpose. / An evil soul producing holy witness / Is like a villain with a smiling cheek'' (I.iii.96–98) denote Puritan use of the Bible for self-justification and insistence upon literal interpretation. And, as Angelo in *Measure for Measure* demonstrates, Puritans were relentless in enforcement of the law and lack of mercy. The imagery of Shylock as "devil" in his house as "hell" (II.ii.1–29 and II.iii.2) can be glossed by "would make a puritan of the devil" (*Pericles*, IV.vi.9). Generally, sin is defined as a bond with the devil, and Shylock is obsessive about his bond.

Some apply the title *The Merchant of Venice* to Shylock, but Antonio's role at the beginning and ending indicate that he is the pivotal figure, and historical details tie him to Catholicism. Jesuit priests, sent to serve loyal Catholics, used the cover of "merchant" when they entered England in disguise, traveled, and sent messages. Antonio is celibate, and his unexplained melancholy in the opening scene, the threats to all his ventures, and later unanswered plea for mercy suit the plight of Catholic priests. Similarly, Bassanio leaves for Belmont, an analog for English recusants in exile. The name of Portia's estate is in *Il Pecorone*, but Belmont is also the name of a home in Hampshire—that of Thomas Pounde, a close friend of Campion, who later became a Jesuit brother in prison, and was a cousin of the young earl of Southampton. Another point is the elaborate favorable reference to monasteries, noted earlier. When Portia leaves Belmont to become the defending lawyer, she is going "to live in prayer and contemplation" at a "monastery two miles off" (III.iv.28, 31). Stephano announces her impending return to Lorenzo: "She doth stray about / By holy crosses, where she kneels and prays / For happy wedlock hours" (V.i.30–32). Her maid and "a holy hermit" accompany Portia (34). In *Il Pecorone* the lady of Belmonte arrives, "pretending that she has been to a health resort" (Bullough I,475). Milward argues contemporary relevance, a veiling of meaning necessary for a practicing dramatist to survive, that Catholics would have recognized as topical allegory. Such reading reinforces a case for the romance habit of mind with its "plots of staggering implausibility."

For *The Merchant of Venice* Shakespeare returns to Gower's *Confessio Amantis* and the *Gesta Romanorum*, edifying narrative collections with characteristics of romance. The choosing of the caskets balances the plot of the bond of flesh, two familiar stories united by the theme of covetousness. As illustration of one of the Seven Deadly Sins the caskets story occurred widely in the Middle Ages; for example, in Vincent of Beauvais's *Speculum Historiale* (1290) and in *The Golden Legend* of Jacobus de Voraigne, a thirteenth-century Dominican, whose collection of saints' legends Caxton printed and de Worde and Notary reprinted. Boccaccio's *Decameron*, and other closer versions in Italian *novelle*, most notably Ser Giovanni Fiorentino's *Il Pecorone* (1558), include the merchant's bond, as does *The Seven Sages of Rome*, and much earlier Indian and Talmudic texts. This indicates a mythic quality, but the situation of the stories as medieval didactic romance especially informs Shakespeare's use.

Like other comedies discussed in this chapter, *The Merchant of Venice* has a theme of friendship and its conflict with the competing virtues of marriage.

But it is a more serious comedy with an emphasis upon the temporal and eternal. Several analogs describe the young man's quest as a simple seeking of fortune; Shakespeare makes the point that Bassanio's economic need to woo Portia stems from his generosity, even prodigality, in the service of companions. Bassanio is like the heroes of *Sir Launfal*, which resembles *Thomas of Ersyldoune* with its fairy lady, and *Sir Amadace*, which resembles *Amis and Amiloun* in potential bloodshed and piety; his fault is *largesse*, giving his fortune too generously and thus finding himself in need. This is directly illustrated when Gratiano says, "I have a suit to you," and without knowing the nature of it, Bassanio replies, "You have obtained it" (II.ii.169–70). He both urges the need for more decorous behavior and, reassured by his friend's promise of respect and at least outward show of piety (181–88), yet allows that in this world it would be a pity not to have mirth, particularly with friends. Here is an illustration of reconciling the claims of earnestness and merriment. Like heroes in romance, and questing knights of history, Bassanio sets out on "a secret pilgrimage" (I.i.120) to resolve his indigence by marrying a woman with a fortune and undertaking a life not rooted entirely in male friendship. Generosity, Antonio's chief trait, is a virtue; the issue, and the play's major theme, is a proper accommodation to the world, without loss of the divine and eternal.

Sir Amadace has, like *Amis and Amiloun*, a didactic intent, and several notable correspondences with the romance in Shakespeare's play. The short poem tells of a knight who leaves home because he has only forty pounds left, and he gives all of this to pay the debt and cost of burial for a knight whose lady grieves beside the corpse in a chapel. Alone and destitute, Amadace meets a White Knight who directs him to a shipwreck where he finds the resources to begin a suit for the king's daughter. Amadace is successful in jousts and love, gains wealth and continues to share it. Ultimately the White Knight reappears to claim the promise made by Amadace to share half of his gains; this includes material goods and also his wife and child. Amadace sadly prepares to cut them in half. The White Knight then identifies himself as the spirit of the debtor upon whom Amadace spent the last of his fortune, and he praises both generosity and keeping a pledge. The medieval poet acknowledges that not all would thus have served, and he argues that there is something higher than human decision:

> But quoso serves God truly
> And his modur Mary fre.
>   This dar I savely say:
> Yette God wille graunte *hom alle **hor wille,   *them, **their
>   Tille hevyn the *redy waye.[23]   (811–16)   *direct

Acknowledging a level of being beyond the worldly is a note sounded in the play's first scene, again explicitly by Gratiano—whose name signifies grace. He tells Antonio, "You have too much respect upon the world. / They lose it that do buy it with much care," and Antonio replies, "I hold the world but as the world, Gratiano— / A stage where every man must play a part" (I.i.74–78).

Consciousness of an earthly role marks Portia's opening scene; she goes a bit beyond Antonio's sadness: "my little body is aweary of this great world" (I.ii.1–2). Portia is much concerned with behavior, admitting "If to do were as easy to know what were good to do" (12) to reveal herself as a person acutely knowing about both moral action and human fallibility. At risk, but obedient to her father's will, and bored by isolation in Belmont, she amuses herself with witty talk, while admitting that "In truth, I know it is a sin to be a mocker" (55). And, of course, she does mock her suitors, indulging in the gossip that is a sin for almost everyone. Only as Bellario, an advocate in a case of life or death and freed from her social role, does she avoid this fault and thus is able to explain "the quality of mercy . . . an attribute to God himself," vastly beyond justice, which would mean that "none of us should see salvation" (IV.i.182–200). The speech contributes much to the number of quotations and echoes from scripture—Ecclesiastes, Psalms, the Lord's Prayer, Proverbs—in the play that often echoes the *Sermons* of Henry Smith. Later Portia urges "charity" (259), and Christian claims intensify until Antonio asks for Shylock's conversion. When Portia returns to Belmont, she has a deeper understanding; she can explain the candlelight in her hall, "So shines a good deed in a naughty world. . . . So doth the greater glory dim the less" (V.i.91, 93). But the immediate future is life in the world, and Portia moves to light playfulness about the rings and chooses the reunion of husband and wife. She is as spirited as she was in the witty analysis of the suitors, but there is a parallel to the trial of Shylock; Portia could be insistent and inflexible upon her bond, since Bassanio and Gratiano have deliberately forfeited by breaking their promises of loyalty. Word count iterates the Christian virtue of charity: *love* appears sixty-six times, only three for Shylock, who says *hate* five of the eight times. Justice faults Bassanio, for he did break his promise when he gave the ring, but he pleads, "forgive me this enforcèd wrong" (240) and "Pardon this fault" (247). Antonio assumes the role of advocate: "I dare be bound again, / My soul upon the forfeit, that your lord / Will nevermore break faith advisedly" (251–53). His earlier pledge of worldly goods is now a spiritual pact. *The Golden Legend* gives the meaning of St. Anthony's name as "holding high things and despising the world," and his story is of fighting devils and helping hermits. Antonio's dedication to friendship continues, but is more distanced; the men will have less singular lives, as marriage wins over friendship. All will live more richly, and the play ends with the wives' teasing their husbands about fidelity and their rueful, and sexy, recognition of how uncertain life is in the world. Portia's "You are all amazed" (266) sums up both the play's action and the human condition, and the news that Antonio's ships are safe merely provides the next example.

Such resolutions may seem arbitrary, but they stem from human choice, a will to follow the good news of Christ, the teaching that out of adversity and suffering come great good and that surface appearance belies reality. Portia and Nerissa know that their husbands are faithful, that the rings are but an outward sign, not the essence and true nature of the marriage. Scholasticism, which dominated much of medieval Catholic thought, distinguishes between accidents and substance, what appears on the surface and inner reality. The caskets scenes demonstrate this theme theatrically, and they contain both didactic teaching and fine entertainment, as is found in such stories in moral collections. Details like the number of caskets vary in analogs, but the point is always that the proper choice is not the superficially advantageous, more specifically that the world's coveting of the riches of gold and silver do not lead to happiness, and that trust in God brings humans comfort and satisfaction. In Gower's *Confessio Amantis* stories that illustrate covetousness center on this sin as the worst for a ruler and his courtiers (Book V.2272–2441). Two include analogous tests; in each two men choose between two items (coffers and pasties) that look the same on the outside but only one contains the wealth that is sought, and those most covetous have least advantage. The moral is:

> That he mai lihtly be deceived,
> That *tristeth unto mannes helpe,   *trusts
> Bot wel is him whom god wol helpe,
> For he stant on the *siker side,   *sure
> (2426–27)

Closer in detail to *The Merchant of Venice* is a story from the *Gesta Romanorum*, a popular Franciscan compilation of fables designed to instruct by combining story with a moral application; the genre dates from antiquity, which explains the medieval title. The stories included, names and places, and the order vary; in the Latin ''The Three Caskets'' is usually CIX, but in de Worde's English translation it is XXXII. The one who hazards is a young woman, the daughter of the king of Naples who fought against the emperor of Rome but in old age sought reconciliation through her marriage to Alcelmus's only son. On the way to the wedding, the vessel is caught in a tempest in which all others perish. Her next threat is a great whale, which she keeps at bay with a large fire until she falls asleep in exhaustion so that the fire goes out and the whale swallows the ship. The plucky young woman beats its sides, makes another fire, and ''grevously woundid the whale with a litille knyfe'' (Bullough I,513). Thus the whale draws to land and dies. Pirius, an earl walking on the shore, has his men strike the creature; the entrapped young woman cries out and he releases her, treats her with respect, and takes her to the Emperor, who insists upon a test to prove that she is worthy of his son. He makes three "vesselles," and they provide Shakespeare's three metals—gold, silver, and lead. The three inscriptions are: "Thei that chese me shulle fynde in me that thei servyd . . . that nature and kynde desirithe . . . that God hath disposid." The lead vessel is thus most significant, and details emphasize the didactic point. The maiden first prays to God for "grace" to choose rightly to have her husband, and she easily selects lead: "Sothely, God disposide never iville; forsothe that which God hathe disposid wolle I take and chese" (514). The tempest and whale derive from Jonas, a type of faith and recipient of God's mercy, a prophet who foreshadows Christ because his delivery from the whale, after three days and three nights in its belly, is a type of the Resurrection. The *Gesta Romanorum* emphasizes trust in God, which is a more religious point than in the original Greek fable of Barlaam, when the king explains "to discern baseness or value which are hid within, we must look with the eyes of the mind" (Bullough I,458). This underlies Bassanio's good sense, acquired through the adversity of loss of fortune and recognition of his own excess. Shakespeare's three possibilities are an alternative articulation of the *Gesta*'s theology: "Who chooseth me shall gain what many men desire . . . shall get as much as he deserves . . . must give and hazard all he hath" (II.vii.4–9). Gold and silver contrast wish and merit, but are tied to the world; lead requires total surrender that is the only way to God. Since eternity is perceived darkly, the choice is hazardous and subject to worldly ridicule—as Morocco and Aragon argue before being forced to accept an alternative value, what lies below surface appearance. The theme of "hazard" unites the play's many episodes of trial and testing of Antonio, Portia's suitors, Shylock, Portia herself, the husbands, Jessica who converts. Risks are not what they are assumed to be, and those who fail do so because they assume knowledge and privilege; those who succeed humbly forego worldly interests and treat others with mercy, as God treats all sinners who accept Him.

Such faith and hazard were the core of religious experience in Elizabethan England; the price of worldly wealth and success, and even of life, was denial of the old religion. The inner concealment in the caskets is pertinent to a major point of theological difference, the doctrine of Transubstantiation. Catholics believe in the Real Presence in the Eucharist, not visible to the human eye; the bread and wine become the Body and Blood of Christ at the Sacrifice of the Mass. The new Established Church argued representation, not reality; the Catholic habit of mind and romance encourage amazement and acceptance.

Two other Scriptural resonances in *The Merchant of Venice* reinforce the unpredictability of human experience and the frequent discrepancy between expectation and event. The parable of the prodigal son in the New Testament (Luke 15) glosses Lancelot and Gobbo his father. Their reconciliation adds to Shakespeare's emphasis upon the family, but also says much about religious debate. The parable concludes with the father's rejoicing in the one who was lost and concurrently delighting in the ever-faithful elder son. The Geneva Bible contains a gloss: "Thy parte, who art a Iewe, is nothing diminished by that the Christ was also killed for the Gentiles: for he accepteth not yᵉ persone, but feedeth i[n]differe[n]tly all the[m] that beleue in him, with his bodie and blood to life euerlasti[n]g." This is cogent for *The Merchant of Venice*, especially that Shylock "presently become a Christian" (IV.1.385). The experience of Jessica, a female Jew, is partially that of Lancelot in Shylock's house, and she decides to reject Shylock and his Jewish tradition to become a Christian. The parable puts succinctly the point of the blindness of Isaac, who blesses Jacob and whose subsequent exile finishes with a meeting with the inadvertently blessed Essau (Genesis 27). Because Shakespeare follows analogs to have men hazard with the caskets, Freud and others note the sexual significance, and a romance motif of questing knight gives male emphasis.

Shakespeare gives the casket test to men, thus changing the gender of the one who hazards in *Gesta Romanorum*, where a daughter triumphs through humility, obedience, and faith. But he tests Portia and Jessica, who are similar in their relation to dominant fathers, in another way. The hazard is beyond worldly wealth and happy marriage, for it is a spiritual test. Both Jessica and Portia are more lively and independent than many of their medieval counterparts, perhaps because their trials are less physically threatening than those of many ladies in romance. There is a prototype for Jessica's conversion—and lively sexuality and independence—Floripas, daughter of the Saracen admiral in the Fierabras story. This Charlemagne *chanson*, favored in English versions, centers on the conversion of a worthy Saracen knight, and is part of Caxton's *Charles the Great* (1485), a composite romance. Floripas, in an engaging episode, releases Christian prisoners from a deep dungeon, bestows lavish gifts upon them, and claims a husband as reward, Guy of Burgundy, "And for the loue of hym I wyl be baptysed & Beleue in the god of crysten men."[24] Like Floripas, Jessica becomes Christian with marriage. Portia obeys, but she too is perky and deliberate in choosing a husband. Yet both recognize authority and, like women in medieval romance, prevail through Christian acceptance and marriage. They model triumphant Shakespearean Woman in romance.

5
UNDERSTANDING THE ROMANCE MODE

The early comedies, as we have seen, combined many elements of medieval romances and native legends with the farce and extravagance of Roman plays that more obviously contributed plots, stock characters, and situations. The achievement of *A Midsummer Night's Dream* and *The Merchant of Venice* is as much dependent upon the romance as it is on comedy. Since the themes of romance are those of marvel, suffering, and restoration, their inclusion explains, at least in part, the essential Shakespearean comic vision that always has a serious underlying quality. Part of his *fin de siécle* experience was to explore both the history of medieval kings in the second tetralogy and to write the early tragedies, plays that explore the limitations of high sentiment and saintly innocence, as well as the disastrous consequences of relentless ambition and sin; these plays lack the reconciliation and joy of romance. But concurrently Shakespeare wrote two of his greatest comedies, *As You Like It* and *Twelfth Night*, both still dependent upon the tradition of medieval romance narratives. In these two plays Shakespeare recapitulates and develops themes of romance explored in the earliest comedies. Thus tyrants, exile, and outlawry; confused identity and disguise; quick reversals; and the amazing happy ending recur. *As You Like It* is heavily dependent on a medieval romance, *Gamelyn*, and has many Catholic references, while *Twelfth Night* includes many romance themes. In both plays Shakespeare introduces the Fool, a figure found in real courts and visual images, as central to humanity. The Fool's complexity was divided into two in *As You Like It*, the commentator-responder to the court and the cynical critic of society, Touchstone and Jaques. More exacting is the role in *Twelfth Night;* Feste is a sage-fool, more perceptive and wiser than those he serves, and a study for Lear's Fool. During these same years, Shakespeare also returned to Chaucer's poetry, from which he derived so many details of romance, specifically the consideration of pagan antiquity. But *Troilus and Criseyde*, Chaucer's great complete chivalric romance proved intractable, and Shakespeare's *Troilus and Cressida* stands as an anti-romance, a relentless reduction of the tradition's high idealism that is concurrent with the period of the great tragedies.

As You Like It

As we have seen, *Two Gentlemen of Verona* contains scenes of outlawry, a role especially cogent for Catholic experience in the sixteenth century, but the outlaw also has a long and prominent role in English literary tradition. The early heroes were the Anglo-Saxon Hereward, whose holding out against William the Conqueror is part of chronicle history, and Fulke Fitzwarin, hero of history and romance, who defended his heritage against the Norman King John. Today Robin Hood, a later type for the tension between Saxon and Norman, epitomizes the outlaw and other exemplars are less well known.[1] Robin Hood was celebrated in many ballads that were part of oral tradition long before they were printed, and Shakespeare often refers to him. But his fullest use of a legendary outlaw is in *As You Like It*, and the inspiration is *The Tale of Gamelyn*, an English legend especially directed against abuses of the social and legal systems. Because of a close tie with Chaucer—the romance survived in twenty-five manuscripts and was printed as part of *The Canterbury Tales*—Gamelyn is the earliest outlaw story for which we have a recorded text, and he was still a parallel to Robin Hood at the start of this century. ''Robyn and Gandeleyn,'' a later ballad, even ties the two together with Gandeleyn as a servant who avenges his master's death. The outlaw or subversive figure fills a significant place in literature both to acknowledge the inevitability of adversity and as the locus for protest against injustice; since the suffering is often not merited, lawlessness becomes a sign of heroism and advocacy for social change, and an occasion of violence. Outlawry is a popular theme in romances sometimes identified as the Matter of England, a land that assimilated many invasions. Its aptness for the Tudor reigns is obvious: violent disagreement between factions and classes of society, vast changes in ownership of lands because of the Dissolution, the forest as a place of refuge for those deprived by political changes and banished by a tyrant, in short a reliance upon the greenwood as a place of escape and regeneration—as in *As You Like it.*

Shakespeare's immediate source, Thomas Lodge's *Rosalynde: Euphues' Golden Legacy* (1590), is identified as a pastoral romance, part of the Elizabethan discourse about courtly sophistication, classical ideas of the pastoral, Renaissance conventions, and stylistic elaboration. Such emphases are appropriate—even though Shakespeare decries the limits of wit and language, while he displays his virtuosity—but there are other points of interest. As was noted earlier, Lodge was an acknowledged Roman Catholic, imprisoned for his belief in 1581: "the black sheep of his family, prodigal, imprudent in all things, and most honourably so in hardly at all disguising his adherence to the old religion."[2] He was a page in the Catholic household of Henry Stanley, earl of Derby, wrote a Catholic pamphlet *Prosopopeia* (1596), and worked on the continent for several years because he was refused a license to practice medicine in England until 1610. Lodge's writings include attempts at almost every form of literature: poetry, plays, *A Defense of Plays* (1580) in reply to Gosson's *The School of Abuse*, and translations. His prose illustrates flamboyant styles, but several topical pamphlets or tracts also usefully gloss religious issues: *An Alarum against Usurers* (1584) warns of the consequences of youthful self-indulgence, *Catharos Diogenes in his Singularity* (1591?) purports to be an Athenian colloquy but relies upon a medieval study of sins, and *The Devil Conjured* (1596) defends asceticism and attacks magic and astrology, one dimension of Elizabethan atheism. Thus many works sign the sober direction of Lodge's religious conversion and later life as a doctor, whatever his youthful adventures. Although he wrote several romance narratives, his fame rests heavily upon *Rosalynde*, which was deservedly popular even without its immortality in Shakespeare's adaptation. Another is of special interest, *Robert Duke of Normandy* (1591), a version of the medieval romance *Robert the Devil*, twice printed by de Worde. This highly didactic and popular story turns on diabolism, violent acts, repentance, a trip to Rome, years of penitence as a fool, and a happy ending in marriage and restored position.[3] Lodge is faulted for eliminating the Devil in his version, but that decision may well reflect the danger of too great a tie to "the old religion" and contemporary anxieties about diabolism. Affinities between *Robert* and *Rosalynde* suggest an attraction to several themes that explore tensions of religious, political, and social conflicts, not least renewed attacks upon Roman Catholics, whose numbers had increased in the 1590s, but here Lodge shows something of Shakespeare's evasive caution in selecting details. *Rosalynde* explores the relation between inward virtue and outward appearance or expression, and concludes "that vertue is not measured by birth but by action . . . that concord is the sweetest conclusion, and amitie betwixt brothers more forceable than fortune" (Bullough II,256). Lodge's combination of a pyrotechnic style on the surface and underlying moral issues mirror the tensions of discernment and suggest the plight of recusant Catholics in Elizabeth's England.

To identify the medieval heritage of narrative, I want to focus on the traditions that underlie *As You Like It*, the story of an outlaw who is a male Cinderella, a younger son who is disinherited and badly treated, but ultimately wins wealth and a happy marriage. This folkloric element is part of the universal success story, especially appealing at a time of extraordinary social and economic change. The losses of the barons in the War of the Roses and the economy of Elizabeth's England make a close analog with the consequences of the Black Death in the mid-fourteenth century when *The Tale of Gamelyn* was written.[4] Sixteenth-century inflation, it has been estimated (and noted in passing earlier), meant that only by doubling income could one maintain one's father's standard of living, and that the number of persons in upper social classes nearly tripled.[5] This suggests a climate of competitiveness and ambition, and ancillary lawlessness. There is also an affinity between the dispossessed Gamelyn and the plight of Roman Catholics during the Reformation. Whatever the humanist antipathy and objections of moralists, the old metrical romances remained popular and even found sophisticated defenders such as George Puttenham, who named *Gamelyn* a popular favorite in *The Arte of English Poesie* (1589); he also accepts other old romances like *Sir Thopas, Adam Bell and Clymme of the Clough*— the latter about an outlaw hero—heard by country fellows and boys in taverns and alehouses and as entertainment for holidays. This robust quality, especially in Gamelyn's several days of feasting and drinking after his victory, is a far cry from the love story that Lodge combines with the virile romance of *Gamelyn* and that Shakespeare develops. But an insistence upon countering the sentimental with skepticism may derive from the medieval romance whose 898 lines show more realism than fancy and a passionate and violent effort to achieve justice. Similarly, the division of *Gamelyn* into six parts suggests an easy transfer to the Elizabethan stage. The minstrel's theatrical injunctions—"Litheth and listneth and herkneth aright / And ye shull heer a talking" (1–2) or "Litheth and lestneth and holdeth your tonge / And ye shull heer talking of Gamelyn the yonge" (169–70)—indicate performance, a "talking" that is to be "heard," just as Elizabethans went to "hear" a play.

Gamelyn's story is one of struggle between brothers over a father's inheritance.[6] The hero's name is related to Scandinavian Gammel-ing (son of the old man); by being almost exclusively devoted to property, runic inscriptions on stones show how crucial is this concern. Scandinavian sagas abound in outlaws, and Gamelyn's elder brother Sir John, who becomes sheriff, declares him "wolves-heed" (700). Also familiar are Things, democratic meetings, antecedent of the shire assembly in "moot-halle" where Gamelyn gets justice by force, a triumphant brawl and summary hangings. Neither Lodge nor Shakespeare uses this primitive way of resolving conflict and tyranny, for they have more sophisticated minds, informed by religious controversy. The most challenging point about Lodge's choice of *Gamelyn* is its central severe criticism of Catholic clergy—abbots, priors, monks, canons (509)—who ignore a fettered Gamelyn's plea for justice, made in the name of Christ's Passion, and support his wealthy evil brother. Adam Spencer, loyal man and servant, first urges disciplined procedure but provides an alternative by secretly loosening Gamelyn's fetters so that he is free to leap to action and with his staff beat his enemies. There is no intervention from the laymen who "hadde no rewthe of men of holy church" (508), whom the poet further mocks by describing Gamelyn's blows as "sprengeth holywater with an oken *spire" (twig 503). Such details are ready made for Reformation anti-Catholicism and justification of the seizure of church wealth, but Lodge deletes this anti-clerical element, no longer credible as an attack on individual failure and abuse in a time of sweeping denunciation of the old religion. Lodge uses the essence of Gamelyn's story—"dismay thee right nought; / Many good mannes child in care is y-bought" (623–24)—that is a poignant description of Catholics under Elizabeth. He concentrates on the family dispute and study of changing fortunes that are prelude to the main love interest of Rosalynde, which is Lodge's addition to a robust medieval romance that had no women and the great appeal of the play.

Gamelyn is rigorously defiant, and he makes himself the instrument of justice. His success begins with a victory in a wrestling match where his weapon is a club, not knightly arms. This victory resembles one in the *Geste of Robin Hood* ballad, or in *Havelok the Dane*, another romance whose hero was deprived of his heritage, a prince exiled to England and part of the local history of Lincolnshire. Lodge keeps the wrestling match but has no weapons, suggesting a sophistication of physical prowess, as Castiglione indicates in *The Courtier*. *Gamelyn* treats only male power and justice, which the hero achieves because he becomes "maister outlawe" and is crowned king, the previous leader having conveniently received word that he can return home safely. A legal reconciliation comes for Gamelyn when the King, who loves his second brother Sir Ote, pardons Gamelyn's offenses and makes him chief justice of the forest. In the last few lines of the poem, Sir Ote names him heir, and Gamelyn marries well— the conventional happy ending and a hint for Lodge's complex plotting of multiple loves and marriages.

Part of the interest of *Gamelyn* for Lodge would have been the concern with justice, so little of which was available to Catholics in the 1580s. No less a personage than Lord Burghley tried to defend the Queen's action, especially physical torture, with two publications, a brief *Declaration* and *The Execution of Justice in England* (1583) that was published in French and Latin as well as English. By changing the names of characters both Lodge and Shakespeare introduce religious allusions. Gamelyn becomes "Rosader," a name that parallels "Rosalynde," both evoking the rose that combines beauty with thorn, and in medieval iconography the Virgin Mary and woman. More obviously he makes the elder brother "Saladyne" to connote pagan evil, which is nicely signed as a contempt for Catholic practices. In *Gamelyn*, the elder brother asks, "Is our mete yare?" (90), and Lodge keeps this as "what, is my dinner readie?" But he precedes it with a chiding, "are you saying a Dirge for your fathers soule?" (Bullough II,167) that is a reminder of the systematic suppression of Catholic services for the dead. The middle brother becomes "Fernandyne," a variation on Ferdinando, the young Catholic aristocrat of the Stanley family whose name Shakespeare evokes in *Love's Labour's Lost* by naming the King of Navarre Ferdinand. Fernandyne, the scholar, returns from Paris with the twelve peers of France to help Gerismond regain his lawful kingship, lost to a usurping Torismond, who is not his relation. The reference to the peers perhaps suggested the names for Shakespeare's heroes, Orlando (Roland) and Oliver, companions in the Charlemagne romances, currently popular in Italian redactions, especially Ariosto's *Orlando Furioso*, that added the hero's passionate love, remedying a defect of the Old French *chanson*, and of *Gamelyn*. Moreover, the two quarreling brothers bear the names of companions who, though briefly at odds, were medieval types of brotherly love and devotion. Thus Shakespeare early signs the reconciliation that is to come in the forest. He keeps the name "John" for the middle brother, Jaques de Boys, and uses it for his own distinctive creation, the melancholy fool Jaques, also a scholar who accompanies the banished duke, and believed by some to be based on Lodge himself. This would make Jaques's decision "to put on a religious life" (V.iv.180) an exact parallel.

The locale in *Gamelyn* is suggested by the identification of "Sir John of Boundis" ("border lands"). But one manuscript has "Burdeux," which is what Lodge uses, and he makes the king of France and places the action in the forest of Ardennes. Most significantly, the good brother Sir Ote, who remains as a landowner and helps Gamelyn, becomes Fernandyne, who is "at *Paris* poring on a fewe papers, having more insight into Sophistrie and principles of Philosophie, than any warlike indeavours" (Bullough II,168, cf.255). His study is thus that of recusant Catholics, many of whom left England to live in France, some to be trained as priests first at Douai and then at Rheims, a location not distant from the Ardennes. Fernandyne appears at the end to tell Gerismond that an army has come to destroy the usurper Torismond; indeed "the Peeres were conquerors, *Torismonds* armie put to flight, & himselfe slaine in battle" (Bullough II,256). Lodge's introducion of a second example of usurpation doubled the plot about justice, and included a king and usurper, a constant political issue for Tudors. *Rosalynde* ends with the death of the tyrant King Torismond and a restoration of the rightful Gerismond, who names Rosader heir apparent, and distributes property and offices. Allegorically, this can be read as an extreme wish-fulfillment for the end of Protestantism, the kind of sentiment that partially explains Elizabeth's view of Catholics as traitors guilty of treason.

Shakespeare is both more moderate and more pointed in his commentary. He makes his forest Arden, in Warwickshire, where, as seen, many Catholics lived and the Gunpowder Plot was planned. The name is also pointedly that of his mother's Catholic family. Moreover, his choice of "Duke Senior" as the usurped ruler who is "exiled" to the forest evokes the old religion. Duke

Senior's first speech (II.i.1–17) is filled with allusions that have a Catholic resonance: "old custom, painted pomp, peril [of] the envious court." His reaction to exiled circumstances is to recognize that "Sweet are the uses of adversity," and he rejoices in the nature of God's creation, finding "good in everything." Amiens agrees and praises the response: "Happy is Your Grace / That can translate the stubbornness of fortune / Into so quiet and so sweet a style" (18–20). This is not simple pastoralism, but the wisdom discerned by the greatest mystic theologian St. John of the Cross (1542–91), a Discalced Carmelite in Spain. Writing with poetic vision, he explains that we cannot determine the events of our fortune, but we can determine our response. When Orlando bursts in with bared sword to demand food for himself and the starving Adam, he perceives the gentleness in Duke Senior. As he asks for the same quality, he evokes an earlier time: "If ever you have looked on better days, / If ever been where bells have knolled to church" (II.vii.112–13). Duke Senior is a good man, tried like Job. Another "conversion" is shown in sinners. Oliver, after entry into the forest, says: "I do not shame / To tell you what I was, since my conversion / So sweetly tastes, being the thing I am" (V.i.136–38). This is easily written off as a convenience to provide Celia with a husband, but the contexts make it a stronger point.

Similarly, the sudden appearance of the middle brother, Jaques de Boys, is often scarcely noticed amidst celebrations of marriages, or it is described as a device to end the story and to unite the parallel plots that focus on justice. Shakespeare's making Duke Senior and Duke Frederick brothers is both a closer analog to Orlando and Oliver, and a gloss upon family within the community. Here is a thoughtful use of a favorite device in medieval romance sometimes called diptych, having two sets of parallel events, and the material gives one of the best insights to how romance influenced Shakespeare. It is also an opportunity for a fuller expression of Catholic interests. The usurping Duke Frederick set out to kill Duke Senior:

> And to the skirts of this wild wood he came,
> Where, meeting with an old religious man,
> After some question with him, was converted
> Both from his enterprise and from the world.
>   (V.iv.158–61)

Shakespeare's modification of the conclusion in *Gamelyn* and *Rosalynde*—in both the killing of the evil brother—is frequently cited as evidence of his generosity of spirit, and this is surely true. But more to be noted is a belief that even the worst of sinners can be saved. Duke Frederick has undertaken to live in a virtuous way; he "hath put on a religious life" (180), which was not possible for him at the "pompous court." Thus the melancholy Jaques evaluates his decision to change. Jaques is one of Shakespeare's most original creations, a thoughtful man so oppressed by the disappointments of the world that he is repeatedly identified as "melancholy" and always risks decline into a harsh lack of charity, so that for him "Out of these convertites / There is much matter to be heard and learned" (183–84). First is the restoration to Duke Senior of his "former honor" because "Your patience and your virtue deserves it" (184–86). Then each of the others—Orlando, Oliver, Silvius, Touchstone—who reflect a range of men in the world, is given a promise of love in his marriage. Duke Frederick and Jaques, whose Christian failure is too great reliance upon intellect, now have time for reflection and sustained conversion. For Shakespeare, then, there is the extraordinary happy ending of romance, but it goes beyond the dance that concludes celebrations of marriage and the play. There is first a confidence in the restoration of the older values, a penitence of the sinner that allows for a better life in this world and joy in the next, and a new effort on the part of those who have been most melancholy and despairing. Some essentials of Catholicism are in Lodge, but he lacked the confidence that leads Shakespeare to affirm it for all. Justice is done, there is still ample opportunity for those who sin and repent, social order is restored, and marriages guarantee the continuity of life.

Generosity of spirit is a crucial theme in *As You Like It*. Like Duke Senior, Orlando and Rosalind suffer not simply because they are victims of injustice but because loss of worldly Fortune only enhances their virtue. Oliver cannot explain his hatred of the youngest brother except "he's gentle . . . full of noble device, of all sorts enchantingly beloved" (I.i.157–59). Adam repeats this evaluation in rhetorical questions: "Why are you so virtuous? Why do people love you? / And wherefore are you gentle, strong, and valiant?" (II.iii.5–6). Then he identifies the qualities in religious terms, as "graces" (11, 18): "Your virtues, gentle master, / Are sanctified and holy traitors to you" (12–13). Adam responds with unpredictable generosity; he gives five hundred crowns to his master's son, who observes in the "good old man":

> The constant service of the antique world,
> When service sweat for duty, not for meed!
> Thou art not for the fashion of these times,
> Where none will sweat but for promotion,
> And having that do choke their service up
> Even with the having.   (II.iii.57–62).

Adam Spencer helped Gamelyn "In hope of advancement that he him *biheet" (promised 418); Lodge's Adam in lamenting Fortune has greater pity for Rosader, but Shakespeare makes the elegiac comment on an earlier way of life, a Benedictine ideal of authority as service, given without being asked for. This

monastic tradition for a thousand years made possible the survival and development of Christianity in Europe. Adam's "truth and loyalty" to the death
(70) is a far cry from the Tudor intrigue, shifting, and betrayal here described.
Orlando's supreme moment is the saving of Oliver's life, a scene from romance. Rosader comes upon a sleeping Saladyne threatened by a lion and debates in a typical meditation what he should do before he slays the lion. A
chastened Saladyne, not recognizing his protector, sorrows over his ill treatment of his younger brother, and this expression of penance leads to reconciliation. In the play Oliver reports the scene (IV.iii.103ff.) in which Orlando
intervened to help "a wretched, ragged man, o'ergrown with hair" about
whose neck "a green and gilded snake" was wreathed ready to enter his
mouth. The forest of Arden has an Edenic threat, made specific when Orlando
recognizes Oliver; "kindness and nature" must triumph over "revenge" for
him to fight the lion.

  Le Beau explains that Duke Frederick is displeased with his niece,
"Grounded upon no other argument / But the people praise her for her virtues /
And pity her for her good father's sake" (I.iii.269–71), and the usurper confirms:
"Her very silence, and her patience / Speak to the people, and they pity her"
(I.iii.76–77). Rosalind's silence and patience are in accepting adversity, not a
restraint of gaiety: she is one of Shakespeare's most articulate heroines, in some
ways the supreme "breeches part." But she is merry as a chosen discipline, a
response to circumstances that she cannot control. Our first encounter is Celia's
"I pray thee . . . be merry" (I.ii.1), and Rosalind quickly devises the sport of
"falling in love." We are reminded of her choice of response in the forest when
she counters Jaques: "And your experience makes you sad. I had rather have a
fool to make me merry than experience to make me sad" (IV.i.25–27). This
statement introduces her virtuoso "wooing" scene with Orlando: a boy actor
plays a girl Rosalind, who pretends to be a boy Ganymede, who is pretending
to be a girl Rosalind—an unmatched exhibition of what seems and what is. The
wit and broad comedy of the play's interconnecting romantic stories fill much
of the action and present a variety of heterosexual attractions, but they are
always placed in serious context by Rosalind, who often directs and at the end
sorts out misunderstandings and wrong choices in her role of "magician"
(V.ii.69). Her qualification for training Orlando as a lover is that "an old religious uncle of mine taught me to speak" (III.ii.337), and Celia protests that
Rosalind's love questions are harder to answer than a "catechism" (225). Rosalind's description of her "cure" is a vigorous outpouring of paradoxes, but
they culminate in the suitor's being driven "from his mad humor of love to a
living humor of madness, which was to forsake the full stream of the world to
live in a nook merely monastic" (406–9). Further, from the age of three, Rosalind "conversed with a magician, most profound in his art and not

damnable'' (V.ii.59–60). Such religious language, from a woman who is inherently serious—however lively her mind and entertaining her speech—leads to a sense that the ''love'' that is the subject of the play is not so much passion as charity. The two are, of course, very closely allied. Shakespeare makes this explicit in an extraordinary image of Transubstantiation in the Eucharist. Rosalind says that Orlando's ''kissing is as full of sanctity as the touch of holy bread'' (III.iv.14).[7] The human and divine are united through Christ, and he is perfect charity, which St. Paul explained: ''And now abideth faith, hope & loue, *euen* these three: but the chiefest of these *is* loue'' (1 Corinthians 13.13). Augustine and Aquinas contribute to a theology of charity that comes only with the absence of cupidity (covetousness), which as the Vostre *Horae* illustrate, is its opposite. Rosalind, Orlando, and Duke Senior early manifest this awareness; others perceive later and move toward true wisdom, which is not what the world sees. This context, considered by Aquinas as the striving for perfection, a state that is the concern of most religious, glosses Duke Frederick's retreat to a monastery.[8]

In Touchstone and Jaques, both identified as fools, Shakespeare considers this. Neither *Gamelyn* nor *Rosalynde* has such figures, though the Fool is familiar as in the household of Thomas More and on the page with the anatomical man in Vostre's *Horae*, which shows the Fool with cap and bells (Figure 1). Medieval stories of those who went from proud position to roles as begging fools, like St. Alexis and Robert of Sicily, were popular, whether in legend, romance, or part of the *Gesta Romanorum*. Having met Touchstone, the loyal servant to Celia and Rosalind who parallels the archetypal Adam, Jaques recounts to Duke Senior sayings of the man in motley, and his startled response: ''That fools should be so deep-contemplative'' (II.vii.31). Jaques goes on to cry, ''O, that I were a fool! / I am ambitious for a motley coat!'' (42–43), yet he quickly lapses into satirical railing, pyrotechnic displays of wit and intellectual suffering. Touchstone, letting William know that Audrey is not for him, offers a saying: ''The fool doth think he is wise, but the wise man knows himself to be a fool'' (V.i.31–32). He demonstrates later a worldly wisdom of the court, ''O sir, we quarrel in print, by the book'' (V.iv.89), and the paradox of the fool. Jaques notes, ''He's as good at anything and yet a fool,'' and Duke Senior replies, ''He uses his folly like a stalking-horse, and under the presentation of that he shoots his wit'' (104–6). Again St. Paul explains:

Let no man deceiue him self. If anie man among you seme to be wise in this worlde, let him be a foole, that he may be wise.
(1 Corinthians 3.18)
And as touching things sacrificed vnto idols, we knowe that we all haue knowledge: knowledge puffeth vp, but loue edifieth. Now, if any

man thinke that he knoweth any thing, he knoweth nothing yet as he oght to knowe. But if any man loue God, the same is knowen of him.''

(1 Corinthians 8.1–3)

Take hede therefore that ye walke circumspectly, not as fooles, but as wise.   (Ephesians 5.15)

Introduction of the two fools focuses Shakespeare's triumph through romance, a medieval habit of mind with faith and hope in a happy ending, often realized through charity.

Twelfth Night

These virtues, and another Fool, inform *Twelfth Night*, and recent performances emphasize the sadness that underlies the festival play's broad humor, which is both amusingly farcical and painful. The play's alternative title *What You Will* encourages diverse readings; it offers a choice for the title itself, suggests that characters or audience may have what they desire, and even introduces the spiritual consolation of our freedom to respond to events that we cannot determine. This is wise, especially in a time of religious turmoil. In the liturgical year the feast of the Epiphany comes on January 6, or twelve days after the Nativity, and the word means "knowing," a revelation of Christ's coming into the world, marked by the homage of the Magi and already making clear that His coming poses hardships as well as brings salvation. Jesus came into the world to save humanity by the Crucifixion; thus religious celebrations and artistic representations of Easter are more developed than those of Christmas. But the somber religious tradition of the holy day coexists with the holiday of Twelfth Night, the end of the Christmas revels with feast and carnival, a time for self-mockery and renewal, as is the Feast of Fools, within the octave of the Epiphany, perhaps the Church's boldest acknowledgment of misrule. The action of *Twelfth Night* leads the principal characters to self-knowledge, and in a sense the play is a similar activity for Shakespeare, for in it he repeats many of the situations of the early comedies.

As in *The Comedy of Errors* there is confused identity; again there are twins but this time not of the same sex—and thus a reminder of Shakespeare's twins Hamnet and Judith. Different sex twins allow amusing play with gender and give a major role to the woman, who defines the romance mode in contrast to the male world of epic. Again a misdirected purse moves the action, and there is an exorcism. Sebastian calls Feste "foolish Greek" (IV.i.17), which is both a reminder of Ephesus and lack of understanding ("It's all Greek to me") and a familiar name for a fool, like Matthew Merrygreek in Nicholas Udall's early Roman comedy *Ralph Roister Doister* (1553, printed c.1567). As in *The*

Comedy of Errors confused identities stem from the twins. Finding himself struck by Sir Andrew, Sebastian defends himself and asks, "Are all the people mad?" (27). But at the end of the scene he allies himself with Bottom, "Or I am mad, or else this is a dream" (60), when he recognizes that his situation is not rational, but yet accepts Olivia's interest and love as readily as Bottom followed Titania. The difference is that Sebastian is not bewitched by Oberon/ Puck, but a careful man who is making a deliberate choice about what to believe. At his first entry Sebastian rightly named himself (II.i.15); this is needed dramatically to establish the family relationships, but it also recalls the frequent moment in chivalric romance when the unknown knight declares himself. In *The Golden Legend* Saint Sebastian, whose feast is January 20, "followed the blessedness of the heavenly city," comforted martyrs, and inspired conversions. He did not die from the myriad arrows shot by Diocletian's archers, so that he "returns to life"; when death comes after a beating with stones, Sebastian's corpse is preserved; following his appearance to her, St. Lucy recovers it, and miracles (and devil possessions) follow.

Later analysis of unexplainable behavior is redolent of Catholic belief. Sebastian holds Olivia's gift, a pearl, associated in the Middle Ages with the "pearl of great price" (Matthew 13.45–46), a symbol for purity and preciousness, and tied to Margaret, a saint especially noted for marriage. Thomas Usk's *Testament of Love* (1387–88) specifies that she "betoketh Grace, learning or wisdom of God, or else Holy Church." The pearl is a token, but more deeply significant than the ring that Orsino sent to woo Olivia or the rings in *The Merchant of Venice* that it recalls. In this story of loss at sea, a pirate has the role of outlaw; and this Antonio is also generous, brave, and loyal. In keeping with the reworking and intensification of earlier themes, he is arrested when he fights for his friend Sebastian. By taking a risk, entering the place where his offense against the state took place, Antonio forfeits his security and satisfying new life as an exile.

Many critics argue that *Twelfth Night* is the serious comedy that marks a transition to tragedy in Shakespeare's writing. It ends with marriages, but not with unmitigated happiness, since sadness is acknowledged. Not found in any of the sources is the character Malvolio (ill-wishes), whose pain and anger are real, albeit self-induced. Although his parting threat, "I'll be revenged on the whole pack of you!" can be read as impotent comic posturing or a throwback to the most primitive of human motives, Olivia rightly observes, "He hath been most notoriously abused" (V.i.378–379) and thus repeats Malvolio's own evaluation "there was never man so notoriously abused" (IV.iii.87). Even proud self-love, confessed and punished, does not justify ill treatment, a Christian advance over Roman satire. There are resonances of the Pharisees, for as noted earlier, Malvolio is "sometimes a kind of puritan" (II.iii.139), and Maria justifies this identification: his "vice" (151) is to be self-righteous and a sycophant. She sees him as a "gull . . . turned heathen, a very renegado; for there is no Christian that means to be saved by believing rightly can ever believe such impossible passages of grossness" (III.ii.67–70). Malvolio's belief is based on the words of the forged letter that he carefully glosses, but the premise that Olivia loves him is his own vain wish. Malvolio's antipathy to the carnival spirit of Sir Toby Belch prompts that gentleman's incisive, "Dost thou think, because thou art virtuous, there shall be no more cakes and ale?" (II.iii.114–15). This food and drink were associated with the feasts of saints and holy days. Thus the rhetorical question evokes the extremes of Protestant reform that attacked Catholicism's acknowledgment of festival and penance, brilliantly illustrated for centuries in medieval Christendom by the inclusion of gaiety in the onslaught against pride, as in depictions of devils in drama and the visual arts, or even in the comic grotesque of the torturers in the York *Crucifixion* play. Faith and play go together, and lack of faith means lack of play, as modern alienation demonstrates. Feasts and saints are crucial in Catholic tradition and practice, not just the Word of Scripture.

Feste's oath "by Saint Anne" is a reminder of Catholic veneration of the Virgin Mary, whose mother was Saint Anne; both are exemplars of humility and strength. Although Sir Andrew Aguecheek resembles Malvolio in pursuing Olivia and being gulled by Sir Toby, he never totally lacks humility and a capacity for enjoyment. He may be a zany, but his self-evaluation rings true: "Methinks sometimes I have no more wit than a Christian or an ordinary man has" (I.iii.82–83). The Church stresses the Ordinary: The Ordinary of the Mass is the unchanging portion, and a large part of the liturgical year is Ordinary Time, the weeks before Lent and after Pentecost or the periods between the two great seasons of Advent and Christmas and Lent and Easter. Sir Andrew delights in revels, but he recognizes their limits. These contexts and characterizations underlie the entrapment and ridiculing of Malvolio by Maria, Sir Toby, Sir Andrew, and Feste.

The encounter between Sir Topas the curate (Feste the fool in disguise) and the imprisoned Malvolio reflects criticism of Puritans, and it also dramatizes the conflict between madness and wit that symbolizes the contrast between the world and the spirit. Feste as Sir Topas the curate wears a disguise of long gown and beard; the plain long gown may suggest a Calvinist, but he first explains that he "will dissemble myself in't, and I would that I were the first that ever dissembled in such a gown" (IV.ii.4–6). These lines suggest that church vestments do not the priest make and that disguise is prudent in a time of persecution. Sir Topas's first words are "*Bonos dies*" which is bad Latin, but Latin nonetheless; and a following reference to "the old hermit of Prague"—usually called an invented mock authority—recalls Catholic experience before the clown identifies himself as "Master Parson" (13, 15) and the exorcism begins. The exchange between Feste and Malvolio turns on who is fool as Malvolio desperately tries to hold onto his conception of himself and secure freedom from his captivity. Feste initially defines his modest role "to be said an honest man and a good housekeeper goes as fairly as to say a careful man and a great scholar" (9–11). Like Sir Andrew's self-characterization as ordinary and Christian, this wise and modest view comes in the midst of apparent foolishness to show how easily the world's values lead to mistakes. Feste urges Malvolio to "be patient" (104), to accept humbly what has happened to him. But the steward insists that he will be all right once he has "some ink, paper, and light" (106–7), since he relies upon intellect and argument, tools of religious controversy but limited. At the end of the scene Feste's song compares himself to "the old Vice" (125), the figure in the morality play that tempts Mankind, who always has an unregenerate quality; and he bids, "Adieu. goodman devil!" (132). The world of *Twelfth Night* is one of confused identities, so that the paradoxical nature of the traditional Fool offers rich possibilities.

Shakespeare's Feste is a provocative catalyst. In his first exchange with Viola, he says, "I live by the church" (III.i.3), an apparent joke and play on words about earning his livelihood and where he lives physically, but also a declaration of faith. Then the exchange centers on dallying with words, which require "bonds" to be trusted and "are so false I am loath to prove reason with them" (21, 24–25), and concludes with Feste's assertion, "I am indeed not her fool but her corrupter of words" (35–36). Yet Viola praises his wit, and skill in eliciting a gratuity, and defines the proverbial nature of the Fool: "This fellow is wise enough to play the fool, / And to do that well craves a kind of wit" (60–61) because he must observe and respond wisely to the moods of those he encounters. Flexible adaptation goes to another level when he becomes "Sir Topas the curate, who comes to visit Malvolio the lunatic" (IV.ii.23–24). The name "Sir Topas" has many connotations, beginning with a relation to topaz, a semiprecious stone thought to heal the lunatic from his lunacy according to Reginald Scot's *Discoverie of Witchcraft* (1584). This is cogent for the questioning of Malvolio's sanity, but the Chaucer allusion applies more aptly, since "The Tale of Sir Thopas" is one that the poet assigns to himself and uses for a consideration of the nature of romance and comic techniques of burlesque and parody. A simplistic reading is restricted to the tale's parodic nature, Chaucer's exposure of the absurdities of romance by writing an example that is itself a horror; but this interpretation ignores the tale's charm and complexity, not least that it is based on a thorough knowledge of romances—which indicates substantial commitment—and is the medieval poet's serious consideration of his craft. Such critical examination and the mingling of genres are analogous to Shakespeare's mixture in *Twelfth Night*. While Lyly's "Sir Topas" in *Endimion*

(1591) is a bragging warrior, Chaucer's knight is an eager innocent, actually called a "child." Chaucer compares him with national heroes like Guy of Warwick and Bevis of Hamptom and with a youthful folk hero Lybeaus Desconus (Fair Unknown) and Percyvell, the Arthurian type of an awkward and unknown knight—who seeks the Holy Grail. Part of Chaucer's subtlety is in the name "Topas," a bright gem connoting superlative excellence in both men and women, and a power against lust—relevant to Malvolio's interest in Olivia. Shakespeare's naming a priest "Sir Topas" has, then, more possibilities than relief for lunacy or parody of chivalric narrative. An eighteenth-century antiquarian, Bishop Richard Hurd, called Chaucer's "Sir Thopas" a miniature of Cervantes's *Don Quixote* (1604), an insight that points to the simultaneous parody of the tradition of romance and great nostalgia for its idealism.

Alternations of behavior are the human condition, and Feste's last song tells of the changes in perception that come with maturity, "For the rain it raineth every day." There are many references to time, and indeed Viola early acknowledges her limitations, "O Time, thou must untangle this, not I" (II.ii.40). As a woman who has chosen to conceal her gender to serve the man she loves, Viola is embarked upon a more costly enterprise than Rosalind, who uses her role as Ganymede to play, to indulge in distraction while instructing her doting Orlando. His love is obvious, and she is but whiling away the time, while Viola has no reason to expect a happy resolution. Yet Viola, like Rosalind, in her page's attire, has a clear sense of her own identity and a deep faith. She promptly wants Orsino as her husband (I.iv.42, II.iv.27, 89, III.i, V.i.132) and dares much to serve him, even though she foresees no way to become his wife. Her faith is also demonstrated when she quickly perceives that Sebastian may be alive:

> Prove true, imagination, O, prove true,
> That I dear brother, be now ta'en for you!   . . .
> For him I imitate. O, if it prove,
> Tempests are kind, and salt waves fresh in love!
> (III.iv.377–78, 385–86)

Viola and Sebastian, twins in appearance and inner reality, embody the habit of mind of romance—in religious terms receive grace—that accepts the happy ending, however improbable. Faith and a willingness to forego control determine the outcome, not gender.

What a difference there is between such abnegation of self and the willfulness of Orsino and Olivia in the opening scenes of the play. In their youthful self-indulgences Orsino loves a woman who wants nothing to do with him and Olivia cuts herself off from society in excessive and reclusive grief for her dead brother; at the end both acknowledge how mistaken they have been, offer forgiveness, and happily move to live more fruitfully. Olivia and Orsino resemble many lovers in many medieval romances, who find pleasure in unrequited passion. But love for Shakespeare, as for Boethius, is a bulwark against time, and the arc of emotion is cyclical. Feste's image of "the whirligig of time" (V.i.376), a spinning top, substitutes for the Wheel of Fortune and is more rapid and unpredictable. Yet both *As You Like It* and *Twelfth Night* cover several months, a longer period of time than do early comedies such as *A Midsummer Night's Dream* or *The Comedy of Errors*, so there is an advance toward the sixteen years of *The Winter's Tale*. Traditionally "a sad tale's best for winter," and the second meaning of "sad" is "serious." Romance lies not apart but at the center of life, and of Shakespeare's work, and he returned to Chaucer's romances to understand more completely.

Anti-Romance: Chaucer Revisited

Shakespeare's plays show an interest in the full sweep of British history. This includes Troy, land of the legendary founders of Britain, whose mythic stories were subjects for many medieval romances. The early quarto and the First Folio identify *Troilus and Cressida* (c.1601–2) as a "History," which can be defined to embrace the legendary. Like many medieval stories, Shakespeare's is in a long line of tales of Troy that form a principal matter of romance.[9] In Chaucer's time London was called "New Troy," and *Troilus and Criseyde* is his greatest completed poem, a philosophical romance of love and chivalry. Fifteenth-century retellings of the Trojan story continued the English literary tradition: John Lydgate in 1412–20 wrote a massive *Troy Book* at the behest of Henry V (pub. Pynson 1513); Scottish Chaucerian Robert Henryson extended the story in *Testament of Cresseid* (pub. 1532 and 1593); William Caxton chose the *Recuyell of the Historyes of Troye* (c.1474) as the first printed English book, and both Wynkyn de Worde and William Copland reprinted it (1502 and 1553), as did T. Creede in 1596 and 1607; George Chapman made a new translation of Homer's *Iliad* (1598–1611). Shakespeare uses something from each, but the result is an anti-romance, the bitter satirical play *Troilus and Cressida,* written about the time of *Hamlet* and expressing a dark and pessimistic mood. Many identify it as a spiritual exhaustion or neurosis that are far and away from the resolution, rebirth, and joy of romance. *Troilus and Cressida* apparently was a contemporary failure, but late-twentieth century performances as antiheroic, antiwar, antiromantic, and absurd have brought some popularity.

A tale of antiquity allows both detached exploration of and calling attention to contemporary issues. Always difficult to place in a genre, *Troilus and Cressida* follows *Henry VIII* in the First Folio, but it is a far cry from the patience and pacifism of Shakespeare's final plays or the resolution in earlier Troy tales. Medieval Christian authors glossed the classical ideals of heroism, aspiration, and fame by viewing such worldly glory in the light of eternity. Thus human failings, explicitly identified as pagan actions and values, become the didactic point, not the vagaries of Fortune. Chaucer's Troilus laughs from the eighth sphere when he looks down on ''This litel spot of erthe that with the se / Embraced is, and fully gan despise / This wrecched world'' (V.1815–18). Chaucer's apotheosis is rooted in a belief in eternity, but the vision comes to the pagan hero only outside the narrative. This separation, like the structural balancing in the *Canterbury Tales*—where *fabliau* follows romance and mock epic follows tragedy—acknowledges both variety of human responses and a faith in God— and suggests the counterpointing by which Shakespeare writes both high idealism and antimyth. Religious belief is explicit in tellings of the Trojan story by two fifteenth-century poets, Henryson and Lydgate, who are more overtly didactic and comprehensive than Chaucer, and thus expand the challenges for Shakespeare. The hardness of his ''problem play'' is blunt in Thersites' epitome: ''All the argument is a whore and cuckold, a good quarrel to draw emulous factions and bleed to death upon'' (II.iii.71–73). Thersites points to *Troilus and Cressida* as anti-romance, but there are other elements.

War and sex are key topics, but also important, and more topical, is treason, the main issue for Roman Catholics, whose faith Elizabeth branded as treason and persecuted. In the Troy story treason is twofold: the civic betrayal through Ulysses' deception that led to the fall of Troy and the personal betrayal in love that is a corollary of the political situation. The severity of Reformation actions and ambitious betrayals at court—notably that of Essex, whom many see imaged in the Trojan heroes—partially explain an interest in Troy, but so do the medieval traditions that infuse it with religious significance. Troy's fall was widely acknowledged in the Middle Ages as an analog to the fall of man that stemmed from pride and lust, spiritual and fleshly sins. While lust is named for the lovers, Ulysses identifies Achilles' ''pride'' (I.iii.371), and Thersites notes the ''envy'' of Ajax (32), ''that fool [that] knows not himself'' (67). In earlier plays Shakespeare refers to the principal figures: Troilus is the name of Petruchio's spaniel in *The Taming of the Shrew* (IV.i.4–6), Rosalind ridicules Troilus as ''a pattern of love'' in *As You Like It* (IV.i.95), Benedict identifies him as ''the first employer of panders'' in *Much Ado about Nothing* (V.ii.31), and Feste offers to ''play Lord Pandarus of Phrygia, sir, to bring a Cressida to this Troilus,'' when Viola comes a wooing for Orsino in *Twelfth Night* (III.i.51). His plea is for another coin, and Viola refers to Cressida's fate as a begging leper unrecognized by Troilus in Henryson's *Testament*. For Shakespeare, as for most Elizabethans, the memorable allusions are to ''a base pander'' (*Henry V*, IV.v.15) and ''Cressid's kind'' (II.i.77). The latter reference is to Doll Tearsheet, who is ''the lazar kite'' and thus both diseased and a bird of prey (Bullough VI,100), a possible allusion to the taking over of Catholic properties, monastic and privately owned, and receipt of fees by men like Tiptoft for betraying Catholics. The leprosy comes from Henryson, who makes a moral judgment, and whose constant theme is spiritual waste. His Cresseid is a leper not because of sexual betrayal, but because she dishonors God in the "kirk": "My blaspheming now have I bocht full deir" (354). In fact, she fulfills the three points of the sacrament of Penance: admission of guilt, contrition, and satisfaction; and Henryson concludes with charity, asking worthy women not to be deceitful.

Although the allusions point to Cressida's fate, Shakespeare denies her the ending. He follows the larger epic treatments—Lydgate, Caxton, Chapman's Homer—to finish with Hector's death. Troilus's lament for the dead, "Hector is slain! . . . Hector is gone. . . . Hector's dead. . . . Hector is dead" (V.ix.3, 13, 16, 22), is both for his brother and the end of chivalry developed in medieval Christendom, and the specifics are not in Homer. Hector courteously gave Achilles a respite in single combat, but the Greek orders his Myrmidons to slay the unarmed Trojan. Betrayal is the point. Opposition to heroic chivalry is also in the two most satirical characters: Thersites' pride in his bastardy and cowardice (V.vii.16–22), and Pandarus's apology for being the servant of traitors and bawds. Both are pragmatic survivors, as the aristocratic Trojans and Greeks are not, but they lack the redeeming virtues of English Bottom. An earlier scene of witty display by Pandarus gives the theological context. Paris's servant says, "You are in the state of grace" (III.i.15). Pandarus denies: "Grace? Not so, friend. 'Honor' and 'Lordship' are my titles" (16–17), and he asserts, "I am too courtly and thou too cunning" (28). This scene can be read as mere clever repartee, or as an allusion to religious circumstances in which Elizabeth's court is set against the crafty survival of religious dissidents. The latter is suggested by the servant's first lines that play with secular and religious devotion: "I do depend upon the lord" and "The Lord be praised!" (5, 8).

Troilus and Cressida lacks a formal happy ending, except that as in Chaucer's romance Troilus becomes a fierce warrior; he is also a wiser man, for he laments Hector and rejects Pandarus: "Hence, broker-lackey! Ignomy and shame, / Pursue thy life, and live aye with thy name!" (V.x.33–34). This is not tantamount to the perspective of Chaucer's hero from the eighth sphere, but it shares a rejection of the worldly values that consume. Troilus's sentence on Pandarus, a life of ignominy and shame, is a wish fulfillment about the fate of betrayers. This is not Shakespeare's last use of Chaucer; he returns to the "Knight's Tale" at the end of his career in a further attempt to assimilate Chaucer's view of pagan antiquity in relation to Catholic faith, in a play that is increasingly given serious consideration.

The Two Noble Kinsmen has only recently been included in *The Complete Works*, and as a collaboration with Fletcher it poses questions about textual authorship, as well as interpretation, although Shakespeare may well be responsible for the overall design. Most agree that Shakespeare was responsible for the opening and conclusion, and this follows the structure of romance that begins in human conflict and achieves resolution through the divine.[10] The play is a composite with many themes and scenes that recall earlier plays, but there are significant points cogent to an ongoing commitment to romance. Just as Shakespeare honored Gower by making him Prologue to *Pericles*, so here the Prologue acknowledges "Chaucer, of all admired," noble, learned, famous from Italy to England, author of a story "constant to eternity" (10–14), and apologizes to Chaucer for scenes "below his art." Native tradition recurs in the reference to Robin Hood. Albeit there is some anxiety about popularizing as in a ballad (21), "the Lord of May and Lady bright" (III.v.128, Robin and Marion) lead the Morris dance, after the Schoolmaster introduces this ancient folk celebration, which is the theatrical heart of the play (III.v) and recalls the native Burgomaster dance of *A Midsummer Night's Dream*. Such local simplicity and energy contrast with the sophistication of the Athenian court and chivalric panoply, also ably translated from narrative to drama.

Two Noblemen Kinsmen follows Chaucer's tale for its main plot, but there are additions, especially an expansion of the role of women, several doublings to enhance the theme of friendship, and a complex characterization of Theseus, who is the continuity with both Chaucer's "Knight's Tale" and the earlier play. For the context of Catholicism Theseus is most significant. The play begins, rather than ends, with a marriage procession of Theseus and Hippolyta that bodes well. But as in Chaucer, those who have suffered, the three grieving queens in black to whom burial of their husbands has been denied, challenge the ruler: "give us the bones / Of our dead kings, that we may chapel them" (49–50), a precise allusion to Catholic chantries and practice. The First Queen exhorts, "For pity's sake and true gentility's," and the Second and Third Queens plead with Hippolyta and Emilia, "For your mother's sake" and for love of possible husband and virginity. The exchange is between the three queens and the Amazon sisters, and it is to the entreaty of the latter that the conqueror Duke Theseus yields and sets out to fight Creon. This augurs that he is not a beneficent ruler by first instinct. Later women's pleas of Hippolyta and Emilia secure mercy for Palamon and Arcite (III.vi).

In the next scene—which is entirely Shakespeare's addition—Arcite and Palamon comment on the corruption of Thebes, which they should flee "before we further / Sully our gloss of youth" (I.ii.4–5). The city has "strange ruins" (130) and the warrior receives "scars and bare weeds" (15), for Creon is "a most unbounded tyrant . . . one / That fears not to do harm; good, dares not" (63, 70–71). His court has "loud infamy," and "the echoes of his shames have deafed / The ears of heav'nly justice" (76, 80–81). Thus the friends fight to escape from tyranny, and briefly after capture Palamon laments, in *ubi sunt* form, the loss of liberty and a warrior heritage. Arcite most regrets that they will never wed and notes that their "banishments" will be lamented, but soon resolves "Let's think this prison holy sanctuary" and thus returns to his original argument for fleeing a corrupt state (II.i.37, 71). As in earlier plays Shakespeare reiterates the themes of banishment and oppression, a Catholic analog.

The resonance expands in the scene in the woods when Theseus confronts Palamon and Arcite, who are fighting because of their competing loves for Emilia. Chaucer's Palamon calls Arcite "false traytour wikke" (I.1580) because he returned in disguise to be near the lady after Theseus had freed him upon condition of avoiding his lands. But Chaucer's Theseus does not call the competing young men "traitor" when he stops their fighting because it is without official sanction. After Palamon identifies them both as "thy mortal foo" (1724, 1736), Theseus accepts their guilt and moves to a death sentence. Again the pleading of his queen and Emelye lead to a different judgment; the offense of Palamon and Arcite becomes a "trespas" that "in his resoun" Theseus must excuse (1762–69), as well as feel compassion for the women's plea for mercy. He concludes, "I yow foryeve this trespas every deel" (1825), and then proposes the tournament of one hundred knights on each side. In *Two Noble Kinsmen* Theseus begins, "What ignorant and mad malicious traitors / Are you that 'gainst the tenor of my laws" (III.vi.132–33). This precedes Palamon's declaration, "We are certainly both traitors, both despisers / Of thee and of thy goodness" (137–38), and he pleads for "justice" that would let the fight continue. Arcite protests that if there is "treason" in love, he will perish "in that faith" (163). As the one who loves Emilia most, he will be most "traitor" (167, 170). The ladies urge "pity" and "mercy," and Theseus's friend Pirithous adds a companion's plea, so that Theseus is overwhelmed, "Ye make my faith reel" (212); but when confronted with male determination to die for love, he also feels "compassion" (270). Emilia asked the gentler sentence of "banishments," but must accept Theseus's compromise of marriage to one and death for the other. When she refuses to choose, the Duke decrees a competition with three supporting knights for each man, a smaller and stageable encounter. The scene may well be Fletcher's, and its Catholic resonances suggest sympathy from this Anglican, Beaumont's friend and collaborator.

Friendship and its conflict with love underlie *The Two Noble Kinsmen*, which expands this familiar theme by increasing the number of examples. In addition to Palamon and Arcite there is the companionship of Theseus and Pirithous, a mature version of loyal warriors. Most interesting is the female friendship of Emilia and Flavina (I.iii.54), the innocent experience of youth cut off by Flavina's early death. After such a soulmate Emilia does not want to love a man, a kind of feminist stance. Her sister Hippolyta counterargues for love above friendship because she, not Pirithous, "possesses the high throne in Theseus's heart" (96–97). Emilia disagrees but quietly concludes, "I am not /

Against your faith, yet I continue mine'' (97–98). This elaboration gives an explanation and contemporary argument to Chaucer's tale in which Emelye moves more quickly to accepting the need to marry. Emilia's prayer to Diana elaborates Emelye's combined devotion to virginity and concession to marriage, for she persists in opposing the marriage for which she is already attired. Shakespeare replaces Chaucer's answers from the gods with theatrical spectacle, but Emilia leaves with a resigned lack of understanding—''unclasp thy mystery!'' (172)—in contrast to the submission of Emelye to Diana's ''proteccioun'' and ''disposicioun'' (1363–64). Emilia refuses to observe the competition and continues her assertion that Palamon and Arcite are interchangeable, and the sorting is by chance: Arcite wins the battle, but receives a fatal injury when he falls from his horse. His dying words to Palamon are, ''Take Emilia,'' and an assertion that he ''was false, / Yet never treacherous'' (V.iv.90, 92–93). The situation recalls the end of *The Two Gentlemen of Verona*, without the second reversal. Thus he who first saw and loved weds the lady, and Palamon can only regret ''That naught could buy / Dear love but loss of dear love!'' (112–13). Chaucer's Arcite gently recommended his friend; also entirely missing is the philosophical reflection of Theseus's First Mover speech that works through to acceptance of the divine (2987–74). The play's Theseus pragmatically notes ''So the deities / hath showed due justice'' (108–9), and that ''Never Fortune / Did play a subtler game'' (112–13); but his religion does not get beyond Fortune, ''O you heavenly charmers, / What things you make of us!'' (131–32). He orders that all look sadly ''a day or two'' for the funeral and then accept what is—''bear us like the time'' (124, 137)—a pagan resignation. A further gloss on the unperceived logic of the plot is the creation of the Jailor's Daughter, a nameless young woman whose love for Palamon is a counterpoint to Emilia's resistance and whose mad scenes—mostly Fletcher's—are a parallel manipulation of a willful young woman.

The Two Noble Kinsmen is a return to Chaucer's ''Knight's Tale,'' but its fuller rendering of the original is less successful than the introduction of a romance mode into *A Midsummer Night's Dream*, where the fusion of several traditions works so brilliantly. As in *Troilus and Cressida*, Chaucer's material proves intractable in *Two Noble Kinsmen*. Both plays lack Chaucer's assimilation of pagan antiquity, its reconfiguration with medieval Christendom. It was too early for Shakespeare to achieve a parallel resolution of Catholic and Protestant differences, beyond praising traditions of the old religion. His successful realization of his own predilection for the romance mode came when he returned to matter that was more deeply mythic and English, but Chaucer's women characters inspired a richer understanding that finds expression in most of his late romances. And the way that began with Portia continues in the last plays with Helena, Marina, and Imogen, culminating in Hermione and Queen Katherine.

6

LOST MEN AND WOMEN: SUFFERING AND TRANSCENDENCE

Concurrent with the satiric harshness and lack of resolution in *Troilus and Cressida* and the dire circumstances of the great tragedies, there are no comedies similar to *As You Like It* or even the darker *Twelfth Night*. But Shakespeare continues to rely upon the romance; its essence is in the title of *All's Well That Ends Well* (c.1601–5), a play with severity but also a confident faith in the alternative vision of healing and restoration. As has been often noted, time plays a large role in the late plays, both as duration and as the way to reconciliation, more acutely needed because of greater suffering. Shakespeare characteristically shows the process in women's lives, and the circumstances are not all the same. It is helpful to divide these plays into two groups: those in which women and men go through major changes in physical circumstances, and experience separation from family and native land; in the other group are women whose situation is constantly domestic. This suggests a contrast between the active and contemplative way, one kind of religious observation. The first plays include vast geographical movement and complex multiple stories. *All's Well That Ends Well* is European, moving from France to Italy, and contemporary; *Pericles* returns to the Greek romance of *Apollonius of Tyre* and sailings in the Mediterranean; *Cymbeline* combines ancient Britain and Rome and interlaces historical eras of emerging Christianity in the Roman Empire and Renaissance Italy; *The Tempest* is set in an imaginative world with allusions to Africa, Italy, and the New World of the Americas; and the protagonist, as in *Pericles*, is male. Prospero, the locus of suffering and transcendence, is removed from his home, like Helena, Marina, and Imogen; but he is also deposed from political rule, a traditional male sphere, to which he returns, as does the self-exiled Pericles. These men share personal suffering and transcendence and a return to a larger political world from which they were exiled while undergoing the transformation. In chapter 7, I discuss a specific and more exactly focused motif of romance, the falsely accused wife/queen, to show how Shakespeare considers it in a great comedy and a great tragedy, *Much Ado about Nothing* and *Othello*. He then makes the topic central to his finest romance, *The Winter's Tale*, which anticipates his return to history in *Henry VIII*, the play that centers on the Catholic queen Katherine of Aragon.

All's Well That Ends Well

Even while Shakespeare's energy was largely given to writing tragedy, there is a strong counter-strain of romance in *All's Well That Ends Well*, with its emphasis upon physical healing and spiritual rebirth, and reliance upon many archetypal elements of story and religion. Discussions identify a single source, Boccaccio's tale of Giletta of Narbonne in the *Decameron*, told on the third day, devoted to stories of lovers who achieve happiness only by overcoming extraordinary difficulties. William Painter made a close English translation of this tale as the thirty-eighth novel in *The Palace of Pleasure* (1566), an exciting collection that shares the role of main source for Shakespeare's plays with North's *Plutarch* and Holinshed's *Chronicle*. Painter, who uses mostly Catholic sources, heightens the idea of pilgrimage and considerations of class, a typically English adjustment. The plot of Helena's story occurs often in folklore, a comment upon both universality and the comparative paucity of plots, so that contexts are as crucial as episodes to an understanding of the play. It is easy to note the bizarre situation of a young woman of modest parentage who heals a king, gains the husband of her choice as reward, is rejected by the young man with the assertion that he will be her husband only if she can present him with the ring on his finger and proof that she is pregnant with his child, and who by the end of the story has accomplished these unlikely tasks. To increase the moral emphasis, Shakespeare alters the source to have a single sexual union, rather than many over months, and no twin sons. Other changes, such as the heroine's name and increased emphasis upon miracles, also suggest religious symbolism.

Sex and secrecy have always been popular topics, and even by late twentieth-century standards "the bed trick" surprises and titillates. But Shakespeare does much more than present a lively play of naughtiness, part of the Italian "vanitie and vice, license to ill living" that Roger Ascham condemned as the continuance of medieval romance in *The Schoolmaster*, written within a year or so of the publication of Painter's *Palace of Pleasure* (1566–67). As I indicated earlier, Ascham censured knights in *Morte Arthure* as killers and adulterers, but he insisted upon greater contemporary danger:

> And yet ten Morte Arthures do not the tenth part so much harme, as one of these bookes, made in *Italie*, and translated in England. They open, not

fond and common ways to vice, but such subtle, cunnyng, new, and diuerse shiftes, to cary yong willes to vanitie, and yong wittes to mischief, to teach old bawdes new schole poyntes, as the simple head of an Englishman is not hable to inuent, nor neuer was hard of in England before, yea when Papistrie ouerflowed all. Suffer these bookes to be read, and they shall soone displace all bookes of godly learnyng. For they, carying the will to vanitie and marryng good manners, shall easily corrupt the mynde with ill opinions, and false iudgment in doctrine: first to thinke nothyng of God hym selfe, one speciall pointe that is to be learned in Italie, and Italian bookes. And that which is most to be lamented, and therfore more nedefull to be looked to, there be moe of these vngratious bookes set out in Printe within these fewe monethes, than haue bene sene in England many score yeare before.   (80–81)

In one of the most absolute and famous denunciations of the "evils of Italy," Ascham goes on to express further grave anxiety about how Italian books— upon which Shakespeare relies heavily, if often in translation—are a threat to the Christian religion. So great is Ascham's distress that he identifies Italian secular texts as the common enemy of Protestants and Catholics:

> shakinge of the motions of Grace, driuing from them the feare of God, and running headlong into alle sinne. . . . They make more account . . . of a tale in *Bocace*, than a storie of the Bible. Than they count as Fables, the holie misteries of Christian religion. . . . For where they dare, in cumpanie where they like, they boldie laughe to scorne both protestant and Papist. They care for no scripture: They make no counte of generall councels: they contemne the consent of the Chirch: They passe for no Doctores: They Mocke the Pope: They raile on *Luther*: They allow neyther side.
>
> (81–82)

I have quoted at some length both to illustrate the emotional fervor of religious argument in Elizabethan England and the complexity of attitudes toward Catholic and Protestant. Reading Shakespeare's plays in this context shows how much his choice of romance went against Protestant sentiment, and close analysis indicates how he added specific religious details and symbolism, typical in medieval romances, in a play like *All's Well That Ends Well*. The second edition of Painter's collection in 1575 marks contemporary interest, and the many plays based on *novelle* are evidence of the popularity of such tales. What is notable about Shakespeare's treatment is his consistent heightening of the moral and religious qualities that were stronger in medieval romances than in Italian *novelle* influenced by Renaissance humanism.

Links to *Troilus and Cressida* come early in *All's Well That Ends Well*, when the fool Lavatch sings of Troy and its sexual indulgence with a turn to misogyny (I.iii.70–79), and the wise counselor Lafew calls himself "Cressid's uncle," when he brings Helena to the King and leaves them alone. These two references contrast alternatives of satiric and positive comedy. The clown Lavatch is clever and bawdy, and seeks personal advantage as fool. Lafew is wise and generous, and his joke eases an initial moment of private meeting, and it concludes with a fuller description: "A traitor you do look like, but such traitors / His Majesty seldom fears" (II.i.99–98). The most famous traitors under Elizabeth were Roman Catholics, so there may be a denial of charges of treason against the monarch. Indeed later Helena wins the King's confidence when she dares venture accusation and slander, even "With vilest torture let my life be ended" (176). Helena is, then, tied to both romance and Catholicism. Earlier Lafew described her healing capacity: "whose simple touch / Is great to araise King Pepin, nay, / To give great Charlemain a pen in 's hand / And write to her a love line" (77–79). One interpretation argues erotic significance, but an alternative is miracles, raising from the dead and creative skill—Charlemagne learned to read as an adult but never was able to write. These French kings are also prominent in romance, most notably in Caxton's *Charles the Grete*, an English composite of the Matter of France.

An elegiac note pervades the play, which begins with Bertram's renewed weeping over his father's death that is quickly followed by an account of the death of Helena's father, Gerard of Narbonne, and the consequent lack of a physician to cure the King's disease. The maimed Fisher King, in Arthurian romance and in Eliot's *The Waste Land*, is a sign of sickness in the kingdom, and Perceval's failure to ask the question and heal the king initiates the awareness needed to undertake the Grail quest, the deeply spiritual strain of this complex narrative. Helena, in the mode of the caregiving female, comes deliberately to heal, and while acknowledging her personal interest in winning Bertram, she identifies herself as an agent of the divine, "the weakest minister" (II.i.139), one through whom "miracles" (143), "the help of heaven" (154), may occur, after greater ones have failed. She urges the King, "Of heaven, not me, make an experiment" (156); and she has faith, "The great'st grace lending grace" (162). The King also perceives a power beyond sense: "Methinks in thee some blessèd spirit doth speak" (175), and he declares her "Unquestioned welcome and undoubted blest.—" (210). Thus from the King's suffering will come renewal, and the court will receive a vision of transcendence, albeit not all will immediately accept it.

Lafew astutely puts the moment of the King's healing in perspective:

> They say miracles are past, and we have our philosophical persons to make modern and familiar things supernatural and causeless. Hence is it that we make trifles of terrors, ensconcing ourselves into seeming knowledge when we should submit ourselves to an unknown fear. (II.iii.1–6)

Renaissance developments in science are the usual gloss for this passage, which describes the man of medicine who in Elizabethan times was much in charge of theory; women traditionally practiced health care, and Helena's low social status, Shakespeare's emphasis, is commensurate with this role. She is very unusual in combining theory and practice, analogous to Catholic combination of faith and good works, unlike Luther and Calvin. For the passage can be read as a contrast between the old and new religion, the moving away from miracles and awe that pervaded medieval Christendom and lingered for Catholic recusants. Lafew's exchange with Parolles, the most distinctive character that Shakespeare added to the story, shows how dire the court can be. Braggart, coward, liar, betrayer of youth and reputations, Parolles lacks ''the privilege of antiquity'' (209) that suggests the chivalry of romance. Lafew explains that the physicians were wrong in declaring the King incurable, and in a lively exchange he cuts against Parolles's pretensions. He reads ''a showing of a heavenly effect in an earthly actor'' (23–24); ''showing'' means print, but it is also a term in mysticism to denote the presence of Christ, as in the *Showings* of Dame Julian of Norwich, a medieval mystic and theologian.

Helena's name, which Shakespeare changed from Giletta in Boccaccio and Painter, has great significance. Saint Helena (c.247–c.330), the mother of Constantine the Great, is a model of humility, acceptance, and ultimate triumph when she discovers the True Cross in Jerusalem, where she had gone on pilgrimage to oversee the building of Constantine's Basilica on Mount Cavalry. Her story is often told. Sermon 34 of Mirk's *Festial* is ''De Inuencione Sancte Crucis'' for May 3 (142–46). Mirk's explanation of the finding of the cross begins with Adam and includes several miraculous preservations and appearances before Saint Helen, in this account ''qwene of Ierusalem,'' sought the Cross at her son's behest and threatened the Jews until Judas revealed the location. Mirk also relates two miracles and counsels ''þat we do reuerence and worschyp to þe cros, for oþyr defence haue we not aðeyne oure gostly enmys.'' Voraigne's *Golden Legend* acknowledges some contradictions in the legends but concludes that Helena led the search, brought a part of the Cross, and some nails, to her son, and ordained celebration of the Invention of the Holy Cross. Mirk says that Helena was born in England, the daughter of a King Ceolus; she married Constantius and had one son. Bede's *A History of the English Church and People* (731) cites Adamnan on places in Jerusalem and Helena's discovery of the Cross of our Lord (V.16).[1] For Bede, she is Constantius's ''concubine,'' perhaps a reflection of a legend of her bearing a child secretly and later revealing him to his father with the contrivance of a ring—analogous to *All's Well*. But Bede's greater interest is her son Constantine's role during the Arian heresy: ''although it was exposed and condemned at the Council of Nicea, the deadly poison of its false teaching nevertheless infected . . . not only the continental churches, but even those of these islands'' (I.8). Helena thus has a very special role. The material wood of the Cross is a valuable relic; its recovery gave the lie to allegorical and symbolic interpretations by countering the arguments of those who were questioning the fundamental dogma of the Church: God became Man Who died on the Cross to bring salvation to all. Modern biography recognizes Helena's exile to Trier—after her divorce by her ambitious husband—and her determined return at a perilous time for the Church to complete a practical task of discovery and help preserve the faith amidst confusion and doubt. Again Shakespeare chooses to remind his audience of Catholic experience of accusation, exile, hardship, humiliation—but also faith and perseverance.

Such a religious reading is appropriate, since the King presents Helena as ''my preserver,'' while she affirms, ''Heaven hath through me restored the King to health'' and insists, ''I am a simple maid'' (II.iii.64, 66). The phrase recalls the Virgin Mary, a simple maid who participated in the miraculous so that God entered the world as Man; thus Catholic devotion to Mary developed during the Middle Ages finds expression in *All's Well That Ends Well.* Shakespeare imbues Helena with characteristics that suggest the Virgin Mary; she is ''a poor unlearnéd virgin'' (I.iii.238), yet she has something more than her physician father's skill, ''a legacy be sanctified / By th' luckiest stars in heaven'' (243–44), and her assurance goes ''knowingly''—beyond simple belief (249). Some readers and viewers fault Helena for her confidence and daring actions, while others judge her Shakespeare's sublime heroine. The difference lies, I think, in whether they perceive the humility that underlies Helena, an analog to Mary's Magnificat and subsequent actions—participating in the divine, while living modestly in the world—and value such female heroism. Helena leaves with the Countess's permission and avowal of faith: ''I'll stay at home / And pray God's blessing into thy attempt'' (252–53). An alternative jaded (''realistic'') reading is of the unparalleled virgin trapped by her passion for a good-looking young man. But heroines of the comedies, like Julia, Rosalind, and Viola, show that Shakespeare lauds the young woman who is confident, virtuous, and sexually confident—as was the pregnant Virgin Mary.

After the miracle of healing come rejection and threat. Bertram denies the consequence of the miracle, his marriage to Helena, who makes her own flight, as a pilgrim to St. Jacques. The choice of pilgrimage is significant. It first suggests Compostella: Spain is Katherine of Aragon's home, and her daughter Mary, the last Catholic queen of England, was married to Philip of Spain. But in the play Helena goes to Florence seeking the church of ''St. Jacques le Grand'' (III.v.33), or St. James the More, as Caxton's *The Golden Legend* names the first apostle to be martyred. Herod beheaded James, and his followers took the body in a ship without sail or rudder; an angel led them to Galicia, ruled by Lupa, which in English is ''she-wolf.'' Lupa tries to destroy the disciples;

but confronted with their miraculous survival, she converts and builds a church in her palace, a wish-fulfillment for the conversion of an evil queen. St. James is a type of exile, and thus especially relevant to English recusants, and many legends of this saint are compelling. Compostella (*campus stellae*) means ''the field of the star,'' a name given because a hermit who found his tomb was led by a star, a mirror of the Magi's finding the Messiah. In the Middle Ages St. James became popular as a champion against the infidel Moors, and the sixteenth century is fraught with charges of heresy. Also cogent are stories in the Compostella *Book of Miracles* that include help for those of humble birth, like Helena, as well as nobility, and accounts of the protection of sea voyagers, a great interest in Shakespeare. Caxton includes a lively story of a young man from Lyon, a fornicator who sets out to Compostella without proper penance; devils tempt him to cut off his genitals and to suicide, but St. James intervenes and takes him to a meadow where the Virgin Mary commands that his life be restored; thus the young man returns and recounts all to his fellows. The relation of sexuality, sin, and redemption is pertinent to the play's treatment of sexuality, its exploitation, human confusion, and often bizarre quality.

Helena's letter explains her need for penitence because of ''ambitious love'' that has put her husband at threat (III.iv.4–17), a parallel to Bertram's snobbery about his low-born wife and anxiety about a woman through whom the divine acts. Here are echoes of Chaucer's Griselda and Walter, the issues of class and the central concept of *gentilesse*. The Countess of Rossillion again relies upon prayer: her son's selfish failure requires an angel's help and ''her prayers, whom heaven delights to hear / And loves to grant'' (27–28). Bertram's challenge to Helena—that she ''get the ring upon my finger, which never shall come off, and show me a child begottten of thy body that I am father to, then call me husband'' (III.ii.57–60)—is as unlikely as a virgin birth. Rings are a familiar means of identification, as in the energetic Middle English romance of *King Horn*, and later ballad versions. This lively and complex tale includes serious considerations of class, exiles, frequent riddles, and an exciting scene in which the ring identifies the hero to preserve his love of Rymenhild. Painter is the immediate source, but *novelle* like his are based on medieval romances that form the habit of mind that is Shakespeare's.

In romance and with God everything is possible, an affirmation that comes at the crucial moment for the Virgin Mary. St. Luke's Gospel concludes the scene of the Annunciation with the Angel's promise of the birth of the Son of God and the pregnancy of Elizabeth, Mary's cousin, in her old age. The Angel says to Mary: ''For with God shal nothing be vnpossible. Then Marie said, Beholde, the seruant of the Lord: be it vnto me according to thy worde'' (I.37–38). *All's Well That Ends Well* affirms the persistence of miracles, and that they rest upon belief and self-abnegation. Mary's faith and humility are a favored medieval model for Christian behavior, as she shows herself both a woman of valor and a devoted servant. This is Helena's profile, when she declares herself a dutiful wife (II.iv.47, 51, 54; II.v.73) and later perseveres to consummate the marriage, having identified her chaste quality: "All her deserving / Is a resolvèd honesty" (III.v.61–62). Just as Helena set out to heal the dying King of France of his physical illness, so she sets out to cure Bertram of his spiritual malady, his egotism and lack of honesty and concomitant sexual pursuit of Diana. Just as Helena attributed her miracle of healing to the divine, so the King explains that she relied upon much more than her ingenuity and courage; to keep his ring, "She called the saints to surety" (V.iii. 109). Portia and Nerissa teased and tested Bassanio and Gratiano with their rings as symbols of marriage truth; Helena must play in earnest. The aristocratic young Venetian and her serving maid acted independently, but Helena moves in a world of supportive and strong women, widows who serve their children—another suggestion of the interceding Mother of God who helps those devoted to her. The Countess loves her son, but honors Helena as a daughter; and the Widow Capilet of Florence is a wise mother who protects and advances her daughter Diana as she aids Helena. Neither is merely self-serving, and their behavior illustrates that nobility is not determined by place in the world; the Countess has wealth, but loves Helena who lacks this, and her salient characteristic is devotion to prayer. Similarly, the Widow, who explains "Though my estate be fall'n, I was well born" (III.vii.4), agrees to help Helena's "deceit so lawful" (38) and instructs her daughter. The substitution in bed validates the marriage made possible by a miracle.

Shakespeare gives to the King of France the role of reaffirming the old faith, as when he warns the proud and scornful Bertram: "As thou lov'st her, / Thy love's to me religious; else, does err" (182–83). Later Helena identifies the King of France as "One of the greatest in the Christian world" (IV.iv.2), pertinent in an age of nationalism and religious controversy. *All's Well That Ends Well* is, like some didactic romances, tied to saints' legends and miracles of the Virgin. An elegiac note sounds through the play, both in its preponderance of older people and in the experience of loss and separation, but Shakespeare reassuringly twice includes the title (IV.iv.35, V.i.25) before the final affirmation "All is well ended" (Epilogue 2). In the resolution scene Diana, a virgin, presents a riddle before the King to answer the riddling demands of proud Bertram: "One that's dead is quick" (V.iii.304). Helena has been reported dead, but she carries a new life within her womb, a promise for the future. Her reappearance is an emblem of resurrection in a scene of last judgment. Bertram recognized and now publicly acknowledges his sinful behavior: "O, pardon!" (309); and he affirms his marriage, "If she, my liege, can make me know this clearly, / I'll love her dearly, ever dearly" (316–317) in words that echo a prayer of St.

Richard to Christ: "may I know thee more clearly, love thee more dearly, and follow thee more nearly."

The King, the Countess, and Lafew are all of an older generation and behave with a kind of medieval chivalry and the charity enjoined in Scripture. Bertram is a Prodigal Son to be taken back, and the elders echo the story of the Woman Taken in Adultery: after Christ forgives her and enjoins those without guilt to throw stones, "they went out one by one, *beginning at the eldest*" (John 8.9, my italics). Such tolerance is expanded, even to Parolles from Lafew: "Though you are a fool and a knave, you shall eat" (V.ii.54). Utterly shamed, Parolles persisted, after acknowledging his fault as braggart, "There's place and means for every man alive" (IV.iii.341). Since "The web of our life is of a mingled yarn, good and ill together" (IV.iii.70–71), there must be generosity and restoration, the habit of romance and religion where nothing is impossible.

In *All's Well That Ends Well* Shakespeare built a greater moral dimension than he found in the tale's Boccaccian original and Painter's translation, and the basis was romance and legend and Mariology. In Helena Shakespeare introduced a woman who suffers much more than his earlier witty and independent ladies like Rosalind and even Viola, and hers is not a breeches part. This representation of a woman as one who suffers greatly, not as a victim, but as a transcendent and heroic figure, is fully developed in Hermione, who unlike earlier heroines is both wife and mother. There was, however, still much to explore in youthful heroines, including further cross dressing, and the depths of the habit of mind of romance. *Pericles* is Shakespeare's earliest fully acknowledged romance, and for this he returned to *Apollonius of Tyre*, well known in Gower's *Confessio Amantis*, which he had relied upon for the romance elements in the superficially farcical *The Comedy of Errors*.

Pericles

Of all Shakespeare's plays *Pericles* most thoroughly resembles a medieval chivalric romance; the events follow those in *Apollonius of Tyre*, and the prominent role of John Gower as Chorus signs the play's closeness to the story in the *Confessio Amantis* and the didactic quality that Chaucer noted when he designated his contemporary poet friend as "moral Gower." My earlier discussion of *The Comedy of Errors* considered some elements of the ancient Greek romance, popular throughout the Middle Ages, and used to mitigate Plautus's comedy, and I argued for Shakespeare's use of romance in the context of sixteenth-century Catholicism. In *Pericles* he attempts a near dramatization of the medieval romance. Characteristic modern critical responses describe the play as "naive," or "deceptively simple" at best, an experiment with an archaic form, and many find its simple antinomies uncharacteristically limited. There is a range of discussion about the play's being Shakespeare's work, perhaps a revision of another's earlier play. Many find a lack of psychological complexity and are taken aback by the idealism of the hero and the virtuous simplicity of the young heroine, who resembles a female saint in her capacity to convert sinners. Marina puts the issue clearly: "If I should tell my history, it would seem / Like lies disdained in the reporting" (V.i.120–21). The word *history* evokes Middle English *storie* (Latin *historia*, French *histoire*), which means a narrative or tale of events that may or may not be true as literal events but show the truth that is beyond such facts. Pericles urges Marina, "Tell thy story" (137), and Gower's frequent appearances keep the audience aware of the focus on storytelling. Gower is Prologue to every act, twice introduces scenes within acts (IV.iv and V.ii), and speaks an Epilogue. Each speech recounts the actions but also points the moral as explicitly as the authorial comments in medieval romances, and the final summary leaves no doubt about the didactic quality of romance:

> In Pericles, his queen, and daughter seen,
> Although assailed with fortune fierce and keen,
> Virtue preserved from fell destruction's blast,
> Led on by heaven, and crowned with joy at last.
> In Helicanus may you well descry
> A figure of truth, of faith, of loyalty.
> In reverend Cerimon there well appears
> The worth that learnèd charity aye wears.
>
> (V.ii.89–96)

I have quoted the positive affirmations, which contrast with the fates of the evil characters, Antiochus who gets "the due and just reward" when he is burned by a fire from heaven "in the height and pride of all his glory" (II.iv.6) and "wicked Cleon and his wife" who are burned by an enraged city. The imagery is of hellfire and the ends come unannounced and quickly, an enactment of Judgment or Doomsday. In contrast, the triumph of good comes through patience, perseverance, and reliance upon the divine, a force beyond the self. Gower's opening words argue the moral role of romance; he comes

> To sing a song that old was sung . . .
> It hath been sung at festivals,
> On ember eves and holy-ales
> And lords and ladies in their lives
> Have read it for restoratives.
> The purchase is to make men glorious.
>
> (I. Chorus)

Here is a recollection of Catholic fasts and feasts through the liturgical year with its observation of suffering and rejoicing, the human condition that Pericles will exemplify. Stories improve the quality of life, they foster healing, and this, it is hoped, will be true even with the increased wit of the present audience. Thus at the outset Gower contrasts past and present, acknowledging the danger of rejection by the overly clever.

Compared to much Renaissance literature, including the elaborately styled pastoral romances of Lyly, Sidney, Lodge, and Greene, *Pericles* and medieval romances seem very unsophisticated. But, as noted earlier, the success of older chivalric stories in the sixteenth century is well established. Survival of such popular literature, a parallel to today's ephemeral paperbacks, magazines, and newspapers, is problematic. But it is notable that *Apollonius of Tyre*, frequently retold in the Middle Ages in many different ways, continued in several prose renderings, the usual change from verse that accompanied printing and the corollary that books were replacing oral literature. Robert Copland translated a French romance, based on the *Gesta Romanorum*, for Wynkyn de Worde in 1510. This Latin collection of illustrative stories for sermons and other edification was also the source for Laurence Twine's *The Patterne of Painfull Adventures*, entered in the Stationers' Register in 1576, but known only in two later editions, c.1594 and 1607. Perhaps the surest measure of the appeal of romance is George Wilkins's *The Painfull Adventures of Pericles, Prince of Tyre* (1608), which announces on its title page "as it was lately presented by the worthy and ancient Poet John Gower." Wilkins interlaces the play with Twine so that the two prose romances are closely related. The narrative events and conclusion in high sentiment in *Apollonius of Tyre* had an audience in Shakespeare's England. Close comparison of texts is informative: *Pericles* favors medieval elements, most apparent in pageantry and color but also crucial in the treatment of suffering and human response, salient in the romance.

The substitution of the name "Pericles" for the hero, whether it was original with or chosen by Shakespeare, suggests a rooting in both history and allegory. The Greek statesman, well known from North's *Plutarch*, is identified with enduring great hardship, so that he embodies the theme of patience in adversity. "Pericles" also hints at "perils" endured, the narrative line of Apollonius's romance and the action of the play. In the reunion scene of father and daughter Pericles speaks of his "endurance" and "suffering," and he describes Marina as looking "Like Patience gazing on kings' graves and smiling / Extremity out of act" (141–42), an otherworldly perspective beyond the vagaries of Fortune in the world. Marina urges "Patience, good sir," and Pericles agrees "I'll be patient" (149–50). Given her story, he considers alternative interpretations: whether she is human or a fairy (158), and whether he is experiencing "the rarest dream" (166). These are recollections of *A Midsummer Night's Dream* in which romance elements of Chaucer's "Knight's Tale" frame the action and inform its themes. Similarly, Marina anticipates Perdita in *The*

Winter's Tale, and in other ways Miranda in *The Tempest*. Shakespeare writes these late romances with psychological and moral complexity, because *Pericles* is so full an exploration of chivalric romance, or alternatively "a preliminary shot in a new romantic campaign" (Bullough VI,373).

The patience urged in the reunion scene is a keeping of the initial advice of the good counselor (steward) Helicanus, who urges his prince "to bear with patience such griefs / As you yourself do lay upon yourself" (I.ii.66–67), when he begins his wanderings after discovering Antiochus's incest. Helicanus keeps his own counsel; when the people of Tyre urge him to become sovereign because Pericles has been so long absent and is probably dead, he asks a year's respite to search for the young prince before "I shall with agèd patience bear your yoke" (II.iv.48). A trusting and supportive relationship between lord and steward underlies medieval social organization; knights were often absent in wars, Crusades, and quests; and the good steward, a figure from Scripture, is familiar in romances. A concern for the community, as much as his own safety, prompts Pericles to leave lest his people be brutalized by the tyrant Antiochus.

Pericles' role as a chivalric knight is manifest when he sets out to win a bride, and Shakespeare alters the sources to make the situation more medieval. Gower's young, fresh, and lusty (pleasant) knight must answer the riddle that Antiochus devised for suitors to conceal his incest. In *Pericles* there is added imagery of gardens and dragons guarding the princess, and the adventurous hero enters the lists "like a bold champion" (I.i.62), but not before he meditates on "frail mortality" and wills himself to confront death and "grip not at earthly joys" (43, 49–50), an early indication of his humility and religious belief. Although early Christianity defined itself in Antioch, in the play it is not a land of Christian chivalry, and thus Pericles flees immediately after solving the riddle of father-daughter incest, quietly avoiding violence. Christian signs are used since Pericles has "forty days" (thirty in the source) respite (I.i.117), and the incestuous father and daughter are "both like serpents" (133). The tempest Pericles must endure leads to further thoughts of death, reiterating his religious quality. Then the fishermen offer some light comedy, but also reminders of religious wonder and church fast and feast: "we'll have flesh for holidays, fish for fasting days, and moreo'er puddings and flapjacks, and thou shalt be welcome" (II.i.82–84). Shakespeare expands the compassion of a single poor fisherman in other versions to create a sense of larger community and respect for the humble, "How well this honest mirth becomes their labor!" (96). Helicanus had earlier tried to dissuade Pericles from melancholy, albeit "princely charity to grieve" (I.ii.102), and the fishermen restore him fully. They find armor for him in the sea, and Pericles acknowledges the change that Fortune makes. He is again lively and describes himself as a chivalric hero, ready to "tourney for the lady," like a young questing knight: "I will mount myself / Upon a courser, whose delightful steps / Shall make the gazer joy to see him tread'' (159–61). These lines sound an idealism like that of *chansons* and romances of Roland and Galahad.

The change from athletic games and tennis match in the sources to tournament in the play makes Pericles a knight of old romance, and he goes before King Simonides of Pentapolis properly to win the princess. The chivalric progress (II.ii) is a theatrical spectacle, reminiscent of the opening in *Richard II* and repeated in the tournament in *Two Noble Kinsmen*. Much is made of heraldry, as the competing knights present their shields of which the devices or Latin mottoes pose characteristics of chivalric endeavor of the suitors, who recall those in *The Merchant of Venice;* Thaisa reads to her father the devices of six knights who proclaim ideals of light, gentleness, honor, faith, and hope. Squires offer the shields of the first five knights, but Pericles delivers his own device, a withered branch with green at the top and the motto *In hac spe vivo* (In this hope I live). Jesting lords wonder at his appearance, but again the ''outward habit'' is no gauge of the ''inward man'' (57). Thaisa subsequently crowns Pericles with a wreath of victory that he modestly claims, '' 'Tis more by fortune, lady, than by merit'' (II.iii.11). At the feast the hero enacts Jesus' advice about seeking the lower room (Luke 14.7–11) and finds among ''courteous knights'' (28) no vying for place. Asked his name and lineage, Pericles like the archetypal unknown knight of romance, claims to be a ''gentleman of Tyre,'' educated in arts and arms, and ''looking for adventures in the world'' (83–85). The hero's modesty prevents his presuming the lady's love that grows when he serves her as schoolmaster in music; Pericles' skills rank him among romance minstrel knights like Tristram and Orfeo. Shakespeare stresses the testing of Pericles as a virtuous suitor, not the wedding festivities, and moves quickly to the next sea adventure and tempest.

In the opening scene of Act III Pericles' suffering reaches its apex; his wife dies (apparently) in childbirth, and the mariners insist that he place Thaisa's corpse in a coffin and toss it overboard to improve their chance of surviving the storm. The nurse Lychorida urges ''Patience'' (19, 25); Pericles accepts his loss, regrets that he lacks time ''to give thee hallowed to thy grave,'' and insists that he ''say a priestly farewell to her'' (59, 68–69), a reminder of Catholic prayers for the dead. The next scene is an extraordinary representation of Resurrection, as Thaisa rises alive from her coffin, an image found in countless medieval depictions of Doomsday, many concealed or destroyed during the Reformation. Cerimon applies medical aids and commands music to help as he awakens the life of one who has lain dead. The First and Second Gentleman who are witness, voice a rational response: ''Is not this strange?'' and ''Most rare'' (108–9).

Absent from Tyre for a year, Pericles prepares to return, leaving his infant daughter Marina (gift of the sea) in Tarsus, with a vow of dedication until she be married. The outward sign is that of a hermit: "Unscissored shall this hair of mine remain, / Though I show ill in't" (III.iii.31–32), a generalization from Gower's detail of an unshaven beard, also familiar in *Guy of Warwick*. Pericles' grieving and penitential observances increase when he returns to Tarsus to collect his daughter, only to be brought to her tomb by the evil Cleon and Dionyza, whose envy led them to order her death. A dumb show mimes lamentation and passionate grief, and Gower explains: "He swears / Never to wash his face nor cut his hairs; / He puts on sackcloth" (IV.iv.27–29). And we next hear from Helicanus that Pericles "for this three months hath not spoken / To anyone, nor taken sustenance / But to prologue his grief" (V.i.25–27).

Gower has alerted the audience to "See how belief may suffer by foul show!" (IV.iv. 23), but Pericles has no reason to doubt his loss of wife and child. In the tragedies Shakespeare shows us men of passion who combine virtue with error, but Pericles is consistently "a perfect gentle knight." What can be argued is that by setting out on adventures he risks life in the world of daring, an explanation of a decline in Fortune, the fall of princes, which is the medieval heritage of Elizabethan tragedy. Pericles' behavior resembles that of knights in popular penitential romances such as *Guy of Warwick* and *Sir Ysumbras*, or the tested innocent women in Chaucer's tales of the Man of Law and Clerk that Shakespeare so often explores. In all there is a strong religious element; the theological question is the most difficult—facing why God, if good and all powerful, allows suffering. Calls for patience and repeated example of endurance show the way of humble devotion, a far cry from the interventions and pride of both classical and Elizabethan tragedy. Medieval imitation of Christ, reflected in the absence of such tragedy, shows the ideal of triumph through suffering, the salvation of the world through the Crucifixion. Pericles thus combines eschewing of his princely role in penitential grief with attempts as a prince to serve the community, while yet he lives. His discernment and duty are paralleled by the response of his wife Thaisa, who assumes "vestal livery," an equivalent of a nun's habit, when she enters the temple of Diana at Ephesus, where the sea cast her coffin and the wise physician Cerimon revived her. At the reunion, Pericles refers to the unrecognized vestal as "the nun" when she faints at his account of their life (V.iii.15).

While the parents serve quietly, circumstances compel Marina to undertake a more active mission. Cast out and nearly murdered, sold to pirates and taken to a brothel, Marina is like a saint in preserving her virginity in spite of the attempts of bawds and various clients to exploit her. While Gower relied upon the appeal of the maiden's human sorrow to protect her, Shakespeare makes Marina an active participant in an evil world, thus giving her a greater glory. Marina's way is to "preach divinity," so that clients put aside their lust "to do anything that is virtuous" (IV.v.4). To the Lord Lysimachus, she speaks "holy words'' (IV.vi.135). Catholic hagiography has many virgin saints, especially among the Romans, and although the obvious exemplar is St. Agnes who was put into a brothel and made it her oratory, equally apt is St. Katherine, of the lineage of Constantine, the bride of Christ who eloquently and successfully disputed philosophers, rhetoricians, and logicians. In Caxton's translation of *The Golden Legend* ''she had in herself all honesty of manners . . . ruled her meiny laudably . . . informed wisely . . . was marvelous in eloquence, for she had fair speech in preaching.'' Many in the sixteenth century saw such traits in one baptized with the saint's name, Katherine of Aragon, also the daughter of a king and renowned for her religious knowledge and piety. Marina's success as a ''teacher'' extends to the city of Mytilene, where she finds ''scholars'' for her skills (''sing, weave, sew, and dance, / With other virtues'' (184–86), and Gower details her accomplishments with ''pupils'' (V. Chorus). One ''other virtue'' is her compassion; the Lords, learning of Pericles' silence, are confident that the ''maid in Mytilene'' will be able to help him. As Pericles won her mother with his singing, so Marina tries to awaken the unfortunate silent man with a song. However, he responds only when she tells her sad story, persisting because ''there is something glows upon my cheek, / And whispers in mine ear, 'Go not till he speak' '' (V.i.98–99). Thus comes the restoration, with ''great seas of joys rushing upon'' Pericles (196). However, he still asks her mother's name before identifying and blessing his child; this makes a subtler dramatic scene and shows a lingering caution in a mutable world.

That voice in Marina's ear means something beyond mortal skill; it anticipates the ''music of the spheres'' (233), ''Most heavenly music!'' (236), which precedes Pericles' vision of Diana, who sends him to Ephesus, in medieval legend the place where Mary died, was buried, and was assumed into Heaven. There Paul had brought the Good News, but while in prison in Rome he heard that the Ephesians followed ''false teachers, who corrupted the true doctrine which he had taught them, by reason wherof he wrote the Epistle to confirme them in that thing, which they had learned of him'' (The Argument). This description resounds in the context of Reformation. Pericles is to ''mourn his crosses'' in the promise of happiness. Music enlivens performance in the theater, but here it also signs an ordered universe. Divine intervention, then, brings an end to sorrow; the reunion of Pericles and Thaisa, not the nuptials of Marina and King Lysimachus, is the right conclusion because the argument is of death and rebirth. The romance's doubling, the assumed death and loss of both wife and daughter, keeps this in focus, amidst repeated adventures and tempests—theatrical spectacle and imagery of the uncertain and unpredictable nature of earthly life. After several exiles and great grief, Pericles recovers those he believed dead, and the manner goes beyond Shakespeare's preliminary use of the conclusion of *Apollonius of Tyre* in *The Comedy of Errors*. The imagery of Resurrection is less dramatic and bold than the statue that comes to life on stage in *The Winter's Tale*, but it hints at what is to come, and Gower's final moral—follow heaven and be "crowned with joy at last"—explicitly promises Redemption.

Cymbeline

The simplicity of *Pericles* gives way to complexity in *Cymbeline*, perhaps the most challenging of the late plays, because of its multiple strands that resemble the interlacing characteristic of many romances, especially Arthurian, and because it shows Shakespeare stretching the boundaries of romance.[2] Although there is a falsely accused woman, who bears similarities to the women and theme considered in the next chapter, Imogen differs in venturing beyond the domestic situation of heroines that I will discuss later. Imogen assumes male guise, albeit she acknowledges, "I see a man's life is a tedious one" (III.vi.1), and she first gains acceptance in exile because of her feminine gentleness and good housewifery at the cave of Belarius and the two young men whom he treats as sons. Moreover, Imogen never indulges in the amusement and confident exploitation of the boy's part that make Rosalind, Viola, and Portia so delightful to modern audiences. Like Helena, Imogen perseveres, weds the man she loves, and remains devoted to her husband in spite of his duplicity. She has a part in the final revelations, but they stem from the war between Britain and Rome; and she defers to father, brothers, and husband, so that she is worrying to many feminists. Imogen is not a "magician"; supernatural forces, not adroit human actions, explain the extraordinary reconciliations and reunions of the final act. Shakespeare alters the Boccaccio story, the *Decameron*, second day, ninth novel, and its English translation as *Frederyke of Jennen* (1518 and 1560), a late fifteenth-century German tale of four merchants, which are his main sources for the wager story. He deletes both the long account of the lady's success as a disguised official at the Sultan's court and the vengeful and horrible execution of the deceiver, the Iachimo figure. This eliminates the tale's orientalism, alters the nature of the heroine, and opens the way to a greater stress upon the power of the divine, the happy ending of romance.

There are many topics in *Cymbeline* in addition to the falsely accused queen: the evil stepmother, treason, two cases of exile or banishment, stolen royal sons, coming of age in the wild forest, war between Britain and Rome, male heroism and affirmation of the warrior knight, duplicity, woman as page, the good servant, riddles, tokens or physical marks of identification, prayer and divine intervention, revenge and forgiveness. These commonplaces of romance indicate that Shakespeare was steeped in the complexities of such narratives, and his inclusion and linkage of apparently separate elements through the theme of forgiveness and joyful reconciliation imitate the romance as secular story in medieval Christendom and the aesthetic of disparate stories that make a didactic point. Indeed the usual readings of the play as rife with improbabilities do not hold once there is an acceptance of limitless possibility with God and an eschewing of the insistence that actions be logical and the consequence of discernible causality, a view of narrative that developed in the eighteenth-century novel and was not challenged until the early twentieth century.

After the systematic dramatizing of a medieval Catholic romance of pagan antiquity in *Pericles*, a richer and more restricted use than in the earlier *The Comedy of Errors* and *A Midsummer Night's Dream*, which have only a frame of romance to underlie stories with other dominant interests, *Cymbeline* is a thorough attempt to enlarge time. Most obviously, the Cymbeline story was at a crucial moment in history, which Dr. Simon Forman, the schoolmaster who recorded the stories of plays that he saw at the Globe in 1611, identified as when "Lucius Cam from Octauus Cesar for Tribut," that is, Britain during the period of emerging Christianity. In contrast, the Imogen and Posthumous story is from the world of Italian *novelle*, established by Boccaccio and widely translated in Renaissance Europe. This dichotomy makes the point that time is not restricted to historical periods but eternal. Medieval cycles of plays tell the story from Creation to Doomsday, they represent Scripture as medieval circumstances and characters, and these are experienced by subsequent audiences who are a third level of participants in the events; similarly, *Cymbeline* brings together different eras as part of time and thus insists upon a perspective of transcendence.

The play combines figures and events from the history of early Britain, readily available in Holinshed's *Chronicles*, as do romances situated in the days of Troy or Thebes, Arthur or Charlemagne, or Athelstan or Etholwold, but defined by later centuries. Two points are pertinent: first, medieval uncertainties about and indifference to evidence and a limited knowledge of the past and much of the world; second and even more telling, in the Middle Ages history and legend are not easily distinguished. This means both the adding of legendary details to factual accounts of established figures of history—a practice that is not unknown today—and presenting heroes of legend as historical personages—like Guy of Warwick, whom Holinshed and other chroniclers include and who was not decried as fictional until the eighteenth century. Shakespeare's history plays show an ease in altering and redefining characters and circumstances in his sources to create a desired "historical account"; for many his medieval kings are more vivid than those in the old chronicles. Cymbeline's era was established by Geoffrey of Monmouth's *History of the Kings of Britain* (c.1135) as a reign of thirty-five years beginning in 33 BC, shortly after Julius Caesar. According

to Holinshed's *Chronicles*, little is known of Cymbeline, but there are two crucial points; he

> was brought up at Rome, and there made knight by Augustus Cesar, under
> whome he served in the warres, and was in such favour with him, that he
> was at libertie to pay tribute or not. Little other mention is made of his
> dooings, except that during his reigne, the Saviour of the world our Lord
> Jesus Christ the onelie sonne of God was borne of a virgine, about the 23
> yeare of the reigne of this Kymbeline.   (Bullough VIII,43)

Shakespeare's combination of the reign of Augustus, the start of Christianity,
with a roughly contemporary story that features a scheming Iachimo is certainly
topical, for it contrasts Rome and Italy in the context of Britain. All would recall
Luke's Gospel: ''And it came to passe in those dayes, that there came a com-
mandment from Augustus Caesar, that all the worlde shulde be taxed'' (II.1).
In *Cymbeline*, Posthumus's friend Philario first notes ''your king / Hath heard
of great Augustus,'' and he reassures the banished man that Cymbeline will
likely respond well to the efficient Caius Lucius and pay the tribute (II.iv.13–
15). Put another way, Britain's ties to Rome are strong. There is a concern about
a curbing of British freedom, but not the eagerness of the somewhat primitive
hero of the *Alliterative Morte Arthure*, abbreviated by Malory, to fight a continental war against Emperor Lucius, representative of the pagan world, rather
than pay tribute. The medieval romance is remarkable in many ways, especially
its rendering of Fortune and the inevitable demise of the epic warrior king and
in its linkage of Britain and Rome. By setting *Cymbeline* in the time of Augustus
Caesar, then, Shakespeare participates in a long tradition in chronicles and in
religious history, and the ethos is medieval.

As in *Pericles*, the details are chivalric. Cymbeline asks the Roman general
Lucius, ''what would Augustus Caesar with us?'' (III.i.1) and welcomes him
courteously: ''Thy Caesar knighted me; my youth I spent / Much under him. Of
him I gathered honor'' (III.i.69–70). After the battle Cymbeline, like a medieval
king, honors those who gave him victory: ''Arise my knights o' the battle. I
create you / Companions to our person and will fit you / With dignities becoming
your estates'' (V.v.20–22). Patriotism made the Britons resist encroachments on
their freedom, but in contrast to the defiance of the Queen and her son Cloten,
Cymbeline is conciliatory, recognizing political differences but reaffirming
''Welcome!'' (85). The King's previous loyalty and benefits from his link to
Augustus, to Rome, as well as his penitent recognition that he has been deceived
by his wicked Queen's beauty, charm, and female inscrutability, and an old-
fashioned chivalry—''It had been vicious / To have mistrusted her'' (V.v.66–
67)—bring him a knowledge of human limitation, and he can only conclude,

"Heaven mend all!" (69). In Cymbeline Shakespeare shows deep humility, a recognition that he depends upon the service of the community to remain king and an understanding that simple nationalism is not a sound response to Rome. A Catholic seeing the play could find an analog to Elizabeth in the evil queen, one who died "with horror" (31), after a full confession of her ill actions, but "repented" only those plots that did not succeed, and "so despairing died" (61). Accounts of the last two weeks before Queen Elizabeth died in 1603 tell of her melancholy and nightmares, understandable in a life beset with plots and executions, many involving recusant Catholics. The Queen's death in *Cymbeline*, albeit not specific like Evelyn Waugh's imaginative account of Elizabeth at the start of his biography of *Edmund Campion*, evokes the terror of the end of a great and relentless queen.

Other characters in *Cymbeline* sincerely repent, confess, and gain forgiveness. Iachimo, vanquished in battle, acknowledges "the heaviness and guilt within my bosom," admits his defaming of Imogen, and judges that "Knighthoods and honors borne / As I wear mine are titles but of scorn" (V.ii.1, 6–7). He even casts himself to justify Tudor condemnations like those of Ascham: "mine Italian brain / 'Gan in your duller Britain operate / Most vilely; for my vantage, excellent" (V.v.198–200); and hearing Iachimo's confession, Posthumus calls him "Italian fiend!" (213). The faithful Pisanio, in Britain, immediately understands his master's plight, prevailed upon by "what false Italian" (III.ii.4), and his father Sicilius Leonatus in the vision questions the success of "Iachimo, / Slight thing of Italy" (V.iv.63–64). Much of Italy's decadence was attributed to the Papacy, especially popes such as Alexander VI (1492–1503), Julius II (1503–13), and Leo X (1513–21), who were Renaissance princes much removed from earlier Catholic ideals, and deeply involved in humanist assimilation of pagan Rome and developing nationalism with the Papal States a major force. A Rome-Italy axis is the current challenge, and Shakespeare's making Posthumus resident with Philario in Rome (I.i.98) is a change from his sources. A geographical link between Augustan and modern Italian Rome eases the interlacing and focuses on some historical continuity. This is unusual, since Shakespeare's classical plays are Roman, but northern Italian cities are his favored contemporary setting. Britain is the main locus; one major theme is its relation with Rome, and decisions are not clear-cut.

The repentant Iachimo, an Italian who sees himself as false, calls Posthumus a "true knight" (188), but that is too simple. Shakespeare makes the Roman Briton an uneasy and uncertain figure. He begins a poor gentleman, elevated when princess Imogen marries him, but Cymbeline banishes the "basest thing" (I.i.127), a typical reaction in medieval romance that usually leads to a proof of *gentilesse*. Pisanio makes this distinction when Posthumus betrays his love: "O my master, / Thy mind to her is now as low as were / Thy fortunes" (III.ii.9–

11). Thus Shakespeare includes some of the chivalric qualities found in thirteenth-century French analogs where nobles, not merchants, wager; and *Cymbeline* is partially a consideration of the nature of true honor. Posthumus professes great loyalty, but confuses his truth as husband and his role as competitive male when he boasts of Imogen's beauty and chastity and makes the wager with Iachimo. Like Othello, he condemns his wife, and all women, on the evidence of a ''corporal sign'' (II.iv.122), but also because Iachimo both ''confirm[s] with oath'' (65) and ''by Jupiter he swears'' (125), suggesting qualities of a chivalric hero even as he lies. Posthumus's chivalric virtues are limited; he knows what they should be, but like Walter in the Griselda story, he lacks the confidence to believe that his wife is truly good; *Cymbeline* echoes the archetypal tale, but transposes the estate and gender of the principals in Chaucer's story. And Posthumus redeems himself, first by repenting the ordering of his wife's murder; and second, having returned with Italian gentry to fight Britain, he defects to fight in Cymbeline's cause. His chameleon quality is theatrically conveyed through his clothes, a metaphor as well as a stage rendering of the unknown knight of romance. Imogen provokes Cloten's vicious plot to ravish her by saying that the Queen's son is not worth her husband's clothes, and she mistakes Cloten's headless torso for Posthumus because of the clothes he wears. The wretched Cloten, faced by a fierce Guiderius, foolishly relies upon outward appearance: ''Know'st me not by my clothes?'' (IV.ii.82). Posthumus returns to Britain in ''Italian weeds,'' but ''suits himself / As does a Briton peasant'' (V.i.23–24). This humility suggests a return to older circumstances, a shedding of the guise of the world, accidents, to return to substance: ''less without and more within'' (33). However, Posthumus fights to find Death, a suicidal Roman ideal that is thwarted. His self-interest contrasts with the heroism of the Britons Belarius, Guiderius, and Arviragus, part of the native Celtic tradition in exile in the Welsh mountains; they made a stand, three against three thousand—''a narrow lane, an old man, and two boys!'' (V.iii.52)—and their epic deeds are the subject for ''rhyme'' (55, 63), even while Posthumus decries the cowards and ignorance of war. Unable to die in battle, he discards his British clothes and identifies himself as a Roman, to make his ransom death (80); he manages to be captured and prays for death. The imagery of clothes comes again in Posthumus's response to the book left by the Leonati of his vision: ''Be not, as is our fangled world, a garment / Nobler than that it covers!'' (V.iv.134–35).

The spectacular masque in which the Leonati appear first to tell the family story and to pray for help from Jupiter, who descends seated on an eagle, uses pagan religious imagery, as was necessary because An Acte to Restraine Abuses of Players (1606) prevented speaking of ''the Holy Name of God or of Christ Jesus, or of the Holy Ghoste or of the Trinitie.'' But the God of the Old Testament sounds in Jupiter's testing those he most loves—the Father testing His Son even to the Crucifixion, suffering repeated by recusant Catholics in a Protestant state. Jupiter appears on an eagle, which is his bird but also the sign of the Evangelist John, whose Gospel, the last written, singularly includes disparate elements of his contemporary world, and his own deep religious experience. Jesus entrusted the care of the Virgin Mary to St. John, "the disciple that Jesus loved," and St. John lived at Ephesus, another link to the city that Shakespeare knew in St. Paul and *Apollonius of Tyre*. Given the prohibition of references to the Christian God upon the stage, such imagery is an alternative, and words like "godhead" and "His ascension" (V.iv.103, 116) evoke Christ in a play that makes much of concealment and how easily deceived are those who rely upon surface appearance alone.

Nowhere is this more effectively presented than in the apparent death and resurrection of Imogen, who as a boy takes the name Fidele (Faith), most obviously stating her trust in her treacherous husband but also describing religious belief in an age of controversy. Shakespeare surrounds his heroine with religious imagery. In the opening scene she answers her father's wrath with a theological pun on "grace" (I.i. 139), and Posthumus's letters are tossed away as "The scriptures of the loyal Leonatus, / All turned to heresy?" (III.iv.81–82); Imogen offers "orisons" for her love as a liturgy of "certain hours," at "the sixth hour of morn, at noon, at midnight" (I.iii.31–32), just as Belarius and his "sons" adore the "heavens" to make "a morning's holy office" (III.iii.3–4). Imogen prays at evening (II.ii.8–10) and meals (III.vi.52), and in the simple life of the Welsh mountains she seems not a pagan fairy, but divine, "an angel" (42–43), and "How angel-like he sings!" (IV.ii.49). Guiderius's expectation that fairies will haunt the tomb is balanced by Arviragus's promise to return often to the grave with flowers in the coming months and a request that they "sing him to th' ground" (238), while Guiderius can only weep. The dirge "Fear no more the heat o' the sun" celebrates freeing from "worldly task" and is a rich intercession for the dead. Belarius insists upon equality in death ("All follow this and come to dust"); thus they place Cloten next to Fidele (Imogen). Once the mourners leave, the audience immediately sees her alive—another staging of resurrection. At the end of the play those who placed her in the tomb see her talking with Cymbeline her father, and Belarius asks, "Is not this boy revived from death?" while Guiderius declares, "The same dead thing alive" (V.v.121, 125). The second witness is Pisanio, who recognizes his mistress and accepts the consequences of her reappearance. In contrast, Posthumus, always the doubter, even after the vision of his family and riddling prophesy from Jupiter, still does not see clearly. Distracted by his anger at Iachimo's confession, he strikes Fidele, who would comfort and explain. Imogen is present because she won the respect and love of Lucius, whom she served, and who asked that the page be spared as a Briton who did not harm his compatriots while serving Rome—the Catholic case against Protestant charges of treason.

Cymbeline's forbearance is the first of many scenes of forgiveness, and such generosity is crucial because he thus spared his daughter, believed to be his only heir. In romance, the world goes round, and "the gods . . . strike to death . . . with mortal joy" (234, 236–37). Cymbeline's joy grows with the restoration of his two sons, as Belarius disputes the charge that he is "a banished traitor." Like Elizabethan Catholics, Belarius is, "a banished man, / I know not how a traitor" (323–34), and he presents visual evidence to legitimate claims— "a curious mantle" embroidered by Arviragus's mother and a mole upon Guiderius's neck, a sign of the future king. The youths are in a long tradition of infants of high birth who are separated from their heritage, reared in wild conditions, but yet manifest their noble blood in brave and direct actions that bring a vitality absent from court. Cymbeline is an intriguing mixture of autocratic, doting, and generous action; he is strongest at the end, and he identifies himself not as father but as mother: "O, what am I / A mother to the birth of three? Ne'er mother / Rejoiced deliverance more. Blest pray ye be" (372–73). There are parallels between *Cymbeline* and the wager in a fourteenth-century French Miracle of Notre Dame, but Mary's intervention to help those devoted to her also recurs in the ideal of reconciliation in dire situations. Great "joy" must be marked by thanksgiving, sacrifice to the gods, and extending of joy to all. Thus a now wise Posthumus spares the life of Iachimo, replacing malice with hope, "Live, / And deal with others better" (423). This is the essential individual penance; Cymbeline, who has learned well that "Pardon's the word to all" (426), takes reconciliation to an international level when he decides

> Although the victor, we submit to Caesar
> And to the Roman empire, promising
> To pay our wonted tribute, from the which
> We were dissuaded by our wicked queen,
> Whom heavens in justice both on her and hers
> Have laid most heavy hand.   (V.v.464–69)

Thus Cymbeline takes a political action that fulfills Lucius's wisdom, "Some falls are means the happier to arise" (IV.ii.406), and the hope of the First Jailer, "I would we were all of one mind, and one mind good" (V.iv.203–4). Cymbeline humbly chooses:

> Laud we the gods, . . . Publish we this peace,
> To all our subjects. Set we forward. Let
> A Roman and a British ensign wave
> Friendly together.   (480, 483–85)

The image is of compatibility between England and Rome, achieved with prayer and putting national power below peace and unity. In Cymbeline's world of romance all is possible, but attention and unselfish devotion to the community are the necessary foundation for such considered mercifulness.

The Tempest

Shakespeare reconsiders exile and service in *The Tempest*, printed first in the First Folio, as the first play in the "Comedies" section. Many esteem it Shakespeare's best "romance," generally agreeing that it was the last written, coming after *Pericles*, *Cymbeline*, and *The Winter's Tale*. Several significant differences from these plays may explain enthusiastic modern responses. *The Tempest* is tidy, reassuringly maintaining classical unities. The time of the action is "three hours" (V.i.136) from the shipwreck plus perhaps another hour for the conclusion; this is close to "the two hours' traffic of our stage" (*Romeo and Juliet*, Prologue 12) that scholars accept as the usual length of an Elizabethan performance, and suggests a deliberate adherence to concepts of classical unities in drama in opposition to romance's extended narration and reliance upon time for resolution. The action takes place entirely on an island, with narrative accounts of previous events, as in Prospero's opening explanation to Miranda of his exile as Duke of Milan, albeit he echoes oral performance of medieval romance in his interruptions—"Dost thou hear?" (I.ii.106)—that keep his daughter, and the audience, alert. Details of the action are varied, especially by spectacle in the opening tempest, banquet, and the masque of Ceres and Juno, and seldom does Shakespeare rely so heavily upon music that, like a strong score in a film, leads audience response as well as movement on stage. All are part of Prospero's dominance, since he controls the elements, including the airy spirit Ariel, who carries out his wishes while waiting for promised liberty. The entire play is like the last act of the other romances in bringing everyone together, so that a showing of suffering or penitence is not the point. Prospero may have modeled patience and endurance in the past, but he was never separated from his library that he valued more than his kingdom—the underlying idea so brilliantly realized in Peter Greenaway's film *Prospero's Books* (1991). Now he shows tolerance and mercy with only fleeting thoughts of vengeance, but there are disturbing indications of his bent to dominance: Caliban calls him "tyrant," Ariel begs for his promised liberty, and the raising of the tempest is to achieve a return to power and vindication. Prospero's exercise of magic, which is closely tied to artistic achievement so that aesthetics vie with ethical issues, seems to explain the improbabilities more than spiritual conversion, and thus in this play the connection to romance is tentative.

The Tempest pleases with spectacle and the exoticism of distant lands, dominant in late romances and here made topical through allusions to the Virginia voyages and New World settlement, even though the island is within Europe. Post colonial theory points out and sharpens understanding of empires emerging in the sixteenth century; the play explores the issue, when the nobles from Naples and Milan discuss the implications of Antonio's marrying his daughter Claribel to the King of Tunis; he chose an African and "would not bless our Europe" (II.i.126–27). Caliban as the native inhabitant evokes sympathy because Prospero took the island from him, and his attempt to ravish Miranda is driven by the necessity to gain people for a revolutionary force against the occupier who has made him a "slave." Caliban both knows the natural wonders of the island and thinks incisively to reject Prospero's attempts to civilize him, and he judges linguistic dominance as useful for protest when he asserts, "You taught me language, and my profit on 't / Is I know how to curse" (I.ii.334–77). An emphasis upon colonial politics has prevailed in *The Tempest* since Jonathan Miller's production (1964), but worldly power has always competed with the magic in the text.

Such arguments and other factors differ from medieval Christendom's romance mode which shows a human pilgrimage of life that moves toward a vision of eternity. In earlier treatments, especially *Pericles* and *Cymbeline* as we have seen, Shakespeare maintains and heightens resonances of chivalric romance that are largely absent from *The Tempest*. No single source has been found for the play; several travel pamphlets, Spenser, and Spanish prose romances are sources for landscape and episodes, some of which belong to the vast storehouse of commonplaces of romance used in the Renaissance. The word "knight," an obvious sign for the Middle Ages, does not appear in *The Tempest*; there are no tournaments or quests, and reassurances are given that danger and hardship are only apparent. Prospero tells Miranda that they came on the island "By Providence divine," well sustained by Gonzalo, who "out of his charity" provided food, water, and "volumes that I prize above my dukedom" (I.i.159–68). Like Emilia tied to the mast of a sunken ship in *The Comedy of Errors* and Thaisa in her coffin in *Pericles*, Prospero and baby Miranda were adrift in "the rudderless boat" of romance and secular hagiography. In Chaucer's "Man of Law's Tale," for example, it carries its occupant(s) to a new destiny in the Mediterranean world, and there are other analogs of the Ship of the Church. *The Tempest* is still about exile in a wooded landscape, but on an island, and the way of entry is by water, which suggests baptism as the sacrament of conversion. This partially explains the simplicity of resolution, brought about by Prospero's "rough magic" which enabled it, not least with "heavenly music" to lead people about the island. Prospero needed these powers to initiate the meeting with his past and to regain his role as ruler of Milan, but he abjures magic, breaks his staff, and drowns his book (V.i.50–57), as his human choice becomes the magic. Before facing his brother the usurper Antonio, he declares, "I do forgive thee, / Unnatural though thou art" (77–78), but when they meet he identifies him as "traitor" (128), only to say "I do forgive / Thy rankest fault" (131–32) without vengeance as he takes back his dukedom. Unlike Alonso—who resembles earlier penitents, such as Valentine or Oliver or Bertram—when he gives up the tribute he gained from the usurpation and unhesitatingly "entreats pardon for his wrongs" (118–19), Antonio neither admits his fault nor asks forgiveness, as might have been expected when Gonzalo noted in him "desperation . . . great guilt, / Like poison given to work a great time after" (III.iii.105–6), even though Antonio rejected "conscience" that inhibited his political and material gains (II.i.277–92). His single comment comes much after Prospero's mercy; he sees the drunken comic figures who tried to displace Prospero with Caliban's help and identifies one as a marketable fish (V.i.268–69).

A linking of Antonio and Caliban is apt; both apparently lack remorse or any unselfish concern; neither Prospero's magic nor his merciful forbearance inspires "this thing of darkness I acknowledge mine" (278–79). Prospero, who regarded some among those he brought to the island as "worse than devils" (III.iii.36), here identifies Caliban, whom Stephano earlier called a "devil, and no monster" (II.ii.98), as a "demidevil" (275). Caliban is the son of "the foul witch Sycorax" (I.ii.259), who knew her island and its earthy charms but imprisoned the airy spirit Ariel. Prospero taught Caliban, but also took the island from him, a usurpation that parallels his own loss of kingdom, and Caliban tries to change masters when he drunkenly follows Stephano and Trinculo, who themselves want to control. Sebastian, who urged Antonio to slay the King of Naples but was thwarted when Ariel waked Gonzalo, who cried out "good angels, preserve the King!" (II.i.309), even charges that in Prospero "the devil speaks" (V.i. 129). Neither nature nor nurture assures, neither force nor kindness insures, virtuous behavior. The island, then, is less a new Paradise—a characteristic paradigm for English writers in the New World like John Smith—than an alternate fulcrum, less like the woods of the early comedies and nearer to the increasingly fanciful places imagined for far away adventures as medieval romances became more escapist and less realistic. Shakespeare uses other religious imagery to describe the island.

The banquet served by many strange spirits leads Sebastian to declare a belief in unicorns and one phoenix (III.iii.22–24). These mythical creatures were in the Middle Ages symbols of Christ. The Unicorn was an unconquerable beast, sometimes pictorially represented as trampling a Serpent associated with the Fall of Man. More frequently the Unicorn is shown with a virgin in the forest, when the beast meekly lays its head on her lap and allows itself to be slain, symbolizing the Incarnation and Passion of Christ. In *The Comedy of Errors* Antipholus of Syracuse takes his oath ''as I am a Christian,'' and his house is called ''the Phoenix'' (I.ii.77, 75). Shakespeare wrote most fully in ''The Phoenix and the Turtle'' of this legendary bird, a symbol of immortality, that is resurrected from its own ashes and finds life through death. The turtle(dove) is a symbol of constancy in love, and in the poem Shakespeare, while writing of a spiritual union of female and male, relies upon the argument of Catholic scholasticism of one essence in two appearances—as in belief in the Eucharist—by which Reason is ''confounded'' (41). But the poem tells how ''Love and constancy are dead'' (21) and concludes with a lamentation for ''Beauty, truth, and rarity, / Grace in all simplicity'' (53–54), and a request that those ''that are either true or fair'' (66) would ''sigh a prayer'' for ''the dead birds.'' As in the ''Bare ruined choirs, where late the sweet birds sang'' of Sonnet 73 that evoked the Dissolution of the monasteries, so there is a poignant sadness in ''The Phoenix and The Turtle,'' a poem about much more than male and female love, that echoes on Prospero's island.

The Tempest contrasts apparently destructive nature with reassurances that all will be well, for Ariel immediately informs Prospero that in the opening storm ''Not a hair perished'' (I.ii.218). Gonzalo, the wise elder who never refuses charity, calls their preservation ''the miracle'' and observes that not even their garments are stained (II.i.6, 64, 71), a fact unnoticed by the other voyagers who ridicule him as they speculate upon the possibilities of easeful life on the island. This evolves into a discussion of the ideal commonwealth, a sixteenth-century preoccupation, as in Thomas More's *Utopia* (1516) and Montaigne's ''On Cannibals'' in the *Essays* (1580). Gonzalo, like More, describes an ideal commonwealth, but gently moves to an acknowledgment of its unreality when he proposes that he would ''with such perfection govern, sir, / T' excel the Golden Age'' (II.i. 170–71). ''Utopia'' means ''nowhere,'' and the ''Golden Age'' is a nostalgic longing for a better time; both concepts come from pagan antiquity, and the Catholic More playfully argued how unlike they are to Tudor England. Prospero's dozen years on the island, time devoted to study especially of white magic but also to recognition of his failure to be a responsible ruler (I.ii.89–151), are a preparation for a return to secular duties, to the Dukedom of Milan, that he neglected for books. Vincentio in *Measure for Measure* found it hard to be a decisive ruler, and Prospero was too detached. Both plays study the ruler with an initial reluctance for involvement in the things of the world followed by a recognition of civic obligation. In Catholic terms, Prospero must return to perform ''good works,'' since for all his study he remains worldly, not contemplative, as do most humans and all but a few heroes of romance. Prospero does not succeed in overcoming Caliban, a quasi-human, the challenging monster, but he has changed and questions his concern with self. Prospero will return as Duke and oversee the nuptials of Ferdinand and Miranda that are the best promise for peace, but he will also tell "the story of my life," an exemplary role. Moreover, he perceives his own mortality: "Every third thought shall be my grave" (V.i.308–15). Caliban also will "be wise hereafter / And seek for grace" (298–99), a pardon from Prospero as he acknowledges his stupidity in thinking a drunkard a god and, in practice, he will be left in control of the island.

Along with many usurpations, Shakespeare includes a tactful love story: Ferdinand and Miranda mutually love at first sight, and Prospero approves and fosters their union, despite his austere treatment of Ferdinand, as he tries and warns against self-indulgence. The carrying of the logs is a test of the young man's devotion, and love transforms labor to an easy burden, but the argument is that marriage requires effort, and the masque promises a rich life in "a most majestic vision" (IV.i.118). Ferdinand exults in Prospero's wonders and Miranda's charms; they make the island "Paradise" (124), but the lovers' game of chess considers playing for advantage, and this leads to conflict. When Prospero restores Ferdinand to Alonso's sight, Sebastian proclaims it "a most high miracle" (V.i.179); and Alonso observes, "These are not natural events" (229). This suggests the world of romance, but Prospero's Epilogue explains "Now my charms are all o'erthrown, / And what strength I have 's mine own, / Which is most faint" (1–3). *The Tempest* is filled with strange but merely magical occurrences, actually a sign of declining faith in the romance habit of mind of medieval Christendom; Prospero's forswearing suggests such artifice is not adequate.

7
THE ROMANCE MODE ATTAINED: ACCUSED WIVES AND QUEENS

Among the most ancient and widespread of folktales is that of the accused wife/queen, which both recurs and is transformed as medieval romance. Folktales, *Märchen*, usually have accusations of witchcraft, infanticide, and animal/monster birth brought against a wife whose existence is resented by her mother-in-law, as in Chaucer's "Man of Law's Tale."[1] This figure, a remnant of matriarchy, appears in *Cymbeline*, when the Queen opposes Imogen, who becomes an exile, albeit with some control of her destiny, and the motif of the rival sons finds its place in Imogen's lost brothers. Romances typically replace the primitive charges of folktales with infidelity and treason; these, as we have seen, preoccupy Shakespeare, as do twins, whose birth often occasions false charges of unchaste or unnatural behavior by an innocent queen. Romances evolve from the folktale's falsely accusing stepmother, the archetypal evil figure in *Cinderella* and *Snow White,* to other villainous accusers—such as a steward or courtier, and then the lover or husband—who are increasingly male, as patriarchy succeeds. Shakespeare's use of the accused woman/queen immediately resounded in the sixteenth century when there were notable examples of such persecution in the fraught religious controversy and politics of the time. He deletes the incestuous father of *Apollonius of Tyre* from the romance frame of *The Comedy of Errors*, but restores the theme in his full rendering of the story in *Pericles*, one sign of his exploration and experimentation with the romance mode. Much medieval fiction is about sympathy for accused queens, and this chapter considers ways in which Shakespeare explores the theme to explain, and honor, the actions of many who choose humility and forgiveness, so advocated by medieval Catholic texts and subsequently deemed "implausible." Not infrequently the stories end in Rome, where the false accusers go as penitents and families are reunited.

Chaucer's "Man of Law's Tale" and "Clerk's Tale" are probably the best known Middle English versions of accused wives and queens, who appear frequently in European and Eastern literature. John Gower also told the story of Constance in the *Confessio Amantis*, and Nicholas Trivet's *Chronicle* version of *Vita Offæ I* seems to have inspired the roof bosses in Norwich Cathedral. Griselda's story was dramatized as a mystery at Paris in 1393, and Thomas Dekker in collaboration with Chettle and Haughton put *Patient Grissil* on the stage in London; it was printed in 1603, and went on to be a popular chapbook. Constance is a more archetypal accused queen, the daughter of the emperor of Rome and a royal wife; the defaming mother-in-law is a primitive form, and the rudderless boat is a stock motif. The issue with Griselda is not lack of chastity but social class, often a concern in romance, and her accuser (tester) is her husband, so that the marriage is more central, as in Shakespeare's plays. Themes of patience and obedience, usually with explicit religious significance, are fundamental both in religious and married life. Thus Griselda evokes the Passion when she bids her daughter farewell, marking her with the cross and commending her soul to Christ, Who "for us deyde upon a croys of tree" (IV. 556–60); and her patience and constancy in adversity are the praised virtues, as they are with Constance, allegorically the human soul. Her several voyages bring Christianity through the limits of the Roman world from Syria to Britain, and there are conversions and miracles, trial scenes and exoneration of the innocent. A surprising number of romances contain similar treatments of heroines, whose experiences—which often anticipate those of Shakespeare's women—belie the false stereotype of women in romance as inspiring, but mostly passive, vain and/or weak beauties.

Persecuted women are catalysts for action in many romances: *Le Bone Florence of Rome*, *Emaré*, *King of Tars*, *Sir Isumbras*, *Octavian*, *Sir Torrent of Portyngale*, *Sir Triamour*, *Sir Eglamour*, and *Lai le Freine*. The woman may be marginal or the central figure, but the theme is a major one; and de Worde, Pynson, and Copland printed many such texts in the sixteenth century. A variety of accusers, circumstances, and resolutions indicates compulsion and resourcefulness in treating the topic. Ambivalent attitudes toward women in the Middle Ages continued in the Renaissance and Reformation, and the accused wife/queen was used for further exploration. On the one hand, the negative judgment and calumniation show contempt that becomes more the province of men as distance from primitive folktales increased; on the other, there is an exaltation of women when they show extraordinary strength and character, and their ultimate triumphs indicate admiration that is often reverential. A significant proportion of these tales can only be described as religious or devotional; there is a close correlation with veneration of the Virgin Mary, a major practice of Catholicism, from the twelfth century when devotion to Mary and to a secular ideal of woman developed concurrently and were a counter argument to less positive views.

Mary is a falsely accused woman/queen. When Mary is found pregnant before she and her betrothed come together, "Ioseph her housband being a iust man, and not willing to make her a publike example, was minded to put her away secretly" (Matthew 1.19). But the Angel of the Lord appears to him in a dream to explain that the child is conceived of the Holy Ghost and is to be called Jesus, "for he shal saue his people from their sinnes" (21). This affirmation did not inhibit the exploration of Joseph's doubts in the apocryphal Book of James and Gospel of the Pseudo-Matthew, and in sermons on the Annunciation. Skepticism about a virgin birth partially explains visual representations of Joseph as an old man. The doubting Joseph figures largely in English medieval cycle plays that also combine the implications of Matthew with secular stories of the old cuckold and the shrew, much developed in *fabliaux*. The *Ludus Coventriae* play about Joseph is a "pagetum de purgacione" (pageant of purgation) and full of challenge, but the angel Gabriel's "Ave Maria" uses the pun, "here þis name Eva is turnyd Ave / þat is to say with-owte sorwe ar þe now," (219–20) that expresses the symmetry of Fall and Redemption. In the *Towneley* play, Joseph has a long monologue and a scene of accusation with Mary. This doubting husband is the natural man in the midst of the supernatural and is also a type for lack of faith. But Joseph in Matthew is a "just man" of compassion and civility; doubting husbands who accuse their wives in countless folktales, romances, legends, and plays are not such men. Few stories were more apt to become Miracles of the Virgin than the saving of the falsely accused queen, and such stories were increasingly numerous. Although Cranmer kept the name of the Virgin Mary in the litany of 1544 when he replaced the invocations of saints with general petitions, subsequent Protestant reformers worked against veneration of Mary. At a time of persecution and charges of treason against Catholics, the falsely accused queen (a role recently lived by the loved Queen Katharine and repeated with the more morally ambiguous Mary, Queen of Scots), a salient part of romance, was a likely subject. There are several types.

The Matter of France, distinguished by its patriotism and strong religious elements, is also dominated by the theme of treason, as in Ganelon's betrayal of Roland and Charles. These stories, though less well told as Middle English romances, were disseminated by early printers—in the "whole life" of *Charles the Great*, *The Four Sons of Aymon*, *Godfrey of Bouillon*, and the *Knight of the Swan*, which was attached to Godfrey's legend, and part of the family history of the earls of Warwick. The composite *Valentine and Orson*, which I discussed in relation to *Two Gentlemen of Verona*, is set in the earlier time of King Pepin; it provides details of brotherhood, forest outlaws, and an apparently inexplicable forgiveness. Here I want to focus on the accused wife/queen and, finally, her lost children. *Much Ado about Nothing, Othello, The Winter's Tale*, and *Henry VIII* are today identified respectively as comedy, tragedy, romance, and history, yet their similarities in treating the falsely accused wife/queen show that a habit of mind is a more helpful description than conventional genres. But before turning to the individual plays, which make a sequence of accused fiancée, bride, wife and mother in romance and in history, it is useful to review cogent models from the medieval heritage.

The prominent characteristic of the accused wife/queen is her innocence, her chastity that is impugned by a male adversary; also salient are her humility and perseverance in adversity. In two other stories with twins, *Emaré* and *Octavian*, the mother, a queen, is calumniated by a cruel mother-in-law; in *Valentine and Orson* the accuser is a lecherous Archbishop, whose advances Bellysaunt repulsed. Emaré flees her father's incestuous advances, mainspring of *Apollonius of Tyre*, and, like Chaucer's (or Gower's) Constance, is put into a boat and drifts, as do Desonell and her twins in *Sir Torrent of Portyngale*. Florence, in *Octavian*, and Bellysaunt are banished from court to forests, where beasts carry the infant boys away, and many adventures follow. The virgin Florence of Rome is persecuted by the brother of her betrothed and a false steward, and a lord who had befriended her but exiles her when she is accused of murder. She suffers both in forests and at sea, as she travels between Rome and Jerusalem.

The beasts that abduct children, especially infants, are quite varied. In *Octavian* they are a lioness, then a griffin, and an ape. Perhaps the work of Thomas Chestre, *Octavian* is a frequent item in medieval lists of popular romances, and the original French story was widely disseminated in Europe; for example, in a German play of Hans Sachs in 1555, as a French miracle play, and in Italian prose romances.[2] The separated twin sons, as in *Valentine and Orson*, provide a consideration of nobility of birth and varied rearing. In *Octavian* the contrast is not between court and wilderness but between the noble upbringing of Octavian (with his mother at Jerusalem) and the bourgeois life of Florent, who is bought by a butcher Clement and taken to Paris. Florent is an incompetent at trade but, like Perceval, acquires whatever arms he can, fights bravely for the King of France against the Sultan, and attracts the love of the Sultan's daughter. Clement is sufficiently convinced by Florent's worth that he assists by stealing the Sultan's unicorn to give the youth a fine mount. Nevertheless, the Sultan captures Florent, the King of France, and Emperor Octavian. The nobly reared young Octavian, still accompanied by his lion, rescues them; victory, recognition, and joyful reunion follow.

Sir Isumbras presents the animal theft of three young sons of different ages—by a lion, a leopard, and a unicorn; after fourteen years of separation the sons, riding upon the wild beasts that bore them away, join their parents in the final fight against the heathen. The widely known *Bevis of Hampton* is on Chaucer's list of "romances of prys" (excellence) in "Sir Thopas," and Shakespeare's friend and fellow Warwickshireman, Michael Drayton tells a bit in *Poly-Olbion* (1598/pub.1613). *Bevis* is a dauntingly complex composite romance, and Shakespeare acknowledges its archetypal quality in *Henry VIII*, when *Bevis*, "that former fabulous story, / Being now seen possible enough, got credit, . . . was believed" (I.i.36–38). *Bevis* has a birth of twins in the forest, but the giant Ascopart carries off not the boys but the mother Josian, whose quality was established in an earlier episode when lions did not hurt her because she was a king's daughter, a queen, and a virgin. These wild creatures, which give much excitement and allegorical meaning, are antecedents for Shakespeare's most famous stage direction, "Exit, pursued by a bear" (*The Winter's Tale*, III.iii.57), when Antigonus leaves the baby girl (Perdita), with treasure, in the "deserts of Bohemia," in one of Shakespeare's richest uses of the long tradition of folklore and romance. The scarlet mantle and gold in *Sir Isumbras* are, like Perdita's swaddling mantle and box, items traditionally needed to identify a lost (royal) child.

All of these romances contain strong advocacy of Christianity, reliance upon prayer, battles against Saracens, sea voyages, journeys in exile as palmers or pilgrims. The *King of Tars* is as much religion as it is romance, although a monstrous birth provokes the action. The accuser is a heathen Sultan, who blames his Christian wife for the deformity; he charges her with insincere belief in his gods when she married him to preserve her father's peace. Each follows respective religious practice. His deities do not respond to prayers; at her request, the formless lump is baptized, and it becomes a handsome boy. The Sultan is thus converted and is washed white in the baptismal water. He joins the King of Tars to lead his vassals to become Christian, or die. The popular *Sir Isumbras* is more filled with exciting adventures, but almost completely pious; it concentrates upon the Joblike trials of the hero. However, some attention goes to his remarkably loyal and brave wife, who gives alms at her castle and ultimately fights in armor at her husband's side—a "breeches part" that anticipates Joan of Arc, or a Spenserian Britomart, or a dueling Viola. The happy ending of a reunited family is a triumph of faith; after initial pride and worldliness, penance and prayer lead to restoration and reconciliation through God's grace. Similarly, an angel, a familiar figure in romances, appears to the long-suffering Sir Isumbras to tell him of God's forgiveness and blessing and direct him to "turne ayeyne" (526–31); the scene evokes the heavenly vision to the falsely accused Catholic Queen Katharine in *Henry VIII* (IV.ii.82).

Editions of sixteenth-century romances that are direct sources for Shakespeare's plays, such as Wilkins's *The Painful Adventures of Pericles, Prince of Tyre*, Thomas Lodge's *Rosalynde*, and Robert Greene's *Pandosto*, do not include the woodcuts that were commonplace in editions of medieval romances printed in early- or mid-century. Particularly rich, and unusually numerous, are the woodcuts in William Copland's *Valentine and Orson*, which Shakespeare knew. There are seventy-two woodcuts in the second edition (1548–58), the earliest to survive (albeit with some imperfection). The third edition (1565–67), set up from the second but more carelessly printed, uses forty-six of its cuts and adds twenty others. The woodcuts are "factotoum," that is images easily applicable to many different stories, as their repeated use (sometimes as copies) in similar volumes indicate.[3] I have chosen five woodcuts, from the unique copy in the Huntington Library, that well illustrate scenes from Shakespeare's romances, especially *The Winter's Tale*.

The first (Figure 12) is the opening page that shows a marriage of a man and woman before a priest and witnesses in an architectural frame; it is a quite conventional scene and often used in romances as well as in devotional books like Vostre's *Horae*, as we have seen, since marriage is a sacrament in the Catholic Church. The religious point is here reiterated in the woodcut of the Trinity, also a popular image in manuscripts and art like English alabasters, for the initial that begins the text. Figure 13 is the most distinctive, for it shows in a wooded landscape as two separate episodes the fate of the twins and the bear. On the left a bear carries away in his teeth a basket with one of the twins; on the right is a man picking up the other swaddled infant. Shakespeare's reference to bears and wolves suckling children in *The Winter's Tale* (II.iii.187–89) is sometimes noted as evidence that he knew *Valentine and Orson*, which he used for details in *Macbeth*. This woodcut, I suggest, is a source for Shakespeare's treatment of the abandoned Perdita: the Old Shepherd finds the single infant, and the bear pursues the courtier Antigonous, who has brought her to the wooded place. The image is repeated twice, so that it would certainly have been noted; and an imaginative response is to make the bear chase the courtier, combining a figure from each section, and to have a single infant awaiting discovery by a local person. The cogency increases with a third woodcut with three scenes: in the background is a woman in bed (following childbirth), on the left a woman presents a baby to a king, and on the right the king ignores a child who seems to be pleading (Figure 14). There could be captions for Hermione, Paulina and the newborn daughter Perdita, jealous and mad Leontes, and poignant little Mamilius. Another image, also used three times in the book, shows a King receiving bad news, an appropriate illustration for the giving of the message of the oracle to Leontes. Figure 15 is a woodcut that appears only as the last illustration in *Valentine and Orson*; it shows Valentine as a hermit

¶ How the kyng Pepyn wedded Berthe a lady of great renowne. Capitulo Primo.

Ualen.j.D?.

Erytably we fynde in the auncient cronicles, that the noble and valiaunt kyng pepyn wedded and toke vnto wyfe Berthe of great renowne, tyscrete and prudent, whiche had and suffred in her tyme greate trybula= cions and aduersities by enuy.

B.i.   fo?

12. Marriage and Trinity initial, *Valentine and Orson* (1550?)

13. Infant abandoned and recovered, *Valentine and Orson* (1550?)

14. Infant presented to the King; child implores the King, *Valentine and Orson* (1550?)

15. Pilgrim penitent, *Valentine and Orson* (1550?)

16. Man and lady outside a city, ship at sea with coffer, *Valentine and Orson* (1550?)

ne Mary.

The martyrdome of D. Cranmer Archb. and Martyr.

❧ The burnyng of the Archbishop of Caunterbury Doctor Thomas
Cranmer, in the Towneditch at Oxforde, with his hand first thrust into the fire, wherewith
he subscribed before.

17. The Burning of Thomas Cranmer, Archbishop of Canterbury, John Foxe's

saint, indicated by the halo and costume, and would serve well for the penitent Leontes. The final woodcut (Figure 16) that I include is somewhat more general, twice used by Copland in this edition, and an apt image for sea journeys in all of Shakespeare's romances. On the seashore stand a man and woman, in the harbor is a ship with men aboard and a prominent chest/coffin on the prow; the city below, some distance from the figures and ship, suggests both journey and exile. Such factotum woodcuts are quite interchangeable, but a direct applicability to a specific romance can also be argued. Moreover, the combination of religious iconography—the opening marriage and Trinity initial and the concluding hermit saint—with episodes of adventure and trial show the affinity of romance and religion, a habit of mind created and sustained for centuries.

False accusations against, and persecutions of, chaste women are a staple of pious tales and saints' legends that closely resemble romances like those I have been reviewing. Early martyrology abounds in persecuted virgins of Roman times, well known saints like Agnes, Agatha, and Lucy—the last two from Sicily. Later, Saint Elizabeth of Hungary is a type of the pious woman who marries but persists in her religious devotion. Caxton tells their stories in his translation of *The Golden Legend*. St. Elizabeth is a likely inspiration for the accused queen, and romances like *Le Bone Florence*; thematic correspondences include persecution, exile, saintliness, healing power, and fame. Some late legends, like that of Genevieve of Brabant, combine marriage, piety, and false accusation. Her accuser is a false seneschal, Golo, and she retreats into a forest to await her repentant husband's coming. The tale, written possibly to glorify a monastery and its founder, is late medieval but found an audience in the early seventeenth century. The Jesuit René de Cersiers (1603–62) published a successful French account, *L'Innocence Reconnue, ou la Vie de Sainte Genevieve de Brabant* (before 1638) that was popular for centuries in folkbooks. A Jesuit's decision to advance piety through a saint's life of the falsely accused wife is a link to the queen whose removal by Henry VIII led to the Jesuit mission to England.

Even so brief an account of accused queens/wives shows how rich was the store of such stories in Europe, and many have Eastern analogs. Anyone who reads such tales is familiar with the improbable, encounters of great danger and hardship, relentless lack of belief and confidence in woman's virtue and thus easy accusation, followed by deep penitence, and ultimately reconciliation. The habit of mind cultivated by such romances favors piety, patience, perseverance, and the triumph that comes through the virtue of women who embody and live these ideals. They are the mothers of the Shakespeare Woman who is increasingly central to the plays; the four now to be considered show an arc of Shakespeare's reliance upon and favoring of the heritage of medieval romance.

Hero in *Much Ado about Nothing*

The attraction of Beatrice and Benedict as Shakespeare's wittiest and most equally matched lovers takes attention away from the play's basic story, which is of a falsely accused woman, the bride Hero, whom Claudio charges with being unchaste and spurns as a "rotten orange" at the church on their wedding day. Like beautiful Florence, Hero is not yet a wife, but does not lack accusers. Both Claudio's friend and mentor, Don Pedro, Prince of Aragon, and Hero's father Leonato support his negative judgment and rejection of the lady. A telling sign of sexual difference is their giving credence to Don John's accusation that "the lady is disloyal" (III.iii.98), even though the prince's brother is a known schemer whom Benedick immediately ties to framing villainies (IV.i.188–89). The two male exceptions to such easy acquiescence to anxiety about sexual betrayal are Friar Francis, an exemplar of the Church, named for the most compassionate of saints, and Benedict, Claudio's best friend, a man who has thoroughly examined his male assumptions and come to regard heterosexual love and marriage as more to be valued than warrior companionship. These two men, a priest and a layman, share the gift of faith, belief in essence whatever the apparent appearance, as Benedict's question to Beatrice makes clear: "Think you in your soul the Count Claudio hath wronged Hero?" (IV.i.327–28). The point is stronger because of Benedict's usual skeptical habit of mind. Claudio sees only "outward graces" and easily believes the charade of a tryst between Borachio and Hero (Margaret) at the window, a scene that is reported rather than shown to the audience. Claudio rejects Hero as "but the sign and semblance of her honor" (32) and berates her "seeming" (55), while arguing the contradictions of human character—"most foul, most fair! . . . Thou pure impiety and impious purity" (103–4).

Claudio is in the tradition of men who cannot believe or simply accept the virtues of a good woman, like Walter in the "Clerk's Tale" who compulsively tests Griselda. Claudio seems incipiently indignant when he rejects Leonato's first confidence in his daughter, "O, what men dare do! What men may do! / What men daily do, not knowing what they do!" (18–20); but he is accurately describing both his own false perception and the anxiety and uncertainty that lead him to mistake. In *Much Ado* the chain of falsely accusing men (Don John, Borachio, Claudio, Don Pedro, Leonato) is a remarkable change from Shakespeare's most direct source, Bandello's Novella XXII, where many events are the same but the response of the family is very different. The rival and rejected suitor Sir Girondo accuses Fenicia and offers "proof," so that Sir Timbreo withdraws his pledge to marry. Her noble father Lionato has never relied upon the match because he knows his reduced economic circumstances. He confidently defends Fenicia, whose name, used by Chrétien de Troyes, means "phoenix'': "It is indeed true that all things are possible, but I know how my daughter has been reared and what her habits are. God who is our just Judge will one day, I believe, make known the truth" (Bullough II,118). And Fenicia is the type of falsely accused bride when she accepts her circumstances:

> "for it is God's will, and we must have patience. . . . Now may God do with me as is most pleasing to Him, and grant that this my trouble may tend to the salvation of my soul. . . . It is enough for me that before the just tribunal of Christ I shall be known innocent of such baseness; and thus to Him who gave it I commend my soul, which longs to escape from this earthly prison and now takes its way towards Him"
>
> (Bullough II,119–20).

She collapses at the end of the speech, but her apparent death brings grief to her family, not relief from shame, and there is great rejoicing when the corpse revives during the burial washing. To Fenicia's momentary despair, her mother and aunt reply, "Child, you must live, since God wills it, and He will set all things right" (121). Seclusion at the house of her father's brother is sweetened by the company of her younger sister. The citizens of Messina believe Timbreo lied, and her funeral elicits their sympathy. Bandello extends compassion: first, the two young men become reasonable and repent, and Timbreo, like Valentine in *Two Gentlemen of Verona*, puts friendship before love; second, the young males set out to restore Fenicia's good name and become penitents at the tomb and then confess to the wronged parents. A year must pass before the reconciliation with two marriages, of the young men and sisters, and the bounty of King Piero and his Queen, giving dowries and making the sisters ladies of the court.

Shakespeare changes Bandello's story of family and support to one of destructive male accusers, but for Beatrice's defense of her cousin, the Friar's support, and Benedict's resolve to believe his love. Accusing men become increasingly difficult and less rational in the sequence of plays about maligned wives and queens; thus the need to rely upon something beyond the human increases. Hero responds to Claudio's charge, " 'True'! O God!" and then "God, defend me" (IV.i.68,77), and she describes her questioning as "catechizing" (78). Her advocate, the pragmatic manager of defense is Friar Francis, who sees innocence, "angel whiteness," and whose defense speech is replete with terms of contemporary religious controversy:

> And in her eye there hath appeared a fire
> To burn the errors that these princes hold
> Against her maiden truth. Call me a fool;
> Trust not my reading nor my observations,
> Which with experimental steal doth warrant

> The tenor of my book; trust not my age,
> My reverence, calling, nor divinity,
> If this sweet lady lie not guiltless here
> Under some biting error.   (163–70)

As we have already recognized, "error" in the sixteenth century is most frequently associated with religious controversy, and the Friar makes this explicit
when he refers to a fire against error, a burning at the stake, the sentence against
heretics (and accused queens of romance), and he strongly affirms his religious
belief and vocation. To be called a "fool" is no minor risk; according to Psalm
14, the fool is the one who does not believe: "The foole hathe said in his heart,
There is no God: thei haue corrupted, and done an abominable worke: there is
none that doeth good." The Friar next refers to reading and observations, ways
of knowing, that connote Scripture and Church tradition, and then gives a final
summary of his reasons for faith—his maturity, reputation, priesthood, and the
divine. Before each reason he speaks of "trust"; faith, whatever fleeting reality
appears, is necessary for human survival, and this is served by the Church. The
rites of burial and prayers for the dead, so elaborate in medieval Christendom
but opposed by the Reformed Church, are to be performed, for they place the
death within the community, encouraging sympathy. The use of the word
"rack" (220), tied to torture of priests like Campion, is another contemporary
allusion; and the Friar's faith that Claudio, as he recalls the beauty and strength
of the one that was cast away, will "wish he had not so accused her" (232),
even though he was sincere, shows the depth of the priest's belief in forgiveness
and hope of reconciliation. When this comes at the end of the play, there is yet
another reminder of Elizabethan religious controversy; Leonato argues innocence for those "who accused her / Upon the error you heard debated" (V.iv.3).
   Devotion to truth in the world means an acceptance of time, not seeking to
dominate events but allowing all to become receptive to God's grace. This is
realized in the play with the scene of lamentation, without which Claudio's
change of heart does not satisfy an audience, as becomes clear when the scene
is cut. Hero, like many other accused or abandoned women, including the Abbess in *The Comedy of Errors* or Thaisa in *Pericles*, will be safe in a convent,
"some reclusive and religious life, / Out of all eyes, tongues, minds, and injuries" (IV.i.243). Her present circumstances are explained; she must "die to
live," and this, the message of the Passion, means life in the next world as well
as this world, where it is necessary to "Have patience and endure" (253), as
did Helena in *All's Well That Ends Well*. The point is reiterated in the final
reconciliation, when the Friar explains, "She died, my lord, but whiles her
slander lived" (V.iv.65). He knows that "all this amazement"—the essence of
romance and life—needs explanation, but this is to come after "holy rites" in

the ''chapel''—following the sacramental practices of the Church. In *Much Ado about Nothing* events happen very quickly, and the gloss of ''nothing'' as ''noting'' is a helpful one to convey the sense of urgency, and the dangers of too hasty action. It is also a reminder that care should be exercised in noting.

The native English element is, as in *A Midsummer Night's Dream*, at the heart of the resolution. Bottom had an ass's ears; Dogberry proclaims, ''I am an ass'' (IV.ii.78) and laments, ''O, that I had been writ down an ass!'' (86). A good performance makes the scenes of the watch an occasion for much mirth, but this should not obscure the fact that simple, bumbling folk bring the calumniators to justice and exonerate the innocent, while the learned and sophisticated merely declaim. As Christ proclaims in the Beatitudes, ''Blessed are the peace makers: for they shalbe called the children of God'' (Matthew V.9); both theology and a Shakespearean pun are possible. Leonato, the shamed and vengeful father, like a knight of old, confronts Claudio: ''Do challenge thee to trial of a man'' (V.i.66), and provokes laughter because he is old and weak. A strong Benedict, echoing Claudio's supercilious put down of Leonato's initial confidence in his daughter, issues a proper challenge to his friend: ''I will make it good how you dare, with what you dare, and when you dare. Do me right or I will protest your cowardice'' (146–48).

But in this world of romance, resolution comes without trial by combat. A faithful Friar and bumbling but sincere keepers of the peace bring a happy ending. Friar Francis's successful intervention is a rewriting of Friar Lawrence's failed attempt to reconcile the Montagues and Capulets in *Romeo and Juliet*, so that in this later comedy Shakespeare allows the helpful priest to succeed according to the traditions of romance, in which hermits and priests restore the health and good fortune of heroes. His two assistants are Benedict, a man who bears the name of the pious and practical founder of monasticism, and Beatrice, a woman who bears the name of Dante's love that leads to the Beatific Vision. In *Othello* Shakespeare shows the horrors that follow when a proud man believes evil, partially inspired by a scheming steward but also generated by his own vanity and insecurity, and falsely accuses an innocent wife. From a Christian point of view, there can never be real tragedy, since Christ's death on the cross brings salvation, the happy ending that reconciles fallen humanity, as in romance. Shakespeare returned to the accused wife to continue exploring the dynamics of that belief.

Desdemona in *Othello*

Othello stands between the mature comedy that is *Much Ado About Nothing* and the richest achievement of romance in *The Winter's Tale*—when Shakespeare again roots a play in the story of the falsely accused woman and relies most directly upon an Italian *novella*, this time the seventh story from Cinthio's *Hecatommithi* (1565), that is a contemporary rendering of subjects developed in medieval romance. Another connection between *Much Ado* and *Othello* is the Turks, the non-Christians who threatened southern and eastern Europe in the sixteenth century and inspired modern Crusades called for by the Popes, not least Pius V. Don John has been identified with the bastard Don John of Austria, whose statue stands before the cathedral in Messina and whose tomb is in El Escorial; he commanded the fleet of the Christian League (between Spain and Venice) that defeated the Turks in the Gulf of Corinth at Lepanto in 1571. This crucial event stemmed the Turkish advances, and the nineteen-year-old James VI wrote a poem, *Lepanto*, about the victory, which is frequently depicted in historical paintings to show the triumph of Christianity. Subsequent popes continued to raise armies against the Turks, Clement VIII in the 1590s to release Hungary, and there were many expenditures to support Catholic forces against emerging Protestants, especially in France. Just as Venice was the favored embarkation port for Crusades to the Holy Land, so the republic of Venice held a crucial position during the Counter-Reformation, when the city resisted papal politics and claimed its own authority, without ceasing to be orthodox and devoutly Catholic. Shakespeare could not have chosen a more pertinent location than Venice to call attention to religious controversy that was moving to crisis when he wrote *Othello*. Pope Paul V (1605–21) excommunicated the Signoria in April 1606, placed the city under interdict, and thus prohibited the celebration of the sacraments. This was quickly recognized as an egregious example of bad papal policy, and Pope Paul lifted the interdict in 1607, but not before the Jesuits, after hard consideration, left the republic. The bias and struggle for power between Protestants and Catholics dominated Europe, and one notorious response is to Pope Gregory VIII's reform of the "Julian" calendar in 1582. Protestant scientists such as Johannes Kepler and Tycho Brahe were pleased, but many others feared and resented the papal Antichrist and refused to accept the adjustments and revisions: in England the Gregorian Calendar was not accepted until 1752.[4] In a world so lacking in reconciliation, the happy ending promised by Christ, and celebrated in medieval romance, seemed uncertain; among such divergent opinions, the falsely accused is an apt paradigm, and Shakespeare reexamined it to show tragic consequences.

Some circumstances surrounding the accused bride in *Othello* resemble those in *Much Ado*, but they do not lead to a happy ending in what is usually called Shakespeare's most domestic tragedy, a treatment of marriage as both erotic and spiritual union. Although a woman's chastity is the occasion of action, the insecure male shown in several guises in *Much Ado* is the focus of attention here. Similarities between Othello and Iago are many, most notably an incapacity to believe in a woman's true worth and a complicity in compulsive testing, the argument of folktales and romances about accused wives and queens that often focus on men. Desdemona is neither angel nor devil, the stringent possibilities in Othello's mind; Iago's bestial imagery and identification of women as whores, his verbal abuse of his wife and assumption that she has no autonomy, as well as his suspicions of cuckoldry, mark him as a man without a sense of worth. Iago's early statement, "Were I the Moor I would not be Iago. / In following him, I follow but myself ... I am not what I am" (I.i.59–60, 67), supports a view that Shakespeare dramatizes the conflict between the ideal and vicious in a single personality by separating the qualities into two characters. In romance the ideal prevails, but the sinister and unredeemed dominate in *Othello*. The closeness of twins in romance is recalled with Cassio, who is casual and confident as Othello and Iago are not. The imagery of Othello's firm rejection, "Though he had twinned with me, both at a birth" (II.iii. 206), echoes the twins separated from accused queens in romance. Cassio is guilty of drunken fighting but repentant; he survives to become Governor of Cypress after Othello's death, and he censures the wounded silent Iago.

Imagery of sin and devils pervades this play that Bernard Spivak discusses as an "allegory of evil," but there is no figure of faith such as Friar Francis, Beatrice, and Benedict in *Much Ado*, and the troublemaking Don John becomes the villain Iago, a "demi-devil" both cleverer and more evil. That Iago's first word is " 'Sblood" (by His [Christ's] blood, I.i.4) marks the blasphemous quality of what is to come, and after an initial success in discrediting Cassio, he swears "By the Mass" (II.iii.372). Othello has avowedly eschewed the pagan magic in his Moorish background; his words, "Keep up your bright swords, for the dew will rust them" (I.ii.60) suggest Christ's response to arrest at the Garden of Gethsemane. But Othello's conversion seems only on the surface, as he quickly reverts to savagery. His mother's handkerchief becomes a supreme token, "To lose't or give 't away were such perdition / As nothing else could match" (III.iv.69–70), and his fall in epileptic seizure (IV.i.50–51) represents possession by evil spirits that, as several Gospel stories establish, need exorcism. Othello's poised apologia before the Venetian senate (I.iii) degenerates into his self-serving defense of his murder of Desdemona, a failure to admit his fault that persists even to a final self-justification and plea for reputation in the last moments before the ultimate pagan act of suicide (V.ii).

Humility is grotesquely lacking, and Othello's pride is similarly great when he confesses Desdemona before killing her. He assumes the role of priest, but not the Christlike servant dedicated to truth and forgiveness. The absoluteness of his behavior is especially horrifying when his wife pleads for "But half an hour! ... But while I say one prayer!" (85, 87), only to be smothered. Emilia's knock comes immediately, a brilliant theatrical showing of irony. Here we see, as Iago warned, "How poor are they that have not patience!" (II.iii.363). Iago is speaking of Roderigo, the rejected suitor who is complicit in his schemes, but he accurately describes the fate of those who lack the Christian virtues exemplified by the accused wives and queens of romance. Early in the play the Duke of Venice urges that "What cannot be preserved when fortune takes, / Patience her injury a mockery makes" (I.iii.209–10), but Brabantio, resisting the message of the Crucifixion, rejects the suffering that accompanies "poor patience" and insists that such "sentences" (maxims) are "equivocal" (218, 220). This anticipates Othello's confidence that he would have had "patience" against many other misfortunes, but that "Patience" will "look grim as hell!" (IV.ii.49–66) when beholding Desdemona's assumed betrayal; he denies her vow of chastity, "as I am a Christian" (85). Patience requires time, an earthly hint of eternity, and in this play there is very little. There is an intervening sea voyage, with a major storm as in so many romances, but Shakespeare limits to a couple of days and nights the time the characters are together. This means that the action is driven; few plays chronicle so relentless an attempt to force behavior, an insistence upon control, with the corollary lack of self-abnegation. There is a terrifying absolutism, as Othello acknowledges when he yields to Desdemona's suit for Cassio: "Perdition catch my soul / But I do love thee! And when I love thee not, / Chaos is come again" (III.iii.98–100). This is not just extreme rhetoric but an accurate statement about the imbalance that comes in a restricted private world of the moment. By the end of the scene Othello declares, "O now forever / Farewell the tranquil mind! Farewell content!" (363–64)" and urges Iago to present "the ocular proof" (377), a sign of his reliance upon appearances in this world that denies substance concealed by accidents.

The play has reminders of the essence of devout Christian community. When Cassio greets Desdemona upon her arrival in Cypress, he echoes the *Ave Maria*: "Hail to thee, lady! And the grace of heaven / Before, behind thee, and on every hand / Enwheel thee round!" (II.i.87–89). But Desdemona practices nothing of the Virgin Mary's response in the *Magnificat* when Mary humbly surrenders self to become open to God's grace. Another Christian virtue, obedience, is a rival theme to jealousy in *Othello*, and Shakespeare explores it in both Desdemona and Emilia. Before the Senate, Brabantio asks his daughter, "Where most you owe obedience?" (I.iii.181). Desdemona's perception of a "divided duty"—like Cordelia's response to Lear or Juliet's conflict of loyalty—fails to acknowledge that her secret marriage has removed the sacrament from the community where it should be celebrated, as she has too intensely chosen to follow her passion for the Moorish general without reconciliation with her father. Like many women, but not the archetypal accused wife or queen, she loses herself to a man's worldly values. Desdemona appears the obedient wife, but challenges her husband when she intervenes in military matters—albeit with the best of intentions. Before Othello's fury Desdemona cowers into submission to him, but not to the truth which accused wives and queens adhere to. Her assertion that Othello is innocent of her murder can be heard as her recognition of her own culpability. But she still lacks understanding when her last words insist, ''A guiltless death I die''—a judgment about nothing except chastity—and that the deed that took her life was done by ''Nobody; I myself. Farewell./ Commend me to my kind lord. O, farewell'' (V.ii.126–29). Desdemona thus dies tragically, in a finish that is a far cry from the vindication of accused wives and queens of romance whose false accusers make public confession to lead to the happy ending. Emilia, a defender of her mistress but herself long deluded about her husband Iago, finally perceives and cries out, ''The Moor hath killed my mistress! Murder, murder!'' (174), and she confronts Iago, ''You told a lie, an odious, damnéd lie!'' (187). Both women have wavered about where obedience is due, asserting themselves and yet becoming victims of male authority, as is clear in the scene when they discuss behavior in marriage. Although obedience is due to husbands, it must be defined by understanding, which is very difficult between the sexes, as Desdemona acknowledges: ''O, these men, these men!'' (IV.iii.62). Emilia is a feisty woman when she claims female sexuality and frailty like those of men, but she denies her own responsibility when she concludes, ''The ills we do, their ills instruct us so'' (106). Desdemona does identify the superior role, ''God me such uses send / Not to pick bad from bad, but by bad mend!'' (107–8), of the falsely accused wife or queen, who in countless romances does just that when she patiently perseveres, accepting the vagaries of fortune, but confident that obedience to God and faith will lead to a worthy life in this world as well as salvation in the next. Sadly, Desdemona does not act upon her perception, but Emilia finally makes the distinction between obedience to a husband and to truth: '' 'Tis proper I obey him, but not now'' (202). And she has a happy death in the theological sense: ''So come my soul to bliss as I speak true. / So speaking, as I think, alas, I die'' (259–60). *Othello* is a tragedy, and thus the accused wife and her attendant cannot end happily. But Shakespeare will soon turn again to romance, whose transcendence he subverted in the anti-romance *Troilus and Cressida* and denied in the tragedies. His last plays are full romances, and the most compelling presents the restoration of the falsely accused queen, who also triumphs in the history *Henry VIII.*

Hermione in *The Winter's Tale*

For many, *The Winter's Tale* is the most implausible of Shakespeare's romances, one that seems to heighten the improbable beyond belief and finishes with pyrotechnic theatricality when the statue comes alive in Shakespeare's most notable addition to the principal source, Robert Greene's *Pandosto; or, The*

Triumph of Time (1588, 1607). The play's title itself seems to ask indulgence, and Shakespeare acknowledges his straining of credulity. About the restoration of an heir the Second Gentleman comments: "This news which is called true is so like an old tale that the verity of it is in strong suspicion" (V.ii.28–29), and the Third Gentleman agrees with the analog and extends the definition: "Like an old tale still, which will have matter to rehearse though credit be asleep and not an ear open" (62–64). Paulina, who has stage-managed the showing of the statue and Hermione's return, repeats the idea: "That she is living, / Were it but told you, should be hooted at / Like an old tale; but it appears she lives, / Though yet she speaks not" (V.iii.116–19). These comments, like the exchange between Hermione and Mamilius, point to the play's origin in the narratives of romance. Hermione asks her son, "Pray you, sit by us / And tell's a tale" (II.i.22–23); they consider whether it should be sad or merry, and the son decides, "A sad tale's best for winter. I have one / Of sprites and goblins" (25). As in the stories of many children, the intent is to pass the time and to be scary; but the modern critic's easy dismissal of such tales, and of old wives' tales, as trivial, fails to recognize the power of folktale and romance, their mythic and religious nature. Shakespeare's deployment of the medieval heritage and habit of mind that take the supernatural very seriously gives the lie to such sophistication, which exalts immediate comprehension and control. Time, as Chorus at the start of the long Act IV, marks the sixteen years' chronological division of *The Winter's Tale*, warns against such limitation, and argues for evolving perception, as does Greene's subtitle. Time will "make stale / The glistering of this present, as my tale / Now seems to it" and urges the audience to "patience" (13–15). The wisdom of old narratives is timeless, transcending any single moment with the perspective of eternity that goes beyond even a sequence of temporal moments. And the Christian vision places life in the world as a mere brief preliminary to what is to come.

The circumstances of the accused wife/queen in *The Winter's Tale* resemble those in *Othello*, but are closer to the folktale and romance archetype of arbitrary charges and affirmative resolution. Desdemona's lack of experience that led her to well-meaning but tactless interference and Iago's evil manipulation somewhat explain Othello's jealousy; Leontes' jealousy and cruelty are self-induced and directly contradict Hermione's many years as "good queen," wife, and mother. The rush of events in *Othello* curtails time, and lack of patience combines with pride to end in tragedy. *The Winter's Tale* rewrites the false charges of adultery in *Othello* and follows fully the model of an insecure male as accusing husband. Shakespeare denies the psychological plausibility of Othello in the intensity of Leontes' feeling and his willful actions that extend to madness as his "diseased opinion" leaps from adultery to denial of sworn friendship to "There is a plot against my life, my crown'' (II.i.47). Jealousy triggers the action, but it is shown as sin, spiritual failing—and this is neither improbable nor implausible.

Delusion brings Leontes to the sin of blasphemy. Unlike Claudio in *Much Ado* and Othello who need ocular proof, and in spite of the court's defense of the ''good queen,'' he is utterly sure in his personal judgment and power and expects confirmation from the oracle to reassure others:

> Though I am satisfied, and need no more
> Than what I know, yet shall the oracle
> Give rest to the minds of others, such as he
> Whose ignorant credulity will not
> Come up to th' truth.   (II.i.190–94)

Like Faustus, Leontes follows the type of Lucifer in his assumption that he does not need the divine. When the oracle declares ''Hermione is chaste, Polixenes blameless, . . . Leontes a jealous tyrant,'' all praise Apollo, but Leontes asserts, ''There is no truth at all i' th'oracle. . . . This is mere falsehood'' (III.ii.132–33, 140–41). Regulations in the theater prohibited references to God, lest there be blasphemy, but Shakespeare here defines the Christian view that sin is a separation from God, and he shows how human error explodes into denial and accusations against the divine. Theology teaches that the sin against the Holy Spirit is most grievous. Jesus describes the choice of those who reject Him: ''Wherefore I say vnto you, euerie sine and blasphemie shalbe forgiuen vnto men: but the blasphemie against the holie Gost shal not be forgiuen vnto men'' (Matthew XII.31), and a gloss in The Geneva Bible notes that the sin comes from striving against what one knows and against one's conscience. As St. Paul explains: ''For if we sinne willingly after that we haue receiued the knowledge of the trueth, there remaineth no more sacrifice for sinners, But a fearful loking for of iudgment, & viole[n]t fyre, which shal deuoure the aduersaries'' (Hebrews X.26–27). In the Elizabethan age of religious controversy few passages are more compelling.

Blasphemy leads to immediate consequences: Leontes learns of the death of his son Mamilius, immediately acknowledges his pride and injustice, and thus prays, ''Apollo, pardon / My great profaneness 'gainst thine oracle! / I'll reconcile me . . . ,'' and contrasts his rust and black deeds with the light of Camillo's ''piety'' that made him forego worldly wealth and position to remain true—an analog for Catholic recusants who went into exile (153–55, 171). Earlier references also sign this comparison; for peace of mind Leontes needs Hermione ''given to the fire'' (II.iii.8), burned at the stake like a traitor—or heretic, as Paulina later points out. When Leontes threatens the Queen's attendant, whose name suggests St. Paul, she asserts: ''I care not. / It is an heretic that makes the fire, / Not she which burns in 't" (II.iii.114–16), and she pursues her role as conscience to the king. At first Paulina would not name Leontes "tyrant," but with the vindication of the oracle, she itemizes his "tyranny" and those he has injured, a way of focusing contrition. His penance begins with Paulina's rhetorical enumeration of the "studied torments" of saints, familiar in the Catholic world of images and texts like *The Golden Legend:* "wheels, racks, fires, flaying, boiling in leads or oils" (III.ii.175–77). Foxe's Protestant martyrs are burned or hanged. These were the tortures of those who would not deny their faith; sometimes the persecutors convert when miracles follow the death of a martyr, and thus provide evidence in the material world that leads to the identification of sainthood. That proof is not easy is hinted at when Florizel acknowledges his need for his father's approval that would be "almost a miracle" (IV.iv.536).

The sixteen years are necessary in the plot to allow the lost child to reach some maturity, but they are also crucial as a penitential time during which Leontes recovers his faith and suffers in atonement for his sins. In early plays framed by a romance mode, the restoration and happy ending come quickly; here the very long Act IV separates Leontes' admission of sin and the recovery of his queen and heir. The time is analogous to the years of Pericles' searching and grief, and to precedents in medieval romances like *Sir Isumbras*, *Valentine and Orson*, or *Guy of Warwick* with a strong penitential element and much suffering. The world away from the court of Sicily, the "deserts of Bohemia," contains shepherds, but also "is famous for the creatures / Of prey that keep upon 't" (III.iii.11–12)—a preparation of the audience for the entrance of the devouring bear. The Mariner who brought Antigonous to the seacoast acknowledges a "conscience" and attributes the pending storm to divine wills displeased by their coming. But in spite of human and natural warnings Antigonous, who did not support his wife Paulina in her defense of Hermione, is skeptical. His long speech explains that he has not believed that "spirits o' the dead / May walk again," but he describes his visit from Hermione, "a vessel of sorrow . . . In pure white robes, / Like very sanctity" who spoke to him to plead for her baby and give her a name. Antigonous accepts that he had a vision. Usually he denigrates dreams as toys, but "Yet for this once, yea, superstitiously, / I will be *squared by this" (directed in my course 39–40). He thinks that Hermione is dead and follows Apollo and Leontes' order to leave the fate of the infant to chance. He pities the innocent infant but declares, "Weep I cannot, / But my heart bleeds; and most accurst am I / To be by oath enjoined to this. Farewell!" (50– 52). Antigonous chooses the values of this world and holds to an oath that is rooted in sin; and the bear eats him. In contrast, the Old Shepherd instantly responds to the bairn with admiration for the beauty of a newly born creature and mercy at its plight, "I'll take it up for pity" (74). Shepherd began with a concern about his son's sexuality and he thinks the baby was probably illegitimate, but he immediately takes it up, an act described by Clown, his son, as "charity" (197). The behavior effectively compares the nature of sins; sex is child's play compared to pride. Clown, like his father, is compassionate; thus he describes the shipwreck in the tempest, "O, the most piteous cry of the poor souls!" (88)—a phrase that evokes the Catholic concern with the cries of the poor souls in Purgatory—and he undertakes to gather the remains of Antigonous, an act that his father calls "a good deed" (128). Father and son will share the task of burial, a reminder of Catholic devotion to observances for the dead. And the scene concludes with a promise of further good deeds as a response to the luck of finding baby and treasure. A contrast is pointed between the charity of the countrymen and the courtier's concern with self, and Clown's oath "Marry" (by the Virgin Mary 131) hints at a devotion already suggested by Antigonus's vision, which greatly resembles the many legends and Miracles of the Blessed Virgin Mary, who intervenes to prevent catastrophe and shows a tender heart even to scoundrels.

A balance between the dying and the newborn is emblematic of life, temporal and eternal, sadness and joy. Shakespeare does not present a lyrical pastoral escapism. Even the sheep-shearing festival, a vibrant celebration that serves to mark change, as do "Merry is the month of May" lyric passages in medieval romances, is not all rejoicing. Polixenes' anger and threats, a recapitulation of Leontes' sinful wrath against his family, mar the occasion, and some imagery has overtones of Christ. Polixenes would have Perdita's "beauty scratched with briers" (IV.iv.427), and Florizel cries out, "But O, the thorns we stand upon!" (588), an inversion of the crown of thorns for the Crucifixion. Autolycus dominates the occasion, and he is a liar and a thief who delights in his own virtuosity and claims to sleep out the life to come (30). The rascal, who charms the audience as well as those at the feast, argues that Fortune would not allow him to be honest even if he tried because simple folk are easily duped in a world where Honesty is a fool and his sworn brother Trust is very simpleminded (598–99)—apt designations for Clown and Old Shepherd. But Autolycus is arguably a good thief; the courtier fallen from grace previously served Prince Florizel, his acts against Shepherd and Clown are ultimately to their advantage, and he contributes to the resolution when he reveals Perdita's identity, albeit unwittingly. In this world of romance, a benevolent place but one that contains suffering and hardship, Autolycus finds that "against his will" he has "done good" (125), and acknowledges that "Though I am not naturally honest, I am so sometimes by chance" (715–16). His muddling through, like that of Dogberry and Verges in *Much Ado*, helps to the happy ending. The crucial point is a surrender of self, in the play signed by Autolycus's changes of clothes, transformations that recall the knight in disguise who best serves when unknown and responding to need rather than seeking fame and wealth. For all his tricks and avowed amorality, there is also in this con-man a spiritual quality that Hamlet identifies as ''the readiness is all,'' an acknowledgment of a power outside the individual and an acceptance that God provides better than anything one can acquire on one's own. This requires flexibility and an absence of urgency. The country celebration marks the renewal of passing seasons, the universal cycle of death and rebirth that in *The Winter's Tale*, for all its surface pagan references, is a Catholic statement of Resurrection. A recorded performance on Easter Tuesday in 1618 is an early acknowledgment of the play's appropriateness to the season.

The final act returns to Sicily and begins with the statement of Cleomenes, a lord:

> Sir, you have done enough and have performed
> A saintlike sorrow. No fault could you make
> Which you have not redeemed—indeed paid down
> More penitence than done trespass. At the last,
> Do as the heavens have done, forget your evil;
> With them forgive yourself.   (V.i.1–6)

Religious imagery pervades; between Paulina's exhortation to the sinner, as in a medieval confession manual, and this recognition of penitent Leontes, there are many reminders, some of which we have seen. Like a spiritual director, Paulina begins with severe censure, urging that the King's guilt in Hermione's death is beyond repentance:

> Therefore betake thee
> To nothing but despair. A thousand knees
> Ten thousand years together, naked, fasting,
> Upon a barren mountain, and still winter
> In storm perpetual, could not move the gods
> To look that way thou wert.   (III.ii.209–14)

When Leontes accepts his guilt, she immediately is sorry for the intensity of the attack, which is not inappropriate to a pagan view of wanton gods that kill for sport but would be blasphemous and a sin against the Holy Ghost in a Christian universe of redemption. The suggested penances are familiar ones in sacred and secular narratives of medieval Christendom, and Paulina furthers this context when she confesses her own sinfulness, ''I do repent'' (220). Moreover, she calls herself a ''fool again'' (228) after she quickly lapsed into an excessive womanly grief over the lost queen; this brings her to a proper spiritual direction: Leontes is to be ''patient,'' and she will say nothing. The scene ends with Leontes' decision to bury his dead queen and son in one grave, his acceptance of "shame perpetual," and promise daily to "visit the chapel where they lie" and shed tears for them as long as he lives (238–40). His faithful office—"said many / A prayer upon her grave" (V.iii.142)—makes Leontes a kind of chantry priest, a celibate who offers perpetual services for the dead, a Catholic practice much resented and prohibited by the Reformers. For Leontes it is "recreation" (III.ii.241), a word that here means restoration more than pastime, and it comes through "sorrows" (244).

The tone and behavior replicate those of the accused queen in romance, and in *The Winter's Tale* she is Hermione, whose trial scene that stands as a testing of humanity is the exemplum and, I think, Shakespeare's finest statement of the Christian life. Jesus was falsely accused and tormented, and His heroic acceptance of the Cross is the model urged in *imitatio Christi.* In the first court scene Hermione protests male nostalgia for lost innocence of childhood and the corollary charge that women as "temptation" destroy it. An eloquent medieval argument against this attack on women is the lyric "Adam lay ibounden" that blesses the time that Adam took the apple because had he not Our Lady would not have been Heaven's Queen. Hermione prays, "Grace to boot!" (I.ii.80), acknowledging that she must trust in God, not men; and she goes farther with her second "good deed" recognized by Leontes. Of this "elder sister" she prays, "O, would her name were Grace!" (99), a personification that is unmistakably a theological allusion, and the feminine suggests the open receptivity to God's gift of grace, a counterargument to the increasing sexual bawdy and insecurity of her husband, whose "diseased opinion" is challenged by Camillo (296). Hermione's trial begins with the touching scene in which the pregnant mother plays with her son, who like Mary's Son and Griselda's children, is taken from her. Quickly Leontes before the court accuses his wife of adultery, just as Claudio shamed Hero at the church with "public accusation, uncovered slander, unmitigated rancor" *(Much Ado,* IV.i.303–4). A difference between young bride and mature queen is that Hermione does not swoon before the false charges; she quietly says, "You my lord, / Do but mistake" (81–82), a generous interpretation of error rather than evil act and a wish for reconciliation. Her concern is less for her shame and vulnerability than for how Leontes will grieve for his actions when he "shall come to clearer knowledge" (97–98). As Christ did not answer accusations before Pilate, so Hermione does not defend herself when Leontes first abuses her and orders her to prison; she accepts the circumstances and knows that she "must be patient" (107). She also recognizes that by not reacting as an emotional and weeping woman she risks a loss of sympathy, so that she asks the lords to use their "charities" to "measure" her (114–15)—an evocation of Jesus' statements forbidding judgment in the passage (Matthew 7.2, Mark 4.24, Luke 6.38) that inspires *Measure for Measure* and in the Woman Taken in Adultery (John 8.3). Underlying Hermione's forgiveness are Jesus' words from the Cross, "Father, forgiue them: for they knowe not what thei do" (Luke 23.34). Her farewell as she goes to prison, accompanied by her ladies, combines a sure sense of justice and mercy with a wish for continued grace and an unshaken faith:

> Do not weep, good fools;
> There is no cause. When you shall know your mistress
> Hath deserved prison, then abound in tears
> As I come out. This action I now go on
> Is for my better grace.—Adieu, my lord.
> I never wished to see you sorry; now
> I trust I shall.   (II.i.119–25)

The dignity of this accused queen is founded on her innocence and truth, and these shine forth in the formal trial scene, where, like Katherine of Aragon, Hermione replies to the formal charges read by the Officer.

Her defense is her own integrity and a belief in divine power that will lead to the triumph of innocence and patience, and she appeals to Leontes' conscience to recognize her honor (III.ii.22–54). Confronted with his madness, she observes, "You speak a language that I understand not, / My life stands in the levels of your dreams, / Which I'll lay down" (80–82). She catalogs her losses and, reviled and suffering, sees no reason to fear death. Her last words recall that she is the daughter of the Emperor of Russia (119), one of the interesting changes of location that shift to northern Europe. In the primary source *Pandosto*, many saints' legends, and the "Man of Law's Tale," the accused queen is daughter of the emperor of Rome. Hermione longs for her dead father's presence, would have him see her misery "with eyes / Of pity, not revenge!" (122–23), another imitation of Christ. The trial allows expression of the high sentiment of romance and history, but Shakespeare saves the religious triumph for the scene that he added to Greene's fiction.

In *Pandosto* the accused queen Bellaria dies; Shakespeare rejects this story to show Hermione come alive, a resurrection from the dead that takes place before the audience's eyes and is much more amazing than the unveiling of Hero and reappearance of Helena in the earlier plays. The theatrical device is powerful, not least by contrast to so much narrative reporting—of the tempest, the oracle, the death of Mamilius, the devouring bear, the meeting and reconciliation of the two kings, the recognition and recovery of Perdita. Sophisticated modern critics describe the ambiguity of the play's language, note a "discontinuity between image and text in Renaissance iconographic structures," and thus posit an audience that "found in incomprehensibility a positive virtue" and to whom the play conveyed "intensity, vagueness, and obscurity."[5] But the statue is a tangible object, unusually substantial on stage, and a familiar image.

Shakespeare identifies it as the work of "that rare Italian master Julio Romano, who had he himself eternity and could put breath into his work, would beguile Nature of her custom" (V.ii.98–100). Guilio Romano (1499–1546) is Shakespeare's only cited contemporary artist and one associated with Rome, as a pupil of Raphael. Although Vasari writes of this artist's sculpture, today he is known for paintings and architecture. There are many speculations about him and the statue. Making the artist one of the Italian Renaissance forestalls easy classical allusions, like Ovid's story of Pygmalion's creation of a statue that comes alive or the wonders achieved by Greek sculptors like Zeuxis. In the context of Catholicism the statue, a clothed female form, means the Blessed Virgin Mary, Mother of God and Queen of Heaven, certainly the most famous and frequently sculptured female figure in Europe; there are stories, Miracles of the Virgin, in which a sculpture weeps or speaks. The woodcut for Edward VI in Foxe's *Actes and Monumentes* (Figure 8, following p. 42) shows a man ready to strike down such a statue, part of the stripping of the altars; and in the magnificent Gothic Lady Chapel—a regular feature of church architecture—in Ely Cathedral the statues have been systematically destroyed or at least decapitated. Hermione's statue is placed in a chapel, not a long gallery, the public space of Elizabethan great houses designed for display, through which the company pass on the way to the viewing in the chapel. Perdita is moved to veneration, while acknowledging skepticism about her devotion: "do not say 'tis superstition, that / I kneel and then implore her blessing. Lady, / Dear Queen" (43–45). Shakespeare's image is one of devotion, not of superstitious worshiping a statue but of finding it an aid to prayer, part of affective piety, as millions of Catholics have through the centuries, whether in stone, stained glass, or illuminations of the Hours of the Virgin in *Horae*. It is not difficult to see Shakespeare's introduction of the Queen's statue as a bold enactment of old Roman Catholic practice—and a wish-fulfillment in the habit of romance.

A statue as a sign of reconciliation of religious opponents was topical at this time. King James, son of Catholic Mary Queen of Scots, commissioned two statues of women in 1605, one of his mother, an accused and executed queen, and one of Queen Elizabeth, whose reign effectively imposed the Protestant Reformation in England. These were effigies for their monuments in Westminster Abbey. They were painted, as was the style in the Renaissance; Paulina describes Hermione's statue as "newly fixed; the color's / Not dry," and warns that a kiss—sometimes a part of religious devotion—would stain the lips with "oily painting" (V.iii.47–48, 83). Reforming iconoclasts destroyed medieval images like the Virgin Queen of Walsingham, Mary's greatest shrine in England. A sixteenth-century lament of farewell, perhaps by Philip, Earl of Arundel, describes the destruction of Walsingham with a repetition of "bitter" and "weep" because of "Blessings turned to blasphemies, / Holy deeds to despites. / Sin is where Our Lady sat.'' Yet Mary still received praise from Reformers (Luther, Zwingli, and Calvin) as a model of faith and the Mother of God. Queen Elizabeth subverted Marian iconography by exploiting her virgin status; an extraordinary range of portraits show her as regal and also youthful well into her old age, and even her white funeral monument continues the appeal.

Othello describes Desdemona as ''smooth as monumental alabaster'' (V.ii.5), and his mode of murder preserves her beauty like a funeral effigy. Cleopatra composes herself as an artifact, a regal image in her monument; she dons her robe and crown, and her attendant Charmian perfects the icon by straightening the crown (*Antony and Cleopatra* V.ii.280, 318). Leontes' first response indicates another artistic triumph: ''O royal piece! / There's magic in thy majesty'' (38–39). Modern audiences and critics usually emphasize aesthetics and theatrical excitement, the demands for a willing suspension of disbelief, even the lure of the occult, a subversion shared with the sixteenth century. But the magic, as when Rosalind styled herself ''a magician'' who had ''conversed with a magician, most profound in his art and yet not damnable'' (*As You Like It*, V.ii.69, 59–60), is not witchcraft. The happy ending comes with self-knowledge and surrender, facilitated by ''an old religious man'' (V.iv.157–61), the hermit of romance; penance, faith, and charity precede the reconciliations, as they do in *The Winter's Tale*.

The statue of Hermione shows a woman aged and wrinkled (V.iii.28–29); this is not what Leontes expected, since his image, a vestigial error in perception that stops with surfaces, is of a youthful Hermione. Catholicism insists upon the material world and also upon seeing inside, substance as well as accidents, as in Transubstantiation, the doctrine of the Eucharist. With Time and Penitence Leontes triumphs over the errors of his false accusations, and the recovery of Perdita gives him an heir after the loss of Mamilius, but *The Winter's Tale*, in the mode of resolution in romance, not the mixture in tragi-comedy, ends with sadness and mystery. Wrinkles, sixteen years of loneliness, the eldest son's death—all part of human suffering in the world—are remembered in the last scene, a necessary prelude to the statue's coming alive in a resurrection that is a sign of grace.

In the opening scenes when Hermione is present the language is of ''grace,'' and Perdita, also the daughter of a king and an accused woman, greets the disguised Polixenes and Camillo at the festival with, ''Grace and remembrance be to you both'' (IV.iv.76). Like her mother, Perdita exhibits social graces, as men request, but as noted, her first response to the statue is quiet piety, and her unwillingness to leave initiates the final resolution when Paulina warns, ''resolve you / For more amazement'' (86–87) and explains, ''It is required / You do awake your faith'' (94–95). What is not required are many words. The deepest spiritual understanding, mysticism, is beyond the verbal because full contemplation of God means no-thing, and words explain things. Paulina predicts Hermione's actions, reassuring everyone that they "shall be holy" (104), and Polixenes and Camillo each have a line to describe her movement toward Leontes: she "embraces" and "hangs about his neck" (112–113). Hermione has no words for her husband; her one short speech is a prayer for her daughter: "You gods, look down / And from your sacred vials pour your graces upon my daughter's head!" (121–22), followed by eager questions about the story of Perdita's life. The mother also explains that she lived because "the oracle / Gave hope" that her daughter lived (127–28). Shakespeare thus associates Hermione with the three theological virtues—faith (assent of the mind to the truths revealed by God, the truths or contents of faith that are believed, and the witness given daily by the believer), hope (a firm trust that God wills our salvation and will give us the means to attain it), and charity (love of God above all things, often designated as grace).

This interpretation comes from a sensibility formed by Catholicism and medieval romance, which may explain why Shakespeare favored superficially implausible and complicated old tales over the less richly episodic Italian *novelle.* No subject served him more often than the accused wife and queen, whose unmerited suffering is at the end followed by a restoration of what has been lost and characters transformed through humility and penitence. Such transcendence comes from a benevolent God Who loves humanity that needs only to be open to grace to receive it. This is the meaning of romance that is also closer to the realities of life than either comedy or tragedy or tragi-comedy, all of which lack its complexity of interlace that best represents the human condition. Significantly, Shakespeare took his final accused queen not from a romance or legend but from history. There is a remarkable similarity between the behavior of King Henry VIII and the response of Queen Katherine of Aragon and that of the men and women of romances about accused wives and queens.

Katherine in *Henry VIII*

Many speculate about Shakespeare's return to the English history play—the current consensus is that the play, included in the First Folio, is not a collaboration with Fletcher—after a decade and a half and about his boldness in writing directly of the Tudors and of some controversial religious, social, and political issues of the sixteenth century. Perhaps as a parallel to *The Winter's Tale* seen as fiction, the play's alternative title is *All Is True*, as Prologue specifies. He begins, "I come no more to make you laugh" (1), promises serious and weighty matters that call for pity and tears and that those who "hope they may believe / May here find truth too" (8–9). Prologue admits a fear that "our chosen truth . . . Will leave us never an understanding friend" (18, 22), yet he exhorts the audience, "Be *sad" (serious 25), and poses a theme of fall from "mightiness" to "misery," the medieval exemplum developed in Lydgate's *Fall of Princes* and in the collection begun in Henry VIII's reign, *The Mirror for Magistrates* (1559), and echoed in Wolsey's "Mark but my fall" (III.ii.440). Such stories inspire reflection, not least upon a good death at the end of a life of error. The play's Epilogue reiterates by giving odds, ten to one, that the play "can never please / All that are here" (1–2), and claims at most "The merciful *construction of good women" (interpretation 10), perhaps a Shakespearean play upon Chaucer's *Legend of Good Women*, certainly an indication that the subject is accused queens. In 1613 there were many to consider. Most critics agree that *Henry VIII* is stylistically different from his other histories, closer to the romances of the last years in staging and verbal language and similarly devoted to themes of patience, repentance, forgiveness, and transcendence.

Holinshed's *Chronicles* (1578), like the King James Bible, is the work of a committee; many believe it to be significant largely because it was used by Shakespeare, who relied more closely upon this source in *Henry VIII* than in other history plays. The antiquarian John Stow was among the many who worked on the three-volume second edition (1586–87); and much of the Irish chronicle was by Richard Stanyhurst, who drew upon the notes of his tutor Edmund Campion, the Jesuit whose gruesome martyrdom is described in the Tudor portion.[6] The first edition provoked the authorities because of references to circumstances in Ireland during Henry VIII's reign, and this led to excisions in the midst of publication; in the second edition there were many excisions, especially about Scotland. But the accused Catholic queens, Mary Tudor and Mary Queen of Scots, and religious controversy got softer judgments than the polemics of John Foxe's *Actes and Monuments* that is a source for the challenge to Cranmer in Act V. Close reading of Holinshed shows no simple favoring of Protestant Reform, and there are passages that express horror about religious persecutions. The joy of the people upon the accession of Queen Mary Tudor is set against public distress over her Spanish marriage; she is censured for religious practices, but given compassion and praise for patriotism. Mary, Queen of Scots, a queen much accused of adultery, gets mostly factual treatment with little attention to Calvinist confrontations and nothing of her execution by order of Elizabeth. The victory of Christians over Turks at Lepanto is followed by distress over conflicts among Christians and a case for freedom of conscience, which Annabel Patterson, a new historicist, reads as evidence of a "proto-liberal" agenda. But this is incidental within substantial medieval traditions of obedience and authority, and a blend of legend and history, that explain why others identify Holinshed as "an old fashioned conservative," whose work found less favor in the seventeenth century. In short, Holinshed's *Chronicles* both gave details of Henry VIII's reign and were free from Elizabethan anti-

Catholic severity. Henry has Catholic traces, when he swears ''By holy Mary'' (V.ii.33), after the council fails to give respect to Cranmer as an ecclesiastic, but their charges against the Archbishop's ''new opinions . . . heresies'' (V.iii.17–18) introduce his long apologia, ''ever to do well'' (37), an advocacy of ''love and meekness'' rather than ''ambition'' as proper to a churchman, and an avowal of his own ''patience'' (62–66). Shakespeare does not refer to Henry's treatise against Luther, cautiously disclaimed in the *Chronicles;* but Wolsey calls Anne a ''spleeny Lutheran'' (III.ii.100).

Katharine of Aragon is never accused of sexual betrayal, and Shakespeare's portrait makes much of her saintliness. She is first seen as a good queen who kneels before the King in compassion for the poor in defiance of Cardinal Wolsey's exploitation (I.ii); she also asks Wolsey to ''*Deliver all with charity'' for Buckingham (tell 142), opposes the Surveyor's slander of him (173–75), and concludes ''God mend all!'' (200). In a Tudor world of ambition, conspiracy, and lies, only God is true. Katherine is thus a Catholic with a conscience, not a superstitious follower of the Church. It is asserted that Wolsey acts ''out of malice / To the good Queen'' to plant a scruple in the King's mind (II.i.156–57), but Henry is ''Ful of sad thoughts and troubles'' (II.ii.15); he finds the divorce attractive only after ''his conscience/ Has crept too near another lady'' (18–19). Anne Bullen becomes the second wife, and the birth of her child provides the concluding pageantry of a baptism of ''the royal infant'' with Cranmer's prophesy of thousandfold blessings from ''the maiden phoenix,'' Elizabeth, who will die a virgin (V.v). Readers of this paean to the last Tudor rarely note that Queen Anne will herself soon be an accused queen, found guilty and beheaded. And Cranmer, whose first acts as Henry's appointed Archbishop of Canterbury were to declare the marriage to Katherine invalid and the secret marriage to Anne Bullen valid, lived a dubious career of justifying Henry's many marriages. He subsequently declared the marriage to Anne invalid (and thus Elizabeth illegitimate), facilitated the separation from Anne of Cleeves, the fourth wife, and acted against wife number five, Katherine Howard, another queen accused of adultery, who was executed. Tried by Catholic Queen Mary, Cranmer wrote six recantations, including his theology that was the basis of the newly Established Church. Usually recanted heretics were not executed, but Mary wanted a public spectacle. She got one, but not what she intended. Before an assembled crowd Cranmer recanted the recantations, and at the fire of the stake plunged in his right hand that had signed the paper. Foxe's account of this heroic martyrdom (Figure 17) is pivotal and rehabilitated Cranmer as a Protestant saint. Also well known from the biographies of recusant Catholics was the death of Thomas More, Wolsey's successor as Lord Chancellor, praised as a learned man and wished a long term to ''do justice / For truth's sake and his conscience'' and a good death (III.ii.394–400). More was the Lord Chancellor for The Order of the Coronation of Anne Bullen (IV.i.37ff), but executed two years later. It seems unlikely that many would have missed the irony of the closing panegyrics in *Henry VIII.*

In such a complex context Katherine emerges as singular; for example, when Shakespeare fully develops Holinshed's statement of her departure:

> without anie further answer at that time, or anie other, and never would appear after in anie court. The king perceiving she was departed, said these words in effect: For as much (quoth he) as the queene is gone, I will in hir absence declare to you all, that she hath beene to me as true, as obedient, and as conformable a wife, as I would wish or desire. She hath all the vertuous qualities that ought to be in a woman of hir dignitie, or in anie other of a baser estate, she is also surelie a noble woman borne, hir conditions will well declare the same.   (Bullough IV,468)

Shakespeare's Henry admires her spirit, "Go thy ways, Kate," and he praises her:

> Thou art alone—
> If thy rare qualities, sweet gentleness,
> Thy meekness saintlike, wifelike government,
> Obeying in commanding, and thy part
> Sovereign and pious else, could speak thee out—
> The queen of earthly queens.   (II.iv.134–39)

Shakespeare reminds the audience of this exemplar just before Anne's Coronation; two Gentlemen speak of Katherine's not appearing for the divorce, her retirement, and ill health (IV.i.22–34). History did not allow Shakespeare to restore Katherine to earthly happiness, as he did Hermione, but he alters dates to have her die before the birth of Elizabeth. And one of the most compelling scenes stages a "vision" that resonates with medieval stories of saints and heroes of romance to whom God gives a foretelling of eternal life and their own nearing death. The stage directions indicate that Katherine "makes in her sleep signs of rejoicing, and holdeth up her hands to heaven" (IV.ii.at 85).

This powerful gesture, like the awakening of the statue in *The Winter's Tale*, is only one similarity of Katherine to Hermione, an innocent and falsely accused queen put aside, who bore her husband's unkindness with great dignity and forgiveness; her son died, and her daughter was denied and passed over for the succession. Queen Mary marked her mother's affinity to a related medieval archetype of romance, as in Chaucer's "Clerk's Tale," when her chaplain William Forrest wrote a rhyme royal poem, "Griselde the Second," in 1558. Katherine's story matches Griselda's especially in the divorce after negotiations with Rome to permit her husband to take a beautiful young bride; Shakespeare's

Katherine describes her Griselda-like wifely strengths—humility, constancy, obedience—before the King's authority and Rome's Cardinals (II.iv.20–39, III.i.125–37), and she echoes Griselda in pleading for her daughter. Finally, Katherine's maid in her last scene is called "Patience"—three times by the Queen (IV.ii.76, 127, 165–66) and once by Griffith (82). The type was first presented on the Elizabethan stage in the early 1560s in John Phillip's *The Commodye of Pacient and Meeke Grissill;* and *Patient Grissil*, by Dekker, Chettle, and Haughton, played in 1599–1600.[7] Chaucer's theme is patience in adversity, and a Church Antiphon for Lent urges, "Armed with God's justice and power, let us prove ourselves through patient endurance." Christ praised the poor widow above men of wealth and power and foretold that His followers would suffer and be hated, but promised, "yet there shal not one heere of your heades perish. By your pacience possesse your soules" (Luke. 21.18–19). The Geneva Bible glosses pacience: "That is, liue ioyfully and blessedly, euen vnder the crosse." Hermione, a figure of romance, and Katherine, a Catholic woman in history, live this spiritual joy, gaining through their experience of suffering greater self-knowledge and "better grace."

The nearest male parallels are men after a fall from the top of Fortune's wheel, like Cardinal Wolsey, who is guilty as accused of greed, vanity, and manipulation. He is also the most complex character, in part because Holinshed juxtaposed condemnation and praise, including the account of his final days in George Cavendish's *Life of Wolsey* and Edmund Campion's summary description. Like the guilty Leontes, Wolsey is a penitent. He recognizes that he fell through pride, expresses his contempt of the world, and finds himself "truly happy" and "out of a fortitude of soul" able "to endure more miseries" (III.ii.362, 366, 378, 387–88). Wolsey relies upon his "integrity to heaven" after regretting that he put his service of his earthly king before God's (454, 456). Griffith's report confirms Wolsey's penitence: he asked for "a little earth for charity" and spent his last three days in Leicester Abbey, where he foretold the hour of his death, and

> full of repentance,
> Continual meditations, tears, and sorrows,
> He gave his honors to the world again,
> His blessèd part to heaven, and slept in peace.
>   (IV.ii.27–30)

This resembles Borromeo's Catholic Last Will, like that attributed to John Shakespeare. Of Wolsey's understanding and penitence, Griffith further observes to Katherine:

> That Christendom shall ever speak his virtue.
> His overthrow heaped happiness upon him;

> For then, and not till then, he felt himself,
> And found the blessedness of being little.
> And, to add greater honors to his age
> Than man could give him, he died fearing God.
>
> (63–68)

Having opposed Wolsey's failures in Christian charity, Katherine now demonstrates her own; she recognizes Griffith's account of his good death as "religious truth" and, in reconciliation, is moved to pray for the man who caused her sorrow, "Peace be with him!" (74–75), as she begins "meditating / On that celestial harmony I go to" (79–80). Act IV balances the Coronation of Anne, and the corollary triumph of Protestantism, with the holy deaths of Catholics, supplanted in this world but blessed in eternity. This vision of medieval Christendom does not pale in the final act that culminates in Elizabeth's baptism, when Henry VIII delights in "this oracle of comfort" (another echo of *The Winter's Tale*) and anticipates his place in heaven, without any evidence of self-knowledge or penitence. His last word is to declare a "holiday" (V.v.77); perhaps this respite is also a holy-day, but the "truth" of *Henry VIII* is an inevitable fall from high place by persons in history who limit themselves to this world's ambition. The alternative is the romance model of the accused queen, the woman who achieves a happy ending through patient endurance and suffering with dignity, an imitation of Christ.

As we have seen, throughout his career, beginning with *The Comedy of Errors*, Shakespeare told stories of women, often falsely accused, who survive—albeit in obscurity and exile—and are restored and reconciled to the world. Many improbabilities may suggest fanciful and wishful thinking and imagining, but "all is true" in the historical person of Katherine of Aragon, for Shakespeare England's last Catholic queen, much loved and lamented. His earliest histories centered on Henry VI, immediately revered as a saint after his death but his cult put aside by the Reformers; *Henry VIII* closes a circle with a holy woman. The accused queen of folktale became in medieval romances and legend a type for suffering that is transcended, with a happy ending, if not long of this world.

CONCLUSION

I n this book I have considered Shakespeare, Catholicism, and Romance—all large topics that are unusually provocative because of centuries of evaluation and volatile and personal judgments. No author has received more critical evaluations than Shakespeare, and it is easy to question whether another view is needed or useful. Attitudes toward religion are today deeply personal, political, and provocative; a disenchantment with religion and denials of religious experience vie with aggressive and divergent claims for particular religious beliefs and groups. And historians of the Late Middle Ages and Reformation have proposed a new understanding of the relationship between Catholicism and Protestantism in Elizabethan England and of the complexities of political and economic conditions. Traditional romance is less respectfully read than the more obvious forms of epic, tragedy, comedy, or the novel; and romance is easily misunderstood and often condescended to or reviled as mere fantasy. The issue and counterargument are tersely made in *The Fisher King* (1991), a film modernization of Arthurian romance. Lydia says of popular romances, ''They're only trash''; and the riposte of Parry, the Perceval figure, is: ''There's nothing trashy about romance!''

Endless possibilities for responding to the plays of William Shakespeare began when John Heminges and Henry Condell offered the First Folio ''To the great Variety of Readers'' with the injunction: ''Reade him, therefore; and again, and again: And if then you doe not like him, surely you are in some manifest danger, not to vnderstand him.'' Liking Shakespeare, as popular films and a plethora of Shakespeare festivals make clear, is not the issue. Understanding is more challenging, a source of endless satisfaction and some frustration. Heminges and Condell freely acknowledged that the responses to his plays would be different: ''to your diuers capacities, you will find enough, both to draw, and hold you.''

Twenty-five years ago, an examination of "Shakespeare, Catholicism, and Romance" would have been unlikely, if not impossible. Without the work of recent historians who have published much previously unexplored data and re-evaluated the assumptions of historical analysis, there was not an adequate context for a subtler understanding of Reformations, the nature of institutions of medieval Christendom, some fundamental distinctions between religious and political changes, the contexts of the community in which Shakespeare lived, the differences between laws to enforce the Established Church of England and responses of parish churches, and of individuals to changes of religious definition. Concurrently, there was a vigorous reaction against the medieval and Tridentine heritage of Catholicism, not least among Catholics in their enthusiasm for changes after Vatican II—like the displacing of Gregorian chant and a "stripping of the altars" that had survived the Reformation. But after thirty years there are some survivals and some restorations, as in the sixteenth century: Latin hymns were occasionally heard, statues of Mary and recitations of the Rosary were returned, and liturgies like the Exposition of the Blessed Sacrament were reintroduced.

As I indicated at the outset, I did not expect to "prove" that Shakespeare was a Catholic; indeed I do not believe that it is possible to do this, even if there were a way of resolving the diametrically opposed possible interpretations of the inadequate formal documentation. What has been shown is a likely affinity between Shakespeare and Catholicism. But as E. A. J. Honigman, who has made the strongest case for the "Shakeshaft theory" that ties the playwright to a Catholic household in Lancashire in "the lost years," concludes: "Let us brace ourselves, then, for howls of anguish about a Catholic Shakespeare." Building upon the work of others and his own new discoveries Honigman saw the link (schoolmaster Thomas Cottom) as converting "a possibility into a probability." Thus he challenged the traditional view of Shakespeare as born a Protestant, wrote some anti-Catholic plays, and 'died a Protestant.' Even an acceptance of some Catholic views in *Hamlet* and *Measure for Measure*, and the use of a Catholic pamphlet of religious controversy in *King Lear*, are open to conflicting interpretations—as are many other points. Although Honigman added substantially to a case for a Catholic affinity, he opts for a modification rather than a full revision, when he concludes with a view of Shakespeare as a "lapsed Catholic," a theory easier to accept than a Protestant who briefly strayed back to the old religion. Park Honan's very recent biography concurs with a judgment that Shakespeare, while very sympathetic to Catholics, accommodated himself to conformity, as did many others, in the 1580s, not least because this allowed him to work in the theater. But one can posit great tension as a consequence to justify Honan's reading of the late romances. He stresses Shakespeare's concern with "the needs of reconciliation, mercy, and forgiveness," but finds in these plays a pessimism, a view of society's corruption and threat. This is perhaps consistent with Honan's attribution to Shakespeare of ''an obscure residual . . . self-contempt,'' albeit the testimony of his friends is directly counter. I use these contradictions as an example of ongoing reading through feeling and inconclusiveness. Peter Milward, as part of a comprehensive study of all available religious backgrounds for Shakespeare, added evidence for the Lancashire and Jesuit connections, made a magisterial survey of publications about religious controversies, and steadily urged ''the Catholicism of Shakespeare's plays,'' but he forbears from making claims about religious commitment. Ian Wilson does argue for a Catholic Shakespeare; he has been accused for tracking down every whiff of Rome to make his case—as though this were an unusual scholarly procedure—and thus criticized. Such partisanship is, I think, inevitable, especially in the present academic and political climate. But the howls are quieter as the difficulties of thinking about Shakespeare and Catholicism have somewhat lessened over the years, and I hope that my argument for a Catholic habit of mind and corollary enthusiasm for romance may prove an acceptable alternative way of reading, not least because the romances are the plays most in need of clarification for a modern and postmodern audience that is much removed from the ethos in which the plays were created.

Definers of the romance habitually note that it is a tale of the improbable or incredible, and when compared to the epic, which antedates it, more exotic and less completely tied to specific historical events and the aristocratic classes, and favored by women hearers and readers. Another crucial characteristic is that whereas the epic tends to be rooted indigenously, the romance has a quality of the alien, a response of adapters who find in romance a way of responding to other civilizations and new ways of thought and behavior. This is especially true of the medieval heritage of English romances, which were mostly translated from French, between 1350 and 1450 usually in verse, and the subsequent prose translations, especially those published by William Caxton, and his successors Wynkyn de Word, Richard Pynson, and William Copland in the sixteenth century, all current in Shakespeare's lifetime. The English romances adapt French originals and intensify their moral concerns or appeals to high sentiment to reiterate that pleasure and profit are not separate entities in encounters with literature. A claim for ''merry adventure'' does not preclude an author's intention to move his audience to serious thoughts, often to piety, as the frequent concluding prayers indicate. The romance's many adventures, martial and romantic, are inspired by a wish for excitement, sexual love, and religious faith, and they define human experience as often not logical. A lasting appeal of romance is wish fulfillment, the achievement of a fuller success than was attained in everyday life and a reaffirmation of an ideal that has been lost. Sir Walter Scott, who both restored the romance from eighteenth-century objections and neglect and concurrently created the historical novel, put the case succinctly: "Life could not be endured were it seen in reality."

To show the ideal, which is fundamental in romance, is to remove the restraints of rationality, and this both requires a surrender of some control and expands human possibilities through an opening of the mind and spirit beyond everyday experience. This happens today in westerns, spy stories, and space epics—with their well-known frame of reference of which the reader/viewer usually has little direct experience. There is a limited resemblance between our known world and the purported societies of such stories, and the accidents vary but the substance remains startlingly similar: an ultimately idealized world, with clear behavior of nobility, honor, and grace to stop imminent threats of evil, which inspire the audience. Much depends upon the hearer/reader who surrenders to this subjective experience and thus has a chance to fulfill desires—heroic, passionate, pastoral, exotic, marvelous, dreamlike, mysterious. Every age has its own tensions, violence, fragmentation, disillusion; the particular focus of conflict in sixteenth-century Europe was distinct because the conflict was religious and within Christendom. Professed believers in Christ accused and killed each other, and religion became an extreme political issue. A nostalgia and need for romance, with its high idealism and urging to ideal behavior are thus rooted in a reality of human incoherence and failure. Stories were necessary.

Many critics find the characters and psychological and political insights of Shakespeare, as well as his fluency and poetic genius, so compelling that the stories become only incidental supports for these qualities. In contrast, the late Victorian Sir Walter A. Raleigh observed: "The story came first with him—as it came first with his audience, as it comes first with every child." There are few surviving contemporary accounts of responses to the plays; but several sheets of a commonplace book of Simon Forman, preserved in Bodleian Library Ashmole Ms. 208, ff. 200–13, *Booke of Plaies*, support a case for the primacy of story. This physician and astrologer saw four plays at the Globe, three by Shakespeare—*Macbeth*, *The Winter's Tale*, and *Cymbeline*, recorded respectively as April 20, 1610 (probably an error in Forman's writing), May 15, 1611, and no date—and someone else's *Richard II*, during visits to the theater in April–May of 1611. Essentially Forman summarizes the action of each play, often beginning a paragraph "Remember," but once, for *The Winter's Tale*, he concludes with a moral: "Remember also the Rog [Autolycus] that cam in all tottered . . . and how he feyned him . . . and cosened . . . and cosened them Again of all their money. . . . Beware of trustinge feined beggars or fawning fellouss" (Chambers II,341). Forman is reacting to both the criminal quality and the uncertainty when trust is lost.

Such didacticism expresses a habit of mind in reading romance, and it echoes medieval literary theory and practice in which the fable is the cover for the truth within, or in the homely imagery of Scripture, the chaff to the grain or the shell to the kernel, cited by Chaucer more than once when he sets forth intentions in *The Canterbury Tales*. By this scheme in *The Winter's Tale* the Pygmalion myth or resurrection myth is the substance; and the characters, motives, and half-hearted attempts at explanation that surround it are the shadow. Circumstances of religious controversy and political constraints led Shakespeare to choose the conventions of romance to present his "improbable possibilities." The appeal of *The Winter's Tale* is documented; it remained in the repertoire of the King's Men for twenty-nine years after it was first performed at court in November 1611. But we do not know what the audience perceived: Forman does not mention in his account the most extraordinary and miraculous event on stage—the statue comes alive. I like to think that the scene was so unusual and astonishing that he did not need a note to "Remember," and I acknowledge that this expresses the habit of mind that I have identified as salient in Catholicism and romance.

Memory was the highest creative power in medieval culture.[1] Romantic privileging of the imagination and modern preference for the documentary obscure the vitality of the earlier way that lasted through the Renaissance. Shakespeare's heavy reliance upon earlier stories and his transformation of these texts, as well as his fluency, indicate that he worked within a medieval tradition, also found in classical Rome, that trained the memory. Accounts of Saint Thomas Aquinas describe his dictation to scribes, sometimes three or four at a time, when he "wrote" with great clarity and precision; these indicate how thoroughly and precisely everything was held in his mind, both his knowledge of texts and his mode of organizing. Moreover, Aquinas's memory was a mark of superior moral quality, as it was for other saints like Francis of Assisi, who, *The Golden Legend* tells us, got the name of Francis "for it is known that he received of God by miracle the French tongue" and "by reason of virtuosity in speaking, for his word carved away the vices like an axe." Memory is, then, not a mere process for communicating but how a person assimilates the thoughts of others.

These stories suggest a model to gloss contemporary accounts of Shakespeare's mind and art. Heminge and Condell in their commendation in the First Folio (1623) wrote: "And what he thought, he vttered with that easinesse, that wee haue scarse receiued from him a blot in his papers." Shakespeare's fellow playwright and friend Ben Jonson analyzed this characteristic with a mixture of praise and irritation, in his posthumously published *Timber; or, Discoveries: Made upon Men and Matter* (1640):

I *remember*, the Players have often mentioned it as an honour to *Shakespeare*, that in his writing, (whatsoever he penn'd) hee never blotted out line. My answer hath beene, would he had blotted a thousand. Which they thought a malevolent speech. I had not told posterity this, but for their ignorance, who choose that circumstance to commend their freind by, wherein he most faulted, And to justifie mine owne candor, (for I lov'd the man, and doe honour his memory (on this side Idolatry) as much as any.) Hee was (indeed) honest, and of an open, and free nature: had an excellent *Phantsie*; brave notions, and gentle expressions: wherein hee flow'd with that facility, that sometime it was necessary he should be stop'd: **Sufflaminandus erat*; as *Augustus* said of *Haterius*. His wit was in his own power; would the rule of it had beene so too. His wit was in his owne power; would the rule of it had beene so too.   (Chambers II,210)

[* imagination   **''He needed the drag-chain'' Haterius was a Roman rhetorician (d.26)].

Jonson's judgment of Shakespeare's mental agility shows an uneasiness that signals a change in the criteria of excellence: ''memory'' has assumed its current most frequent meaning of a memorial, not the older trained memory so often noted and highly lauded in Aquinas. Jonson praises Shakespeare's excellent imagination (*Phantsie*) and insists that such easy facility needed to be slowed. The Latin quotation is an early, similar judgment, an authority, and the culprit is a rhetorician who would have been trained in memory.

Shakespeare's control of rhetorical devices is very evident, whether in an early play like *Love's Labour's Lost* with its comic deployment of school exercises, the excesses of the pedant Holofernes and the phrase maker Don Adriano Armado, who is a parody of Euphuism, or in the patterns of *Richard III*, or in his creation of one of the most famous of orators, Mark Antony, who brilliantly demonstrates skills of memory in a seemingly spontaneous threnody in *Julius Caesar*. Part of Invention is Memory, and his friends testify to Shakespeare's capacities. The Middle English word *male* means a traveling bag, but Chaucer also uses it figuratively to refer to a small leather-covered box with internal compartments so that it becomes a metaphor, Carruthers argues convincingly, for an organized space for the riches held in memory that could be drawn out as needed. Stephen Hawes describes the orator's *male* in *The Pastime of Pleasure* (1517) as a place for ''sundry tales and sundry images,'' well ordered according to the matter they treat and thus ready to be used. Pictures as an aid to memory are basic, as the myriad images of medieval Christendom testify. Images tell a story as do words, and manuscripts and churches, as we have seen, combine the two. The woodcuts from Vostre's *Horae* show how this works in a book for devotion; those in *Valentine and Orson* illustrate the same intent in a printed secular romance. In both examples, many of the images are *factotum*, that is they give a broad applicability and point a specific text. Only in the mid-twentieth century did books, particularly fiction, generally not include pictures—except for children. The theater combines spoken words and seen images, and we remember both; in fact, the one aids us to remember the other. The statue in *The Winter's Tale*, with its memory of the Virgin and saints, and Christ's Resurrection, boldly repeats this favored process; and the story of the accused queen voices an experience with many glosses through the centuries. Shakespeare thus looks back to the past when Catholicism and Romance were the modes that gave substance to society; and he makes that past present, which is ours to recover even as we praise the present that he created.

Notes

INTRODUCTION

1. Collected works; e.g., David Bevington's updated fourth edition of *The Complete Works of Shakespeare* (1997), xix–xx, usually promulgate the old view of the Reformation, typified by restricted historiography and more limited data. Bevington introduced "Shakespeare on Religion" after the third edition of 1980, noting "partisan" and then "various" claims for Shakespeare as "a Catholic sympathizer or a loyal moderate Anglican." He concedes that "We can certainly say that Shakespeare consistently avoids the chauvinistic anti-Catholic baiting so often found in the plays of his contemporaries," but urges the non polemical nature of his art and "avoidance of extremes," xxiv–xxv. The latest bibliography includes Fripp's biography, a Puritan view, but still not books with Catholic sympathies; e.g., Peter Milward or Ian Wilson.

2. Schoenbaum favors Protestant biographers, such as Fripp and Rowse, and asserts that "The religious training provided for Shakespeare by his community was orthodox and Protestant" (47). He either denies or denigrates details that suggest Catholic interests (46, 36): John Frith at Temple Grafton is an "unsound priest" (71); the leader of the Jesuits is "notorious Father Parsons" (53); Davies receives attention for the poaching story and Anthony Wood's note on his drinking (79–80), so that "we need not find too puzzling chaplain Davies's claim that he died a Papist" (50). Rather revealingly, Schoenbaum asserts that "Probably Shakespeare remained a tolerant Anglican—after all, he could imaginatively comprehend, if not condone, a Shylock" (50). He admits that "one may conform outwardly as a matter of convenience, to avoid the law's importunities, and still privately nourish heterodoxy or indifference. Thus the scattering of Jews in Elizabethan London survived by conforming to the Anglican Church, but for some at least the conversion must have been prudential." Others think that many Catholics behaved so.

3. Ronald Bridges in *The Bachelors* (London: Macmillan, 1960) and Barbara Vaughan in *The Mandelbaum Gate* (London: Macmillan, 1965). See my *Muriel Spark* (New York: Frederick Ungar, 1984).

4. Eugene Vinaver, "Form and Meaning, The Presidential Address of the Modern Humanities Research Association, 1966," urges that we read medieval romances without classical, humanist preconceptions; he develops this thesis in *The Rise of Romance* (Ox-

ford: Oxford University Press, 1971). See my *The Popularity of Middle English Romance* and "The Humanist Rejection of Romance."

5. See my *The Legend of Guy of Warwick*, 163–236. Ronald S. Crane early established the persistence of the romance tradition in "The Vogue of *Guy of Warwick* from the Close of the Middle Ages to the Romantic Revival," *PMLA* 30 (1915): 125–94, and *The Vogue of Medieval Chivalric Romance during the Renaissance* (Menasha, WI: George Banta, 1919).

6. Although licensed for printing in 1617, and prefaced by a commendatory sonnet written by John Milton, the poet's father, the "Corrected Historie" was never published.

7. See my "*Guy of Warwick*: A Medieval Thriller," *The South Atlantic Quarterly* 73 (1974): 554–63. Ralph Harper's *The World of the Thriller* (Cleveland: Case Western Reserve University, 1969) brilliantly argues the spiritual dimension, relating existential categories in plots of thrillers with concerns of the reader and arguing that the purpose of such modern fiction—that follows from romances and adventure narratives—is "transfiguration" (ix–x).

8. Northrop Frye, *The Secular Scripture: A Study of the Structure of Romance* (Cambridge, MA: Harvard University Press, 1976), 15.

CHAPTER 1 MEDIEVAL CHRISTENDOM

1. Leah Marcus, "Renaissance/Early Modern Studies," in *Redrawing the Boundaries: The Transformation of English and American Literary Studies*, ed. Stephen Greenblatt and Giles Gunn (New York: Modern Language Association, 1992), 41–63. Frank Kermode explores ideological significances of changes in "The Discipline of Literature," *The Modern Language Review* 93 (1998): xxxiii–xxxv. A salutary reminder of the role of personality and the moment in history is Norman F. Cantor, *Inventing the Middle Ages: The Lives, Works, and Ideas of the Great Medievalists of the Twentieth Century* (New York: William Morrow, 1991).

2. *The Medieval Heritage of Elizabethan Tragedy* (1935; Oxford: Basil Blackwell, 1956).

3. In *Medieval Secular Literature: Four Essays*, ed. William Matthews (Berkeley: University of California Press, 1967), 2–4.

4. A good example is Elizabeth Salter, *Piers Plowman: An Introduction* (Oxford: Basil Blackwell, 1962). John Fisher, "To teche hem letterure and curteisye," *The Chaucer Newsletter* 10 (Fall 1988): 1–3, well illustrates changing expectations.

5. *Instructions for Parish Priests by John Myrc*, ed. Edward Peacock, EETS 31 (1902; Kraus Reprint, 1969); *Mirk's Festial: A Collection of Homilies*, ed. Theodor Erbe, EETS ES 96 (1905; Kraus Reprint, 1975).

6. *Religious Pieces in Prose and Verse*, ed. George G. Perry, EETS OS 26 (1867, 1914), 2.

7. This passage illustrates the issue of religious interpretation. Bevington's edition glosses "holy bread" as "ordinary leavened bread that was blessed after the Eucharist and distributed to those who had not received communion" (312). The Variorum notes explain that this is a post-Reformation reading. Catholics have an alternative experience.

8. M. D. Anderson, *History and Imagery in British Churches* (London: John Murray, 1971), 147–48, 263 note 12. G. L. Remnant, *A Catalogue of Misericords in Great Britain* (Oxford: Clarendon Press, 1969) has representative pictures. Illustrated booklets are available in many cathedrals and parish churches; e.g., Mary F. White, *Fifteenth Century Misericords in the Collegiate Church of Holy Trinity, Stratford-upon-Avon* (Stratford-upon-Avon: Philip Bennett, 1974). C. J. P. Cave, *Roof Bosses in Medieval Churches: An Aspect of Gothic Sculpture* (Cambridge: Cambridge University Press, 1948) is a survey with photographs, such as the Jew of Bourges at Norwich.

9. H. S. Bennett, *English Books and Readers 1475 to 1557*, 31–32.

10. Like manuscripts, early printed books use many Latin abbreviations, which I have expanded in brackets, following A Cappelli, *Dizionario di Abbreviature Latine ed Italiane* (Milano: Ulrico Hopeli, 1954).

11. Eamon Dufy's *The Stripping of the Altars*, 227–29, cites a Vostre edition of Sarum usage. Plates 91 and 92 show the same woodcuts that are in my edition of Rouen usage, but they are arranged and placed in different ways and less consistently appropriate.

12. The most famous sequence was at the Cemetery of the Innocents in Paris, made in 1424–25; John Lydgate saw it in 1426 and translated the verses for the pictures that were imitated in the cloister of Pardon Churchyard at St. Paul's. John Stow in *A Survey of London* (1598) gives a crisp account of its destruction in the Reformation: "In the year 1549, on the tenth of Aprill, the said Chappell by commaundement of the Duke of Summerset, was begun to bee pulled downe, with the whole Cloystrie, the daunce of Death, the Tombes, and monuments: so that notheing therof was left, but the bare plot of ground, which is since converted into a garden, for the Pety Canons." Since both Dominicans and Franciscans popularized the Dance of Death, there were many others in Europe, including several mural paintings made in England in the fifteenth and sixteenth centuries. See Florence White, *The Dance of Death*, ed. Florence Warren and Beatrice White, EETS OS 181 (1931; Kraus Reprint, 1971).

13. Holbein completed the woodcuts as a self-imposed work, not a commission, in 1526; but it was not published until 1538, when he was already at the court of Henry VIII, and then anonymously at Lyons, not Basel, where the paintings in the Dominican cemetery were part of his inspiration. Between 1538 and 1562 eleven authentic editions were printed at Lyons and many spurious ones, five between 1555 and 1573 at Cologne. This story indicates the complexity of religion and politics in Tudor England. The fifty-one woodcuts, more separate groups than dance, are reproduced in James M. Clark, *The Dance of Death by Hans Holbein* (London: Phaidon Press, 1947). My discussion draws from the introduction.

14. Helpful on chapbooks are Victor E. Neuburg, *The Penny Histories* (Oxford: Oxford University Press, 1968), Margaret Spufford, *Small Books and Pleasant Histories* (Athens, GA: University of Georgia Press, 1981), and John Ashton, *Chapbooks of the Eighteenth Century* (1882; New York: Benjamin Blom, 1966).

15. Philippe Ariès, *Western Attitudes toward Death*, trans. Patricia Ranum (Baltimore: Johns Hopkins University Press, 1974) uses Roland as the archetype for early medieval "composed death." In *The Hour of Our Death*, trans. Helen Weaver

(New York: Alfred A. Knopf, 1981), Ariés develops the conceptual argument more fully.

16. I am indebted for several references to Peter Milward's two essays on *Hamlet*, in *The Catholicism of Shakespeare's Plays*, 34–47, and *The Medieval Dimension*, 61–73.

17. Pearl Hogrefe, *Tudor Women: Commoners and Queens* (Ames, IA: Iowa State University Press, 1975), xiii, distinguishes between greater numbers of women carrying on their own businesses before 1485–1500 and larger numbers of women acquiring a classical education after 1500. Juliet Dusinberre, *Shakespeare and the Nature of Women* (London: Macmillan, 1975) finds a shift of feminism from courtly to middle class between Elizabethan and Jacobean. Louise Schleiner, *Tudor and Stuart Women Writers* (Bloomington, IN: Indiana University Press, 1994), in a series of case studies, includes comparisons between Protestant and Catholic women writers, finding some of the Catholics to be humanists with a ''much more open-ended and internationalist'' attitude developed as a corollary of exile from the Protestant community. Anticipating such writers was the most distinguished medieval woman of letters, Christine de Pisan (1365–1429?). Caxton printed her *The Book of Fayttes of Armes and of Chyualrye* (1489), which he translated, and *The Morale Proverbes of Cristyne* (1478), translated by Earl Rivers; Wynkyn de Worde published a third edition of the latter in 1528. Bryan Anslay translated and published *The Book of the City of Ladies* (1521); this defense of women against male myths contains, e.g., a version of *Le Bone Florence*, one of the romances of accused queens, as a Miracle of the Virgin.

CHAPTER 2 REFORMATION CHANGES AND LINGERING IMAGES

1. The data are interesting. Each page of the *Concordance* has three columns for a total of about 355 entries to the page. A cluster of *law, lawful, laws* fills an entire page, as does *just*, while *judge* and *judgment* take two columns, and *trial* about half a column. In comparison, *church* takes a column, *religion* and *religious* take less than half a column, and *priest* and *priestly* about two-thirds.

2. *The New Oxford Book of Sixteenth Century Verse*, ed. Emrys Jones (Oxford: Oxford University Press, 1991), 550–51. The lyric (Bodleian Library MS Rawl. Poet. 219, fol. 16) may be the work of Philip, Earl of Arundel. For Shakespeare's relation to monasticism, see de Groot, 204–9; Mutschmann and Weltersdorf, 291–98; Milward, *Shakespeare's Religious Background*, 179–81. De Groot's detailed comparison of *King John* with *The Troublesome Raigne*, 180–224, shows it as not anti-Catholic. Honan, who does not mention this interpretation, reaffirms Shakespeare's sympathy with Catholics but distance from youthful pieties and consequent sharpness in the play.

3. Madeleine H. Dodds, *The Pilgrimage of Grace, 1536–37, and the Exeter Conspiracy, 1538* (1915; London: F. Cass. 1971) describes the circumstances. Dickens stresses social and economic motivations; Haigh, an expert on Lancashire, urges religious inspiration.

4. D. Cressy, *Literacy and Social Order: Reading and Writing in Tudor and Stuart England* (Cambridge: Cambridge University Press, 1980), 104–69. See also J. W. Ad-

amson, "The Extent of Literacy in England in the 15th and 16th Centuries; Notes and Conjectures," *The Library* 10 (1929): 186, that includes surveys of literacy.

5. Quoted by Duffy, 533.

6. Alan Keen and Roger Lubbock, 14. The scope of the annotation is substantial: 406 notes, equaling 3,600 words, as well as "sundry crosses and underlinings," (7, 9).

7. Duffy, 573–86, citing from *English Church Furniture, Ornaments and Decorations at the Period of the Reformation: As Exhibited in a List of the Goods Destroyed in Certain Lincolnshire Churches, AD 1566,* ed. Edward Peacock (London, 1866), and the continuations by C. W. Foster, Lincolnshire *Notes and Queries* 14 (1917): 78–88, 109–16,144–51,166–73.

8. Haigh, *The English Reformation Revised,* 24, quoting from *Yorkshire Diaries and Autobiographies* (Surtees Society, LXV, 1877), 137.

9. *Toxophilus* in *English Works of Roger Ascham,* ed. William Aldis Wright (Cambridge: Cambridge University Press, 1904); *The Scholemaster,* ed. Edward Arber in English Reprint Series (1870).

CHAPTER 3 THE SHAKESPEARES OF STRATFORD

1. Jaroslav Pelikan, *Mary through the Centuries: Her Place in the History of Culture* (New Haven: Yale University Press, 1996) and Bertrand Buby, *The Marian Heritage of the Early Church* (1996) are recent surveys. Less conservative analyses are Geoffrey Ashe, *The Virgin* (London: Routledge & Kegan Paul, 1976), Marina Warner, *Alone of All Her Sex: The Myth and the Cult of the Virgin Mary* (1976; New York: Vintage, 1983); and Maurice Hamington, *Hail Mary? The Struggle for Ultimate Womanhood in Catholicism* (London: Routledge, 1995).

2. As noted previously, Chambers accepts the Will as authentic (I, 16); de Groot reviews the arguments thoroughly, 64–110. He includes, e.g., Sir Sidney Lee's declaration that it was "a forgery," in *The Life of Shakespeare* (1898–1915), and the denigration of C. R. Haines in *The Quarterly Review* for October 1921: "the so-called will of John Shakespeare, an absurd rigmarole found like a dead mouse behind the wainscot of the birthplace, still meets with ardent champions among Roman Catholics"; and a list of sixteen biographers who do not mention the will. Something more than Catholic partisanship became clear with the discovery in the British Museum in about 1923 of the first version of Cardinal Borromeo's *Testament or Last Will of the Soul*; this was followed by the identification of other versions that prove the will a formula of devotion. de Groot, 64–110, prints the texts and reviews issues; Mutschmann and Wentersdorf, 54–62, supply additional details and modernized texts. Schoenbaum, *A Documentary Life,* 41–46, has facsimiles of Malone's transcript in *The Plays and Poems of William Shakespeare* (1790) and of Carlo Borromeo, *The Testament of the Soule* (1638), the "unique copy" of the "only authentic English text" acquired by the Folger Library in 1966. Schoenbaum perpetuates the denial of authenticity: "For clues to Shakespeare's religion we must turn to other sources, and as regards his father's Spiritual Last Will and Testament settle (as on other occasions) for a secular agnosticism," 46.

3. Malone had investigated the will's authenticity through a series of inquiries, but he changed his mind and in 1796 denied it. His memorandum about William Shake-

speare's legal will states: "It commences with a pious declaration of his religious principles, but affords not the slightest countenance to a notion which has been started, of Shakespeare being a Roman Catholick. To this supposition, I myself may have given some support by the publication some years ago, of a singular manuscript, purporting to be the confession of faith of John Shakespeare, . . . I am now convinced that I was altogether mistaken." James Boswell included this note, but not the will, in the posthumous *Third Variorum*. Here is another tantalizing example of the thriller dimension of scholarship.

4. I quote from the version with modern spelling, Mutschmann & Wentersdorf, 394–95.

5. Emrys Jones, *The Origins of Shakespeare* (Oxford: Oxford University Press, 1977) and H. A. Kelly, *Divine Providence in the England of Shakespeare's Histories* (Cambridge, MA: Harvard University Press, 1970). Cf. Ian Wilson, 100–110.

6. Many argue that Shakespeare's living with a Huguenot family at Silver Street, Cripplegate, in the city of London, after moving from Southwark—where there is no evidence of his participation as an Anglican—supports the case for his being Protestant. But there is an alternative: Huguenots were free to practice their religion and not required to attend Anglican services, so that being in the household could have been a way of avoiding forced attendance at the Anglican Church. The lawsuit of Belott-Mountjoy in 1612 shows that the association between Shakespeare and the family, for more than ten years, was a close one (Chambers II, 90–95). Cf. J. J. Walsh, "Was Shakespeare a Catholic?" *The Catholic Mind*, XIII (1915).

7. Chambers II, 169–80, and Mutschmann and Wentersdorf, 186–95, review the implications. Schoenbaum, 243–49, has a facsimile. His discussion sustains his secular view: he identifies the opening as a "pious declaration," but then asserts: "To find here a confession of personal faith is to consider the matter too curiously. The preamble is formulaic, following almost word for word . . ." (246). By this logic any recitation of a prayer—Pater Noster, Credo, Ave Maria—or the words of a ritual or sacrament would also not be a sign of piety. Moreover, many literary critics do not regard the use of formulaic expression as an uncertain or limited choice.

8. Frank Kermode, "The Discipline of Literature," incisively describes changes of recent years and sounds an urgent warning against current dominant trends.

CHAPTER 4 THE ROMANCE MODE: MEDIEVAL ORIGINS AND SOME REWORKINGS

1. *The Romance* (London: Methuen, 1970), 37–38.

2. Quotations are from *The English Works of John Gower*, ed. G. C. Macaulay, EETS ES 81 and 82 (1900; rpt. 1957).

3. See Elizabeth Archibald, *Apollonius of Tyre: Medieval and Renaissance Themes and Variations, Including the Text of the Historia Apollonii Regis Tyri with an English Translation* (Cambridge: D. S. Brewer, 1991). The daughter's flight from an unnatural father is also in the Constance saga, told by Chaucer and Gower from Trivet, and *Emaré*.

4. Douai is explicit: "Now all these things happened to them as a *type*." (my italics).

5. Two analyses illustrate the wide variety of ways of reading texts: R. Chris Hassel, Jr., *Renaissance Drama & the English Church Year* (Lincoln, NE: University of Nebraska Press, 1979), documents the relation of performance to feast, and Scriptural relevance for *The Comedy of Errors* and Holy Innocents Day, 37–42; Patricia Parker, *Shakespeare from the Margins: Language, Culture, Context* (Chicago: University of Chicago Press, 1996), concludes that the most apt description of the play, even with its heavy use of Biblical matter and structural analog, is "post-Christian" (82).

6. Peter Milward, "Shakespeare and Elizabethan Exorcism," reviews the playwright's continuity of interest in the subject in *The Medieval Dimension*, 46–58.

7. J. Dover Wilson, ed. *The Two Gentlemen of Verona* (Cambridge: Cambridge University Press, 1921), xvi, following the lead of Arthur Quiller-Couch, argues a "botcher's hand," a badly transmitted, mutilated text used by the printer.

8. Robert G. Hunter, *Shakespeare and the Comedy of Forgiveness*, 85–87.

9. *Sir Eglamour of Artois*, ed. Frances E. Richardson, EETS OS 256 (1965).

10. *Valentine and Orson*, trans. from the French by Henry Watson, ed. Arthur Dickson, EETS OS 204 (1937). See also Arthur Dickson, *Valentine and Orson: A Study in Late Medieval Romance* (New York: Columbia University Press, 1929) and my *Popularity*, 105–18.

11. *Amis and Amiloun*, ed. MacEdward Leach, EETS OS 203 (1937). Leach's thorough review of the sources and folk motifs is a useful introduction to the nature of romance. He argues that the romance is fundamentally a testing of friendship, in contrast to the Christian meaning in the hagiographic versions. William Calin, *The Epic Quest: Studies in Four Old French Chansons de Geste* (Baltimore: Johns Hopkins University Press, 1966), 57–111, argues the poem's doctrinal core. See my *Popularity*, 92–105.

12. Floris Delattre, *English Fairy Poetry: From the Origins to the Seventeenth Century* (London: Henry Frowde, 1912) and Minor White Latham, *The Elizabethan Fairies: The Fairies of Folklore and the Fairies of Shakespeare* (New York: Columbia University Press, 1930). Shakespeare's friend Michael Drayton most elegantly develops the tiny size in *Nimphidia*. Nineteenth-century painting richly explores fairies; well presented in *Victorian Fairy Painting*, a catalog for the Royal Academy of Arts Exhibition (London: Merrell Holberton, 1997), including the exquisite, fanciful, richly detailed paintings of Alan Paton, *The Quarrel of Titania and Oberon* (1849) and *The Reconciliation of Titania and Oberon* (1847), both now in the National Gallery of Scotland, Edinburgh.

13. My discussion is based on the text in *Select Remains of the Ancient Popular and Romance Poetry of Scotland*, collected and ed. David Laing and re-ed. John Small (Edinburgh: William Blackwood and Sons, 1885), 137–66. This is the version in the Thornton Manuscript, Lincoln Cathedral 91, a mid-fifteenth-century collection that combines romances and devotional pieces in its sixty items. Texts have significant differences, and Laing included from other versions lines missing in Thornton. *The Romance and Prophecies of Thomas of Erceldoune*, ed. James A. H. Murray, EETS OS 61 (1875: facsimile rpt. Llanerch Publishers, Felinfach, 1991), prints four parallel texts and illustrative fifteenth- and sixteenth-century prophecies.

14. J. Q. Halliwell [Phillipps],"Illustrations of the Fairy Mythology of *Midsummer Night's Dream*," *Shakespeare Society* 26 (London, 1845): 58, noted the metrical romance's aptness.

15. "An English Prophecy of Gladsmoor, Sandisford, and Seyton and the Seye, Predicted of 1553," in BL Sloane MS 2578, tells of Pole's coming out of Rome to win London, fighting at Charing Cross, freeing prisoners from the Tower; of the King's riding to London and the slaying of priests and their servants, warnings of a hermit of France to Englishmen, and so on. Printed as Appendix III in Murray, 62–63.

16. See my "Pacience in adversitee: Chaucer's Presentation of Marriage," *Viator* 10 (1979): 323–54.

17. *Records of Early English Drama: Coventry*, ed. R. W. Ingram (Toronto: University of Toronto Press, 1981).

18. David Wallace, *Chaucerian Polity: Absolutist Lineages and Associational Forms in England and Italy* (Stanford, CA: Stanford University Press, 1997), in "Chaucer as Bottom the Weaver" ties *A Midsummer Night's Dream* to a declining crafts culture and offers a Chaucerian view of the play as "politically pusillanimous" (123) that is slightly offset by Act V's "intuitive, even restorative, understanding of Chaucerian poetics" (124). Wallace reads by way of "modern Marxist historiography, gender theory, and cultural studies" (jacket), in which Catholicism does not enter. But his "Conclusion" observes: "Shakespeare's evocation of the culture that dies with Sir John [Falstaff] is so potent that we might want to connect it with memories of Catholic and guild-rooted Stratford and Coventry, worlds but recently vanished," 383.

19. Quoted in *Chaucer: The Critical Heritage, Volume I, 1385–1837*, ed. Derek Brewer (London: Routledge and Kegan Paul, 1978), 98.

20. Jay L. Halio's "General Introduction" to the Oxford World's Classics ed., *The Merchant of Venice* (New York: Oxford University Press, 1993), 1–13, suggests the restricted nature of Elizabethan interpretation of the Judaic tradition.

21. James Shapiro, *Shakespeare and the Jews* (New York: Columbia University Press, 1996) develops this point in Chapter 5. This book puts the Jewish case aggressively.

22. "The Religious Implications of *The Merchant of Venice*," in *The Medieval Dimension*, 29–45, and a fuller analysis in *The Catholicism of Shakespeare's Plays*, 13–21. Also helpful is his *Shakespeare's Religious Background* .

23. *Sir Amadace*, 811–16, in *Six Middle English Romances*, ed. Maldwyn Mills (Totowa, NJ: Rowman and Littlefield, 1973).

24. *The Lyf of the Noble and Crysten Prynce Charles the Grete*, ed. Sidney J. H. Herrtage EETS ES 36 and 37 (1880 and 1881; rpt. 1967), 96.

Chapter 5 Understanding the Romance Mode

1. There are many studies of the Robin Hood tradition and outlawry. Current, accessible, and comprehensive is *Robin Hood and Other Outlaw Tales*, ed. Stephen Knight and Thomas Ohlgren, Medieval Institute Publications TEAMS series (Kalamazoo, MI: Western Michigan University Press, 1997), with primary texts, including *Gamelyn*, and introductions.

2. C. S. Lewis, *English Literature in the Sixteenth Century Excluding Drama* (Oxford: Clarendon Press, 1954), 409. For a recent evaluation see Sarah Hilsman, "Thomas Lodge," in Hager, *Major Tudor Authors*, 309–15.

3. *Robert the Devil* is one of the most famous of European legendary romances with more than a hundred texts surviving. See my *Popularity*, 68–75.

4. The Black Death traversed and decimated England in 1348–49, but lesser outbreaks continued in the sixteenth century, and indeed were the occasion for the closing of the theaters. Key periods during Shakespeare's working career were: June 1592–May 1594, when theaters were closed most of the time; March 1603–April 1604, when they were open only occasionally; 1605–09, when there were occasional closures.

5. F. W. Bateson, *A Guide to English Literature*, 2d ed. (New York: Anchor, 1968), 44–48, argues an economic approach. Lawrence Stone, *The Causes of the English Revolution, 1529–1642* (London: 1972) finds that between 1540 and 1640: "The number of peers rose from 60 to 160; baronets and knights from 500 to 1400; esquires from perhaps 800 to 3000; and armigerous gentry from perhaps 5,000 to 15,000," 72.

6. See John Scattergood, "*The Tale of Gamelyn*: The Noble Robber as Provincial Hero," in Meale, *Readings*, 159–94, and Nancy Mason Bradbury, *Writing Aloud*, 23–64.

7. Peter Milward has some helpful readings in *The Catholicism*, 22–33.

8. *Summa Theologica*, 2d part of the 2d part, Question 184.

9. Medieval French *chansons* identified three "matières"—France, Britain, Rome the Great—and the Normans assured that tales of Charlemagne, Arthur, and Troy, Thebes, Alexander were part of the literature in conquered lands. The many romances about heroes with Northern origins have led modern critics to identify a Matter of England, to which Shakespeare responds.

10. The usual attribution to Shakespeare is Act I, Act II.i, Act III.i and ii, Act IV.iii, Act V except ii. See Bevington, 1559.

CHAPTER 6 LOST MEN AND WOMEN: SUFFERING AND TRANSCENDENCE

1. Bede, *A History of the English Church and People*, trans. Leo Sherley-Price, rev. ed. R. E. Latham (Harmondsworth, England: Penguin Books, 1968), 300–1.

2. J. M. Nosworthy, ed. "*Cymbeline* as Experimental Romance," The Arden Edition of *Cymbeline* (Cambridge, MA: Harvard University Press, 1955), xlix–lxiii, sets out challenges, and concludes that Shakespeare's attempt is "prone to partial or total failure" (xlix).

CHAPTER 7 THE ROMANCE MODE ATTAINED: ACCUSED WIVES AND QUEENS

1. Early and still useful are Margaret Schlauch, *Chaucer's Constance and Accused Queens* (New York: New York University Press, 1927) and Laura Hibbard [Loomis], *Medieval Romance in England*. Marijane Osborn, *Romancing the Goddess: Three Middle English Romances About Women* (Urbana: University of Illinois Press, 1998) reevaluates the subject, as "castaway queens," and employs feminist and anthropological theories;

she includes her modern verse translations of *Émare, Le Bone Florence of Rome* (Part II), and Chaucer's "Man of Law's Tale."

2. The text is one of *Six Middle English Romances*, ed. Maldwyn Mills, which also has *Sir Isumbras* and *Emaré*.

3. Dickson, *Valentine and Orson*, EETS OS 204, xliv–li, has a useful descriptive list of the woodcuts, including how they are repeated, and a selected list of other books in which they appear. But his descriptions are brief and not always adequate; e. g., #5 "A bit of landscape" does not mention the crucial lost infants, bear, and human.

4. For the broad context, see Duffy, *Saints and Sinners*, 167–81.

5. Stephen Orgel, ed. *The Winter's Tale* (New York: Oxford University Press, 1996), 1–12.

6. See Louis A. Gebhard, "Raphael Holinshed," in Hager, *Major Tudor Authors*, 245–53, and Annabel Patterson, *Reading Holinshed's Chronicles* (Chicago: Chicago University Press, 1994).

7. Helen Cooper, *Oxford Guides to Chaucer: The Canterbury Tales* (Oxford: Oxford University Press, 1989), 422–24, discusses the likely influence of Chaucer on Shakespeare.

CONCLUSION

1. Mary Carruthers, *The Book of Memory: A Study of Memory in Medieval Culture* (Cambridge: Cambridge University Press, 1990) gives many examples, beginning with a comparison of contemporary descriptions of Aquinas and Einstein to show their similarities. "The difference is that whereas now geniuses are said to have creative imagination which they express in intricate reasoning and original discovery, in earlier times they were said to have richly retentive memories, which they expressed in intricate reasoning and original discovery," 4. Murray J. Evans, *Rereading Middle English Romance: Manuscript Layout, Decoration, and the Rhetoric of Composite Structure* (Montreal: McGill-Queen's University Press, 1995) describes twenty-six manuscripts and how their iconographic devices for memory work, especially the problematic secular/religious distinction.

A Bibliographical Note

The materials for the study of Shakespeare are quite overwhelming in variety and bulk. Here I indicate only some of the studies that I have especially relied upon; almost all have extensive bibliographies for further reading. The standard sources for the biography are E. K. Chambers, *William Shakespeare: A Study of Facts and Problems*, 2 vols. (Oxford: Oxford University Press, 1930) and S. Schoenbaum, *William Shakespeare: A Documentary Life* (Oxford: Oxford University Press, 1975). F. E. Halliday, *A Shakespeare Companion 1564–1964* (Harmondsworth: Penguin Books, 1964) is a very helpful reference, as is *Four Centuries of Shakespeare Criticism*, ed. Frank Kermode (New York: Avon Books, 1965). Marvin Spevack, *The Harvard Concordance to Shakespeare* (Cambridge, MA: Belknap Press of Harvard University Press, 1973) greatly facilitates study.

Important biographies are: Edgar I. Fripp, *Shakespeare, Man and Artist*, 2 vols. (London: Oxford University Press, 1938), which is knowledgeable about Warwickshire and written from a strongly Protestant point of view, as is Thomas Carter, *Shakespeare: Puritan and Recusant* (Edinburgh: Oliphant Anderson & Ferrier, 1897). John Henry de Groot, *The Shakespeares and "The Old Faith"* (New York: King's Crown Press, 1946) focuses on John Shakespeare's religion and will (not mentioned by sixteen biographers), the religious training of Shakespeare and increasing Protestant elements in the Established Church, and Catholicism in the plays, especially *King John* that he argues is not anti-Catholic or anti-Papal. Heinrich Mutschmann and Karl Wentersdorf, *Shakespeare and Catholicism* (New York: Sheed and Ward, 1952) is more comprehensive and a forceful argument with a systematic identification of Catholic dogma and its exact application to biographical evidence, including the Catholicism of friends and people in the theater, and of the plays. Peter Milward's *Shakespeare's Religious Background* (London: Sidgwick & Jackson, 1973) is a broader survey of religious issues and practice, including Anglican and Puritan as well as Catholic, the political contexts of the Reformation, and analyses of theology and ethical viewpoints. Ian Wilson, *Shakespeare: The Evidence. Unlocking the Mysteries of the Man and His Work* (London: Headline Book Publishing, 1993) reviews previous studies, makes the connections, and advances the most aggressive argument for Shakespeare's Catholicism. Park Honan, *Shakespeare: A Life* (Oxford: Oxford University Press, 1998) interlaces biographical materials with social history and evidence in the works to show a Catholic affinity; he concludes that Shakespeare was, like most, a lapsed Catholic.

Crucial to the argument for Shakespeare's affinity to Catholicism is the relation to Lancashire. Oliver Baker, *In Shakespeare's Warwickshire and the Unknown Years* (London: Simpkin Marshall, 1937) first made the connection between Shakespeare and the "Shakeshafte" mentioned in records of the recusant Houghton family in Lancashire and implied that Shakespeare was a practicing Catholic as a teenager. E. K. Chambers, *Shakespearean Gleanings* (Oxford: Oxford University Press, 1944) developed the theory. Alan Keen and Roger Lubbock, *The Annotator: The Pursuit of an Elizabethan Reader of Halle's Chronicle Involving Some Surmises About the Early Life of William Shakespeare* (London: Putnam, 1954) added data about Catholic aristocracy in Lancashire, on the Continent and in London; they made Shakespeare connections, and even posited that the youth might briefly have gone to Douai with Hunt, as did his schoolmate Debdale. E. A. J. Honigman, *Shakespeare: the "Lost Years"* (Manchester: Manchester University Press, 1985; rev. 1998) most fully presents the connection of the recusancy of Lancashire and Shakespeare's biography; it centers on the Houghtons of Houghton Tower. Richard Wilson reasserted and developed the arguments in "Shakespeare and the Jesuits," *TLS*, December 19, 1997, 11–13; and Peter Milward commented, *TLS*, January 2, 1998, 15. Christopher Haigh, *The Last Days of the Lancashire Monasteries and the Pilgrimage of Grace* (Manchester: Chetham Society, 1969) and *Reformation and Resistance in Tudor Lancashire* (Cambridge: Cambridge University Press, 1975) present essential data.

Eamon Duffy, *The Stripping of the Altars: Traditional Religion in England 1400–1580* (New Haven: Yale University Press, 1992) is a monumental study of the lasting strength of medieval Catholicism. He addressed the question, "Was Shakespeare a Catholic?" in *The Tablet* 27 (April 1996): 538, to make several points: that Shakespeare grew up in a community saturated with Catholic sympathies, consistently treated Catholic themes with sympathy, and was certainly not a Protestant writer. The systematic political suppression of a vital Catholic community experience is charted in Harold Gardiner, *Mysteries' End: An Investigation of the Last Days of the Medieval Religious Stage* (New Haven: Yale University Press, 1946). Eamon Duffy's *Saints and Sinners: A History of the Popes* (New Haven: Yale University Press, 1997), written to accompany six television programs about the Papacy, gives many perspectives about the workings of Rome through the centuries. *The Christian Faith: Doctrinal Documents of the Catholic Church*, ed. J. Neuner, S. J. and J. Dupuis, S. J., 5th ed. (New York: Alba House, 1990) is an important source, while *Medieval Liturgy: A Book of Essays*, ed. Lizette Larson-Miller (New York: Garland, 1997) discusses the Eucharistic liturgy, other rites, and some controversies.

A. G. Dickens, *The English Reformation* (1964; rev. Cambridge: Cambridge University Press, 1987) was the dominant view that gave greatest emphasis to evangelical Protestants and little to Catholics; see also his *Reformation and Society in Sixteenth-century Europe* (London: Thames and Hudson, 1966) and *The Counter Reformation* (London: Thames and Hudson, 1968), both in the Library of European Civilization. J. J. Scarisbrick, *The Reformation and the English People* (Oxford: Oxford University Press, 1984) redressed the balance to show opposition, already demonstrated by G. R. Elton, *Policy and Police: the Enforcement of the Reformation in the Age of Thomas Cromwell*

(Cambridge: Cambridge University Press, 1972). *The Reign of Elizabeth I*, ed. Christopher Haigh (Athens, GA: The University of Georgia Press, 1985) includes his study of "The Church of England, the Catholics and the People," as well as an introduction and conclusion, and Patrick Collinson's "The Elizabethan Church and the New Religion," in a volume that challenges reflexive and unmitigated enthusiasm for the Virgin Queen. *The English Reformation Revised* (Cambridge: Cambridge University Press, 1987), ed. Christopher Haig is a collection of articles, most reprinted, that indicate the range of topics: Stephen Lander, "Church Courts and the Reformation in the Diocese of Chichester"; Margaret Bowker, "The Henrician Reformation and the Parish Clergy"; D. M. Palliser, "Popular Reactions to the Reformation during the Years of Uncertainty, 1530–70"; Ronald Hutton, "The Local Impact of the Tudor Reformations"; R. H. Pogson, "Revival and Reform in Mary Tudor's Church: A Question of Money"; Gina Alexander, "Bonner and the Marian Persecutions"; Haigh, "The Recent Historiography of the English Reformation," "Anticlericalism and the English Reformation," "The Continuity of Catholicism in the English Reformation," as well as the introduction and conclusion. Haigh's *English Reformations: Religion, Politics and Society under the Tudors* (Oxford: Clarendon Press, 1993) is a longer, more conceptual study. Helpful among studies of Catholics in pre-Reformation England are: David Knowles, *The Religious Orders in England*, 3 vols. (Cambridge: Cambridge University Press, 1959) and Anne Hudson, *The Premature Reformation: Wycliffite Texts and Lollard History* (Oxford: Clarendon Press, 1988) that makes the case for the opponents of the Church; and in post-Reformation England, *The Other Face: Catholic Life Under Elizabeth I*, ed. Philip Caraman (1960), John Bossy, *The English Catholic Community, 1570–1850* (London: Darton, Longman, and Todd, 1975), and Peter Holmes, *Resistance and Compromise: The Political Thought of the Elizabethan Catholics* (Cambridge: Cambridge University Press, 1982).

Extremely helpful are Peter Milward, *Religious Controversies of the Elizabethan Age: A Survey of Printed Sources* (London: The Scolar Press, 1977) and *Religious Controversies of the Jacobean Age: A Survey of Printed Sources* (London: The Scolar Press, 1978), annotated bibliographies with a topical organization and the starting point for investigation. H. S. Bennett, *English Books and Readers 1475 to 1557* and *English Books and Readers, 1558–1603*, 2d ed. (Cambridge: Cambridge University Press, 1969 and 1965), explain much about printing and audience. There are a vast number of books and pamphlets, many surviving in single or few copies. Very evocative are contemporary writings like *The Miracles of Henry VI*, ed. Ronald Knox and S. Leslie (Cambridge: Cambridge University Press, 1923); *Autobiography of an Elizabethan Gentleman John Gerard*, trans. Philip Caraman (1960), a Jesuit account; and William Allen's *A True, Sincere and Modest Defence of English Catholics that suffer for their faith both at home and abroad, against a false, seditious and slanderous libel, entitled: "The Execution of Justice in England,"* 2 vols. (St. Louis: B. Herder, 1914), with modernized spelling. A good sampling of texts is John R. Roberts, *A Critical Anthology of English Recusant Devotional Prose, 1558–1603* (Pittsburgh: Duquesne University Press, 1966) that has a general introduction. Ceri Sullivan, *Dismembered Rhetoric: English Recusant Writing, 1580 to 1603* (Madison, NJ: Fairleigh Dickinson University Press, 1995) considers devotional texts to show how they were rhetorically skilled and a part of missionary efforts.

---

228   *A Bibliographical Note*

Several biographies of Tudor figures illuminate and evoke the circumstances of Catholicism, e.g., Philip Caraman, *Henry Garnet, 1555–1606, and the Gunpowder Plot* (London, 1964). Particularly memorable are Evelyn Waugh, *Edmund Campion: Jesuit and Martyr* (1946: Garden City, NY: Image Books, 1956) that includes a description of Campion's mission, including the move toward Houghton, where he had stayed previously and left papers; and most recently Peter Ackroyd, *The Life of Thomas More* (New York: Nan A. Talese, 1998), which reflects revisionist Reformation history. Alan Hager, *Major Tudor Authors: A Bio-Bibliographical Critical Sourcebook* (Westport, CT: Greenwood Press, 1997), has current evaluations, and the editor's remark that "When I saw what I had, I was initially surprised by the number of Roman Catholic authors" (xi).

Quotations are from David Bevington's *The Complete Works of Shakespeare*, updated 4th ed. (New York: Longman, 1997). Single play editions have helpful notes, especially the Variorum Shakespeare, Arden Shakespeare, and Oxford Shakespeare World's Classics. I often cite Geoffrey Bullough, ed. *Narrative and Dramatic Sources of Shakespeare*, 8 vols. (London, 1957–75); and romances, plays, and other medieval texts published by Oxford University for the Early English Text Society (EETS), with details in the Notes. I quote from *The Golden Legend; or, Lives of the Saints as Englished by William Caxton*, ed. F. S. Ellis, 7 vols. (London: J. M. Dent, 1900). *Gesta Romanorum; or, Entertaining Moral Stories*, trans. and ed. Charles Swan and Wynard Hooper (1876; New York: Dover, 1959) has many more stories than Bullough. Passages from Scripture are from the most popular sixteenth-century English translation, highly influential for sermons and literary works, and frequently echoed in Shakespeare's plays, *The Geneva Bible: A Facsimile of the 1560 Edition*, intro. Lloyd E. Berry (Madison, Milwaukee, London: The University of Wisconsin Press, 1969). Comparisons can be made with the Douai-Rheims Old and New Testaments, which were published later.

Among many books of literary criticism about Shakespeare and romance are: G. Wilson Knight, *The Crown of Life: Essays in Interpretation of Shakespeare's Final Plays* (1947; New York: Barnes & Noble, 1966); E. C. Pettet, *Shakespeare and the Romance Tradition* (London: Methuen, 1949); Derek Traversi, *Shakespeare: The Last Phase* (New York, 1954); *Later Shakespeare*, ed. John Russell Brown and Bernard Harris, Stratford-upon-Avon Studies 8 (London: Edward Arnold, 1966); R. A. Foakes, *Shakespeare: From the Dark Comedies to the Last Plays* (Charlottesville, VA: University of Virginia Press, 1971); Douglas L. Peterson, *Time Tide and Tempest: A Study of Shakespeare's Romances* (San Marino, CA: The Huntington Library, 1973). Leah Scragg, *Shakespeare's Mouldy Tales* (London: Longman, 1992) and *Shakespeare's Alternative Tales* (London: Longman, 1996), urges Shakespeare's subversive use of traditional stories. Some books especially concerned with religion are: Robert G. Hunter, *Shakespeare and the Comedy of Forgiveness* (New York: Columbia University Press, 1965); Northrop Frye, *A Natural Perspective: The Development of Shakespearean Comedy and Romance* (New York: 1965); Alan R. Velie, *Shakespeare's Repentance Plays: The Search for an Adequate Form* (Madison, NJ: Fairleigh Dickinson University Press, 1972). Harry Morris, *Last Things in Shakespeare* (Tallahassee, FL: Florida State University Press, 1985) uses eschatology to make a case for Shakespeare as a medieval poet; there are many good illustrations. Peter Milward's knowledge of religion and controversy, and of the role of the Jesuits, informs his critical readings in *The Medieval Dimension of Shakespeare's Plays*, Studies in Renaissance Literature 7 (Lewiston, Queenston, Lampeter: The Edwin Mellen Press, 1990) and *The Catholicism of Shakespeare's Plays* (Southampton: The Saint Austin Press, 1997).

Tudor interest in romance stems from a great medieval tradition, and there are a number of studies, with a favoring of both secular and religious interpretations. Laura Hibbard [Loomis], *Medieval Romance in England: A Study of the Sources and Analogues of the Non-cyclic Metrical Romances* (New York: Oxford University Press, 1924; rev. 1963); Dieter Mehl, *The Middle English Romances of the Thirteenth and Fourteenth Centuries* (London: Routledge and Kegan Paul, 1969); John Stevens, *Medieval Romance* (London: Hutchinson University Library, 1973); and W. R. J. Barron, *English Medieval Romance* (London: Longman, 1987) are overviews. Thomas J. Heffernan, *The Popular Literature of Medieval England* (Knoxville, TN: University of Tennessee Press, 1985) includes reviews of romances and several of religious literature. Andrea Hopkins, *The Sinful Knights: A Study of Middle English Penitential Romance* (Oxford: Oxford University Press, 1990) has a narrower focus on theme. Susan Crane, *Insular Romance: Politics, Faith, and Culture in Anglo-Norman and Middle English Literature* (Berkeley: University of California Press, 1986); Carol Fewster, *Traditionality and Genre in Middle English Romance* (Cambridge: D. S. Brewer, 1987); Carol M. Meale, ed., *Readings in Medieval English Romance* (Cambridge: D. S. Brewer, 1994); Nancy Mason Bradbury, *Writing Aloud: Storytelling in Late Medieval England* (Urbana, IL: University of Illinois Press, 1998) reflect contemporary theories not evident in earlier studies.

My last reference is to my own work. I first wrote about the relation between romance and Elizabethan drama in *Laments for the Dead in Medieval Narrative* (Pittsburgh: Duquesne University Press, 1966). In *The Popularity of Middle English Romance* (Bowling Green, OH: Bowling Green University Popular Press, 1976) I argued that romance is part of a Catholic (and subsequently English moral) tradition, rejected by Renaissance humanists and Protestant reformers; the organization was thematic, and I discussed especially popular romances, including some here related to Shakespeare: *Émare*, *Robert the Deuyll*, *Amis and Amiloun*, *Valentine and Orson*, *Paris and Vienne*, and *Guy of Warwick*. Two essays, "The Humanist Rejection of Romance," *The South Atlantic Quarterly* 77 (1978): 296–306, and "Guy of Warwick: A Medieval Thriller," *The South Atlantic Quarterly* 73 (1974): 554–63, consider Renaissance attitudes and analogous modern genres. *Geoffrey Chaucer* (New York: Continuum, 1996) has discussions of his romances. *The Legend of Guy of Warwick* (New York: Garland, 1996) is a comprehensive study of texts in historical contexts from Anglo-Norman to today; "Renaissance Diversity," 163–236, shows both the wide interest in Shakespeare's local hero and how religious changes affected his legend.

Index